BODY TALK

USING GESTURES TO RETHINK HUMAN-CENTERED PRODUCTS

Dane DeSutter
Stephanie Scopelitis

Rosenfeld

NEW YORK 2026

"The most meaningful innovations come from seeing what others overlook. *Body Talk* helps product teams move beyond words to better understand human needs, making it an invaluable resource for anyone committed to human-centered design."

—Nick Smarrelli
Author, *The Next Two Steps*, professor, Butler University

"If the precariousness of today's tech and business environment has you looking for a place to stand, Scopelitis and DeSutter offer a slab of solid bedrock. The timelessness of their message stems from its grounding in human principles that will be relevant as long as people have bodies and interact with each other in the world. (If you don't think they will or should, this book is probably not for you.) The practical advice they provide is addressed to product development professionals, but it will be useful to anyone who wants to make good stuff with people and for people."

—Siri Mehus
User experiencer consultant, Bottle Fly Research and Strategy

"In the age of AI, *Body Talk* is a timely reminder that truly human-centered products still begin with human observation, including the gestures we often overlook. This is a must-read for all experience designers who are navigating the world of designing for humans and machines."

—Beth Ard
CEO, Customer Thrive Consulting

"*Body Talk* provides a compelling new lens for human-centered design, showing how gestures reveal the needs, intentions, and insights that words alone often miss. Drawing on decades of research and practical experience, DeSutter and Scopelitis illuminate how the body supports thinking, communication, and collaboration, offering a powerful new approach to understanding people and designing experiences that truly fit human needs."

—Thérèse Dugan, PhD
Research leader and learning scientist

"Arriving at a time when contextual data is more important than ever, *Body Talk* is a perspective-shifting resource for researchers, designers, and product teams alike. It brings us back to the most intimate source of meaning: what the body knows before we do."

—Vera Haussler
Anthropologist and design research lead

"*Body Talk* starts with advice I've seen issued to boards and elite awards juries around physical gesture and its role in communication, and it expands that to help you become a better designer. The authors of *Body Talk* will help you understand how transformative it is not just to design for gestures, but also to swipe right on gestures as a rich source of human behavioral insight."

—Cheryl Platz
Author of *Design Beyond Devices* and
The Game Development Strategy Guide

"*Body Talk* makes a compelling case that the body has been the main character all along. By expertly refocusing our understanding of interaction on the gestures and physical behaviors that shape our lives, Scopelitis and DeSutter have created an essential guide for anyone creating immersive experiences, designing embodied technologies or seeking to build truly human-centered products and teams."

— Michelle Cortese
Design Director of Input and Interaction at Meta Reality Labs,
author of *Embodying the Machine*

Body Talk

Using Gestures to Rethink Human-Centered Products

By Dane DeSutter and Stephanie Scopelitis

Rosenfeld Media, LLC
125 Maiden Lane
New York, New York 10038
USA

On the Web: www.rosenfeldmedia.com

Please send errata to: errata@rosenfeldmedia.com

Publisher: Louis Rosenfeld

Managing Editor: Marta Justak

Interior Layout: Danielle Foster

Cover Design: Heads of State

Illustrator: Dane DeSutter with assistance from Nano Banana Pro

Indexer: Marilyn Augst

Proofreader: Sue Boshers

ISBN: 1-959029-25-8

ISBN 13: 978-1-959029-25-0

LCCN: 2026930286

For my family, broadly and dearly defined,
who gave me the time, space, patience, and conversation
to follow an idea wherever it led.
Thank you for living with my curiosity,
engaging with my questions,
and helping me keep asking why.

—Stephanie Scopelitis

To every person who believed in me,
you made this work worthwhile.
Thank you for the long philosophical conversations,
tolerating the half-baked ramblings,
and never doubting that my ideas were worth pursuing
to their fullest. You shaped how I think,
and I know you'll see yourself in these pages.

—Dane DeSutter

HOW TO USE THIS BOOK

Who Should Read This Book?

Do you talk to users and customers, drive product design or strategy, or facilitate the teams that do? Whether you call yourself a researcher, designer, engineer, or product manager, you've probably got stories of a product or feature that seemed really promising but failed to land.

It's rarely the execution that fails first. It's the foundation. Products are only as good as your understanding of the people they're built for and how well you build together as a team. Sometimes, the gap shows up as a single bold decision that turns out to be wrong. More often, it accumulates quietly, at decision points scattered across the entire product journey.

Products fail for many reasons. But there's one failure mode that shows up everywhere: a shallow connection with the people you're building products for and with.

Most human-centered approaches overindex on what people say. Listen to words alone and you'll find that "it's over there" or "no, it's like this" are vague, imprecise, and contradictory. Words don't work alone. People think, communicate, and coordinate their world through gesture and language together. They move their hands, shift their posture, and gaze with intent. Yet the body rarely shows up in how product teams build empathy or work together.

And that gap costs you. Your research misses critical insights. Your team doesn't align. Your products miss the mark.

Gestures are essential to how people work together. It's where thinking happens. It's where meaning gets made clear. It's where coordination takes shape. You already use them. Your users and customers use them. Your team uses them. But you're not using them deliberately. When you do, your research surfaces what language alone won't capture. Your meetings produce faster alignment and surface misunderstandings earlier. Your products work because they're grounded in how people actually understand and act in their world.

This book shows you how to use gestures intentionally across research, collaboration, design, and innovation. It's a craft you already have the instincts for. This book helps you dial in to those instincts and use them deliberately, and that makes the difference between a product that almost works and one that truly does.

If you're a leader, educator, healthcare professional, or facilitator whose work depends on understanding people and getting things done with them, this book is for you, too. Pull up a chair and listen to what the body has to say.

What's in This Book?

This book treats gestures as actions. Not signals to decode, not behaviors to classify, but things people do in order to think through problems, communicate what words leave out, and coordinate with others toward a shared goal. That framing runs through every chapter. The question the book returns to goes beyond "what gesture happened?" and instead asks the deeper question "what did that gesture make possible?"

The book moves in four broad arcs.

Chapters 1 through 3 build the foundation. You will learn what gestures are, how they work alongside speech, and how they help people think, communicate, and coordinate. These chapters train your eye so you can begin to see the gestures that matter in your work and learn which ones you can let fade into the background.

Chapters 4 and 5 are about understanding users. You will learn how to surface mental models in interviews and observations, how to use gesture-speech mismatches as openings to push conversations deeper in the moment, and how to move from those observations through analysis to grounded design directions.

Chapters 6 and 7 are about building and working as a team. You will learn how to create the conditions where people feel safe enough to bring their best thinking into the room, and how to channel that energy into developing ideas together from early sparks through to a prototype that can be tested and built. Gestures here are not just something to observe but are something to use.

Chapter 8 looks at the long relationship between the body and computing—and what lessons it holds for innovation. Through the history of interfaces, gaming, body-tracking technology, and robotics, the chapter traces a consistent push and pull: the most successful technologies are those that align with how the body already moves. As AI and robotics accelerate, this chapter asks innovators to dial into the way that the body shapes what resonates with people.

Throughout, you will find examples, methods, and practices that help you bring gestures into your everyday product work. The aim is not to become a gesture expert. Rather, it is to tap into a richer understanding of people by making use of everything that makes us human, which includes the body and how it acts on the world.

What Comes with This Book?

This book's companion website (https://rosenfeldmedia.com/books/body-talk/) contains the book's diagrams and other illustrations—all available under a Creative Commons license (when possible) for you to download and include in your own presentations.

FREQUENTLY ASKED QUESTIONS

Is gesture only about the hands?

No. Gestures can happen anywhere in or across the body; it's a whole-body thing! It includes what you do with your hands, of course, but also your posture, gaze, how you orient toward or away from someone, and even the way you sit. A turned shoulder, a lifted chin, or even a cocked eyebrow in context are a type of gesture.

In this book, gestures refer to any visible bodily action that helps make meaning when people think, communicate, and coordinate with others. (See Chapter 1, "The Need to Go Deeper.")

Are gestures just body language?

Not quite. Body language books are about reading personality, detecting deception, or projecting confidence. This book is about something different: the work that gestures actually do. Gestures help people think (Chapter 2, "How the Body Talks") and reveal their mental models (Chapter 4, "Understand Users' Gestures"). Gestures communicate what words can't capture (Chapter 2). Gestures build belonging in teams (Chapter 6, "Build Strong Teams That Belong") and enable richer collaboration and design (Chapter 7, "Design Everyday Things Together").

Do I need special training to see gestures?

No. You already read gestures naturally in everyday life. When someone shakes their head side to side, you instantly know it means "no." When a colleague leans forward in a meeting, you sense engagement. You're doing this all the time without thinking about it (Chapter 2). This book takes that natural skill and makes it intentional and reliable for your product work. You can cultivate a sharper, more deliberate way of noticing the gestures that matter. It's a skill you can develop, not a special talent you either have or don't have (Chapter 3, "How to 'See' Gestures").

How much extra time does this add to my process?

Usually, very little. There are two ways this book asks you to work with gestures.

The first is in-the-moment attention: noticing and using gestures as they happen. This adds almost no time at all. You're already talking to users, customers, stakeholders, and teammates as they think, talk, decide, and work together. This book lets you become more intentional about what you already notice naturally (see Chapter 3 for a field guide for understanding gestures and what they contribute) and use gestures deliberately to drive conversations deeper—whether in a user interview (see Chapter 4) or a team meeting (see Chapter 6).

The second is formal gesture analysis on video data. It does take more time, but you don't need to analyze every gesture. (See Chapter 5, "Analyze Your Gesture Data," for guidance on when a quick scan is enough.)

The payoff: a little attention early catches confusion, missed needs, and costly misunderstandings before they become harder to fix.

Can't AI or software just do this for me?

AI and software can help. They can locate movement at scale, make video easier to search, and point you toward moments worth a closer look. But detection is not interpretation. A gesture matters because of what people are trying to do, what came before, who responds, and what happens next. Understanding context requires knowing your goals (Chapter 3), the relationships at play (Chapter 6), and how ideas move through collaboration (Chapter 7). That still requires human judgment. This book treats AI and software as useful aids, not replacements for your attention. They can help you narrow the field. You still need to make sense of what you see.

Why should technology and product design care about the body?

Because the most successful products you use today were shaped by the human body. Computing has always been built on metaphors that bridge the physical and digital—you organize files, you drag and drop, you swipe and tap. This reliance on the body isn't accidental, but foundational (Chapter 8, "The Body Points the Way")! As technology evolves and innovation accelerates, especially in the age of AI, understanding how people move and think becomes more critical, not less. The body is your constant anchor for keeping design human-centered (Chapter 8). When you lose sight of it, products feel clunky and people abandon them. When you design with the body in mind, technology feels intuitive, reachable, and genuinely human.

CONTENTS

FOREWORD

Long ago, I began my career in user research while working at an industrial design agency. Once the internet became a thing (I said it was long ago!), people were more likely to think of product designers (as they were also known) only in terms of digital user experiences. But when I started, my colleagues and I focused on the design and engineering of *physical* products: laptops, network servers, pulse oximeters, livestock medication systems.

Listening to my colleagues talk to each other, I got a sense of their intimate familiarity with the physical world that we all inhabited. An edge was chamfered. A shelf was buttressed. A form was extruded. A device had visible parting lines that revealed how it was manufactured. They had mental models of—and language for—not just the built environment but also the space that people and objects moved in together.

As a researcher, my emphasis has often been in how people talk: words, emotion, ideas, hidden meanings. Sure, I've watched people use prototypes, clutch a favorite item to their chest, laugh while pointing out an item in their kitchen, or use extra steps when operating a piece of machinery. I suspect I'm like many people who do research. We collect what people say, and if we're good, we gather what people do, and if we're *really* good, we also make note of what people say about what they do. But we are lacking awareness, let alone literacy in how people say what they say and do what they do. We're lacking that intimate familiarity with the physicality of people, as well as the mental models and language to unlock the insights that are right there, if only we realized.

So, how fantastic that not too long ago I saw a brief conference presentation from Dane DeSutter where he explained the benefits of gathering and analyzing this rich data—the physical movements of people as they talked, explained, worked, and communicated. I was, like [*hands curved beside each temple, eyes and mouth opened, hands pulled slowly away from head, fingers widened and palms flattened, lips pursed and exhaled a "ka-pyewww" sound, eye roll, small head shake*]. Yeah, my mind was blown.

Now, Dane and Stephanie Scopelitis have taken the work so much further *[arms push out from shoulders, palms forward, repeat twice]*. This book is an immensely helpful guide for you to build a richer understanding of people. Stephanie and Dane really break things down *[short karate-chop]* and show you the way with stories, comics, case studies, and plenty of examples. You can immediately put the tools in this book to work *[hands wide beside head, pull down, rotate slightly, right hand snaps fingers, and index finger points forward]*.

You, readers of *Body Talk*, are in *good hands*.

—Steve Portigal
Author of *Interviewing Users*, 2nd ed. and
Doorbells, Danger, and Dead Batteries

INTRODUCTION

Dane's Story

When Dane was just a few months into his graduate studies, he knew he needed something new for a sticky problem: improving pass rates in organic chemistry. The subject was notorious for its demands on spatial thinking. Yet, students had to simultaneously visualize, rotate, and internally deform these unseen, three-dimensional molecules and consider their interactions with their chemical environment. But they were most often presented as flat diagrams on a page alongside cryptic letters and symbols.

Trying to clear his mind and get inspired, he took a walk across campus. *Maybe I could... no, that won't work. What if...* Then he saw a tree (yes, really). He slowed and fixed his gaze on it as he walked and thought.

He had passed this tree countless times. He had seen it in every season: bare-branched in winter, flowers opening in spring, their smell hanging in the air. He knew the sharp feel of the bark, the way it creaked and swayed when the wind moved through it. *How is it that I understand something spatial about this object? I've seen thousands of trees. I've moved around them on walks and hikes. I climbed into their canopies as a kid. I understand it through experience.*

Dane realized he understood the spatial world not because he had studied it in diagrams, but because it was a rich sensory experience he could draw on from everyday life. He saw the gap between understanding the three-dimensionality of molecules and the value of experiencing them with the senses.

Stephanie's Story

Early in her teaching career, Stephanie partnered with educators to implement a curriculum to improve descriptive language and fluency. The classroom teachers brought the pens and the paper. Stephanie brought her lived experience of being in her body.

A student named Izak wrote eleven words in his journal: *When they tried to beat my brother up, I was angry.* The task was to write about a particular moment and how it made you feel. Izak's statement was clear. But there was no personal story there. Not yet.

Stephanie asked Izak to put down his pen and stand up. "Show me how anger feels in your body." He did. His body became rigid. His face tightened. His breath was audible. He picked up his pen and began to write: *My eyebrows are scrunched. I feel my breath huffing and puffing.*

To push the exploration further, Stephanie showed him what anger looked like in her body. She clenched her jaw, balled her fists, and crossed her arms strongly over her chest. Izak watched and then scribbled down more words, *My fists are like rocks in my hands. I feel like the chains inside my body are going to burst.* He looked up. His eyes seemed to ask permission. Stephanie nodded and Izak's pen hit the paper again. He added, *I could hear my mother's voice in my head telling me to calm down.*

Stephanie realized that the experiences people hold in their bodies can build understanding. Through the exchange of gesture for gesture, body for body, Izak's writing didn't just improve; his awareness sharpened. As his anger came into view, as it took shape and became shareable, he understood what to do with it. The story transformed and so did Izak.

Our Story

Our paths first crossed as learning scientists studying how students learned chemistry at the University of Illinois–Chicago. We brought two different vantage points. Dane was interested in what gestures revealed about cognition. Stephanie was interested in how bodies supported interaction and learning. When Dane watched a hand rotate an invisible molecule, he saw thinking made visible. When Stephanie watched the same gesture, she saw a student and teacher building understanding together. Both were true.

That experience clarified something for us. Human-centeredness is more than surface-level empathy. It is about understanding the whole person: what people say, what they do, how they move, what they notice, what they struggle to express, and what their bodies reveal before their words catch up. The body is an important source of insight into human needs and a driver of human experience, but it is often not meaningfully considered in design iterations or roadmap decisions.

And this problem we realized was not unique to our particular industries. Every product team claims to be human-centered, and many genuinely aspire to be. But most are still working with only part of the picture.

That gap has never been more consequential. AI tools now surface patterns and generate insights at a speed no researcher can match, but they don't probe, they don't notice when words and body tell different stories, and they can't ask a follow-up question rooted in what they just saw. Agentic development means software products can be built and shipped faster than teams can understand who they're building them for. And after years of remote work, many teams are returning to physical spaces together, relearning how to read a room. The body is back in the room. The question is whether you know how to pay attention to it.

That gave Dane an idea: what if the gesture lens could be translated for product teams? He thought of Stephanie and the work they had done together previously. Then he made his pitch. What if researchers, designers, and product managers could learn to read what users were actually showing them?

That question became our presentation. And as we built it together, we noticed something in our own practice. Ideas were taking shape in our hands before words caught up. Gestures weren't just the subject of what we were making, but they were the medium and tools we used to advance our ideas together.

This reminded us that gestures are not just trailing signals to interpret after the fact. They do something much larger. Gestures do meaningful work across the whole product development journey: in research, collaboration, design, and innovation. At every stage, gestures can move work forward.

That was the story we needed to tell. And that became this book.

I just need to optimize the route...
...and that's basically what the Bauhaus movement got wrong about embodied experience, if you think about it.
Stephanie, the sidewalk is here. What are you doing?
What is all this?
If we follow the sidewalk around the quad, then cut left at the...
Let's just walk, I'm good with directions. You know I actually knew Tom of TomTom...
You don't say... Hold up, wait for me, I've got the map!
This path is here because people just knew where they need to go. Their feet wrote the story before anyone could pave it! It's called a desire path.
Thoreau or Rousseau came up with the name.
...neither of them said anything about— I think we're lost...
Maybe he knows how to get to Espresso Yourself?

CHAPTER 1

The Need to Go Deeper

It started with a hand. Sam Farber, creator of OXO Good Grips, watched his wife Betsey struggle with a vegetable peeler. Arthritis had turned a simple kitchen tool into daily frustration.

"This is hard to hold," she said. As she set the peeler down, she instinctively grasped her wrist, flexing her fingers to stretch out the ache. A team relying solely on the words "hard to hold" could have started crafting a product solution that missed the mark entirely. Maybe they would have proposed changing the grip material or adding some additional texture to the handle. However, these well-intentioned solutions would have overlooked what Betsey really needed.

But Sam looked beyond the words. He saw his wife's flexed fingers and noticed her massaging her wrist. He then observed the tense, full-fisted grip she had been forced to use. This key observation of the body revealed the real problem: the shape of the handle was forcing her hand into an unnatural posture. That insight, found through observing the body, is in no small part why the iconic, wider Good Grips handle exists today.

This principle that the body reveals needs that words may not reveal is universal. It applies whether you are designing a physical tool like a vegetable peeler or a digital interface. At the end of the day, all human-centered design needs to be grounded in and informed by the body, because every experience is lived through physical actions and reactions.

You Need to Go Deeper

Working in product, design, or UX, you entered this field to create products that genuinely help people, whether to delight them, solve everyday frustrations, or make their lives easier. Fulfilling that mission requires driving at a deeper understanding of what people need.

To achieve this, you may talk to top customers, observe people on the job, or look at analytics to see where people spend their time. You might also read forums, run focus groups, or conduct in-depth interviews. Maybe you're starting to even leverage AI to parse social media posts and customer support tickets at scale.

You already use this information and apply tools to make sense of it to build a clear path for product development. Product teams rely on an arsenal of tools to understand people, communicate clearly, and collaborate effectively. You've probably used many of them: journey maps, personas, wireframes, and even the classic "How Might We" exercise. These tools help teams structure ideas, surface assumptions, and keep miscommunication in check in order to guide roadmap decisions with intention.

But a bias runs through nearly all of these tools: it's the primacy of language. Written or spoken, words pave the pathway for the product development journey. They carry insights from research, fuel ideation, and frame design choices.

Words are crucial and informative. Yet even with all these well-intentioned tools and processes, products sometimes still miss the mark. The reality is that it's not always about *failing to listen* closely to the words; it can also be about failing to *listen to the body.*

To build human-centered products, you need to understand humans fully, not just through what they say, but also through what they do. The way that people move their hands and bodies, shift their posture, adjust their gaze, and react through facial expressions is part of how they think, communicate, and coordinate their actions. To build products that truly fit people's needs, you have to look beyond language to the way the body talks. And that applies to everyone in your work: the people you build *for,* and the people you build *with.*

NOTE **GESTURES DEFINED**

> Gestures are part of the spontaneous and intentional physical actions that people make. They include hand movements, body posturing, and shifts in gaze. More than just emotional expressions, gestures are active participants in the thinking, communication, and coordination that drive product development.

Go Beyond Words

To supercharge how you create products for people, you need to supercharge how you understand people holistically. Going beyond language and making use of what the body "says" can help you.

HOW MUCH IS "SAID" NONVERBALLY?

You're probably familiar with the claim that 80% of human communication is nonverbal. While widely cited, this figure is likely an overgeneralization that stems from psychologist Albert Mehrabian's "7-38-55 rule."[1] Mehrabian's research focused on how people interpret feelings and attitudes when verbal and nonverbal cues are incongruent. He found that in cases where words and body language didn't match, people relied on verbal content only 7% of the time, while tone of voice accounted for 38% and facial expression for 55%. This led to the common estimate that 80-90% of communication is nonverbal, although this interpretation overlooks the specific conditions of his study.

The idea gained traction, particularly in public speaking seminars and communication training. Mehrabian himself later clarified[2] that his findings do not mean that words are insignificant; rather, nonverbal cues play a significant role in resolving ambiguity about emotional intent. The research numbers may vary depending on how gestures are utilized. For example, Adam Kendon suggests that gestures account for as much as 50% of the meaning conveyed in conversations.[3] What remains true is that gestures are not an adjunct to talk; they are an essential part of it.

---

1 The so-called "7-38-55 rule" traces back to two experimental studies by Albert Mehrabian and colleagues (1967). These studies looked specifically at how people judge emotional attitudes when verbal and nonverbal cues conflict, producing the well-known weighting of verbal content, vocal tone, and facial expression. The popular summary was later condensed into the 7/38/55 proportions.

2 Mehrabian later emphasized in *Silent Messages* and subsequent interviews that these findings apply only when interpreting feelings under ambiguous conditions. He cautioned against using the percentages to describe communication more broadly.

3 Adam Kendon's work (e.g., *Gesture: Visible Action as Utterance*, 2004) provides a more nuanced view, showing that gestures can contribute substantial semantic content in conversation, particularly when speakers describe spatial layouts, actions, or abstract ideas.

Consider the universal usability test. A user is shown a prototype and clicks through. A researcher or designer asks for feedback on the prototype, and the user says that it was "easy to use." (That's what the transcript captured as well!) However, they also noticed a hesitation in the user's voice that was coupled with a furrowed brow and hesitant mouse movements. Though never articulated in language, the unspoken aspects of this session hinted at a more nuanced interpretation of this user's experience. The design concept is likely not, as the words state, entirely "easy to use." There's more work to do!

Although words are essential in how people share thoughts, communicate ideas, and work together, the words people share don't always tell the entire story. Relying solely on words might risk overlooking crucial information that is embedded within nonverbal cues. Hand gestures, facial expressions, gaze, and body posture often significantly enhance talk, adding critical meaning and essential understanding when words alone fall short.

The Case for Gestures

Gestures are not just hand waving. They aren't mere decorations, nervous fidgets, partial fill-ins for words, or simply learned cultural habits. They are something more.

Gestures do more than add kinetic flair. Just as a knife cuts and a wrench tightens, gestures do something.

When you are planning out the argument in an essay, and you stack imaginary ideas in the air, you are using your hands to organize your thinking before you write a single word. When you are planning what to say in a meeting, you might move your hands in front of you as if laying out points in space—placing one idea here, another there, and then circling back to the first. Your hands help you organize the sequence of your thoughts before you say a word. When you raise your arm and lean forward on the sidewalk to hail a cab, your action stops a two-ton vehicle. When you use your finger to stand in for a wood peg and then motion how it joins the back and side of an IKEA bookshelf, you're explaining how to complete a step in the instructions (and hopefully not fighting with your significant other).

Gestures provide a visceral channel of insight and action and serve as a silent invitation for exchange that propels everyone forward.

GESTURE-LANGUAGE LINK: EVIDENCE FROM APHASIA

The connection between language and movement is deeply rooted in human biology. Research in embodied cognition shows that understanding action-related language engages parts of the motor system, overlapping with the neural circuits used for action execution.[4] One striking piece of evidence that established the gesture-language link comes from patients who have suffered strokes. Aphasia, a disorder caused by localized brain damage, can result in selective linguistic deficits depending on the location of the damage. Clinical researchers working with these patients have also extensively documented correlated impacts on gesture production.[5] This distinction is particularly clear when comparing Wernicke's and Broca's aphasia (see Figure 1.1).

Wernicke's aphasia (also known as *fluent aphasia*) occurs when people experience damage to the brain's *language comprehension* center. Patients with fluent aphasia are able to produce fluent speech, but often what they say is not coherent. Interestingly, researchers observed that these patients produce gestures that also lack conceptual depth. Rather than producing illustrative or meaningful gestures, they primarily rely on pointing, suggesting a disruption in their ability to encode cohesive ideas into both speech and movement.

Broca's aphasia (also known as *nonfluent aphasia*), by contrast, occurs when people experience damage to the brain's *speech production* center. While these patients struggle to control the muscles that move the tongue and vocal cords to produce vocalizations, their ability to comprehend language remains intact. Though difficult, these patients can produce speech that is coherent and logically organized. Notably, their gestures remain unaffected, often serving as a compensatory tool to express meaning when words fail.

---

4 Gallese and Lakoff (2005) synthesized evidence from neuroscience and cognitive linguistics to argue that conceptual understanding—including abstract concepts—is embodied, relying on distributed sensory, motor, and affective systems rather than abstract symbols.

5 McNeill (1985) reviewed evidence from Broca's and Wernicke's aphasia showing that gesture and speech exhibit parallel patterns of impairment and preservation following brain injury. Broca-type patients retain referential words and iconic gestures but lose the ability to combine elements linguistically or gesturally, while Wernicke-type patients preserve fluent sequencing and beat-like gestures but produce few meaningful iconics. McNeill argued that these parallel breakdowns indicate a shared computational stage underlying speech and gesture production.

FIGURE 1.1

Patient with Wernicke's aphasia uses simple pointing gestures that provide little additional meaning to the language (left); patient with Broca's aphasia struggles to verbalize the number "60" and uses gestures to compensate for missing language (right).

When language comprehension and production are selectively disrupted by damage to the brain, parallel deficits emerge in gesture. The contrast between these two types of aphasia reinforces that gestures and language originate from the same neural system[6] and share a deep network for representing meaning across both modes.

6 McNeill (1992, 2005) and Goldin-Meadow (2003) argue that gesture and speech are co-expressive components of a unified meaning-making system. Evidence from aphasia supports this view, showing that gesture and language remain fundamentally integrated rather than functioning as separate channels.

When you notice someone pointing left while giving directions and saying, "...then you'll make a right," it's a signal that prompts you to ask for clarification before you get lost. Similarly, if a friend tilts their head while you're explaining the rules of a new board game, you might recognize the need to backtrack and provide a simpler explanation. When a choreographer points to a spot on the stage during a school play rehearsal, they shift every child's gaze to the same location, coordinating their action and completing their understanding of the director's vision.

This seamless interaction between language and gesture elevates human engagement, transcending words alone to build shared understanding. Gestures, along with the words you speak, expand meaning. Gestures in collaboration with the sentences you exchange develop ideas. And gestures partnered with the thoughts you process build understanding. Ignoring the connection between language and gestures can lead to incomplete inquiries, misunderstandings, and inaccurate conclusions.

When thoughtfully employed and perceptively observed, gestures become a powerful resource to

- Support thinking.
- Enhance communication.
- Coordinate people, things, and actions.

Gestures work so well because they are inseparable from the people using them. They are always present, easy to access, and flexible enough to adapt to whatever the moment requires.

How Gestures Support Your Product Journey

The path of product development follows a familiar trajectory, from uncovering a human need to shipping a solution that meets it. It's a journey that takes you from research and discovery, through definition and ideation, into design and delivery. At every step, gestures can help you.

But this journey isn't just a series of technical steps, it is a complex social endeavor of designing with people, for people. Products aren't just objects! They are the outcome of a complex, messy, and sometimes circuitous journey of teams moving together. This process is filled with human interaction, collaboration, and creative sparks.

When you start to attend to gestures as tools for thinking, resources for communication, and a means for coordinating people, things, and actions in your product development journey, you will open up opportunities to do the following:

- Understand users and communicate their needs.
- Create inclusive teams that collaborate effectively.
- Build innovative solutions that center on human experience today and in the future.

But how you make use of gestures depends on where you are in that journey. In the early stages of discovery, gestures help you understand users by revealing what they really think and clarifying their mental models. A hesitant hand movement during a user interview can expose a hidden source of friction far better than words.

As you move to define the problem, gestures help you convey user needs to stakeholders with impact. Re-enacting a user's struggle by mimicking their posture and frustrated movements creates a visceral, shared understanding that a slide deck would struggle to achieve.

During ideation, gestures help you foster belonging in teams and invite the full participation that unlocks creativity. A quiet designer tracing an idea in the air can be invited to contribute, ensuring their perspective isn't lost. And as you design and prototype, gestures help you test ideas. The seamless swipe of a finger across a prototype confirms an intuitive design, while a fumbled grasp reveals a flaw long before a user can articulate why it feels wrong.

Each of these moments—from discovery to delivery—is a step on your path. Attending to gestures doesn't just make each step more effective, but it also ensures that the entire journey carries you toward your North Star: building something human-centered that delights people and makes their lives better.

Gestures Look Back and Forward

Gestures support every stage of the product journey. At their foundation, they are sense-making tools that drive action: they help you understand where you've been, where you are, and where you're going. They link parts of the journey that might otherwise feel separate. Think of them as a bridge.

GESTURES AND THE TRACES THEY LEAVE

For cross-functional product teams who are designing human-centered solutions, pay attention not only to what people do, but what they have done as well. *Desire paths*—those well-worn shortcuts across the grass, the muddy trails that cut past pristine sidewalks—are everywhere. You've probably seen them in parks or on college campuses, quiet but visible signs of how people actually move through a space. These informal paths zigzag around congested spots, shorten distances between locations, or sidestep areas that become treacherous in bad weather. (See Figure 1.2.)

FIGURE 1.2
A desire path carved between the walkway and adjacent parking lot behind a building.

At first, these unplanned trails might just look like inefficiencies: people bypassing carefully laid-out paths in favor of their own. They emerge when enough people share the same impulse to step off the paved route, eventually carving a new trail that reveals a gap between intended design and real-world behavior. It's tempting to see desire paths as a result of a failure of design. Or to only see them through the clarity of hindsight: *How could they have gotten that so wrong!* In reality, every product is just a hypothesis frozen in time, an informed attempt to address users' needs based on the available information. And like hypotheses, products are tested continuously. People, often without intending to, expose mismatches between design intent and lived experience (see Figure 1.3).

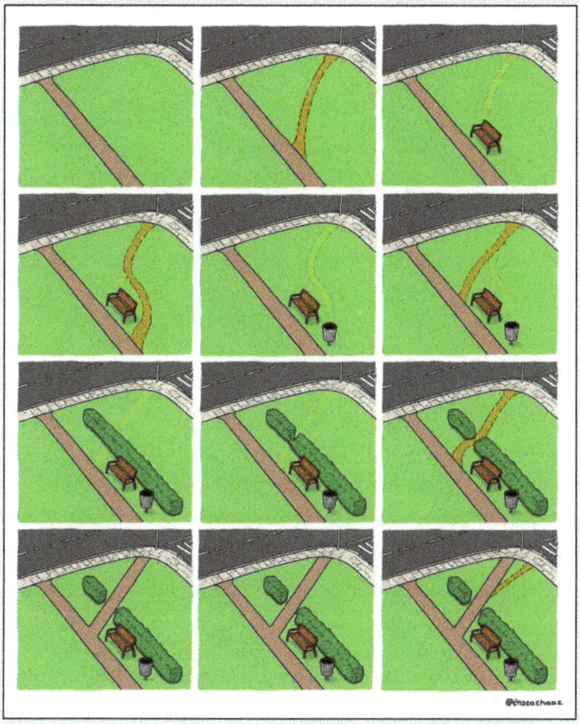

FIGURE 1.3
The work of design is never done because human needs are in constant flux and so designs evolve.

The traces that actions leave behind tell a visible story of human needs. When people fold the corners of a book page into a dog ear, they are marking their place in a novel. When someone tapes over a laptop camera, they are trying to improve their personal security. When someone slings their legs over the arm of a chair into an indentation, they reveal how they like to relax. These residues of human action can also become signals for change. When needs aren't fully met, people leave behind evidence of their adaptations. Although some might abandon a product or experience, others create their own shortcuts. These symbolic and physical desire paths aren't just signs of unmet needs, they are opportunities. They offer a chance to uncover what changed, where friction exists, and what gaps might need to be examined in your understanding of people's needs.

Keep this in mind! Physical actions leave a trace. People's past behaviors constantly reveal something about their needs and underscore opportunities. The body talks in many ways, so listen!

Gestures bridge your organization and your users, helping your team develop empathy for the people you are designing for. They bridge people and ideas, turning a creative spark into a shared reality. They bridge diverse expertise, perspectives, and priorities by linking members of different teams. They even bridge the past and the future, connecting a user's past frustration to better design decisions.

Seen this way, gestures aren't just isolated events; they are the through line in the journey from nothing to something. Using gestures well means consciously integrating what makes this process human. You live in and through a body. You engage the world with it, and you challenge the world through it. By attending to the body, you bring that fundamental human reality into the enterprise of making things for other people.

When leveraged effectively, gestures add a valuable layer of information, giving them a unique ability to enhance human-centered design throughout the entire product development process, from discovery to delivery. By incorporating gestures into your product toolbelt, you gain a new superpower that opens up creative avenues for developing products that meet real needs, enrich lives, and, if you're fortunate, stand the test of time.

Gestures, simply put, do something for you in the product journey.

Navigating the Product Landscape

One important way that gestures drive action is that they help you navigate the twists and turns of product development. Product development isn't a single road leading from an idea to a finished product. It's a network of paths, filled with convergence, divergence, and realignment as teams work toward a shared goal.

The metaphor of a product roadmap may make the journey seem linear and well-understood, but in reality, product teams are constantly shifting between exploring new directions and coming back together to make decisions. This complex terrain is often a tangle of overlapping efforts (see Figure 1.4).

Some teams run ahead, scouting what's possible. Research might be gathering insights for a feature that won't be built for months, while engineering builds out technical capabilities. Other teams move in parallel, tackling different aspects of the same problem. And at key points, teams must converge to align on a shared direction before work can move forward.

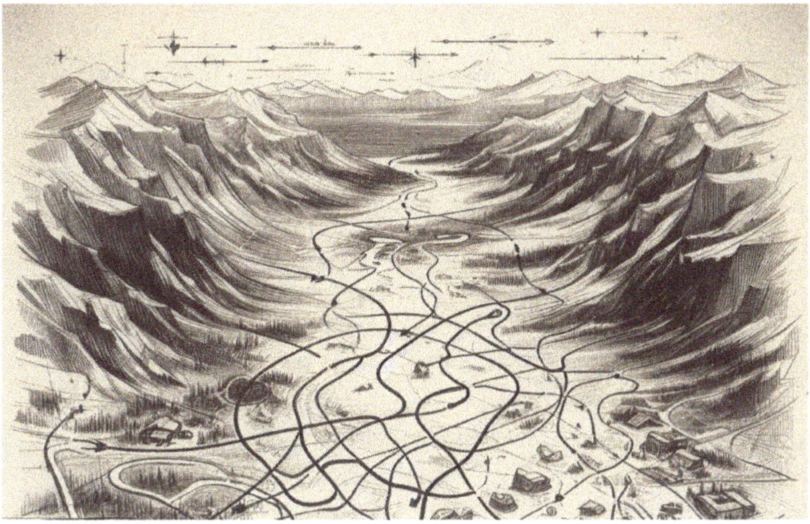

FIGURE 1.4
Reaching the goal of a product requires navigating a tangle of pathways.

To move forward effectively, you need to not only know what path you're on but also be open to the paths that emerge. The main paths you will navigate in the broader product journey are the following:

- **Research path:** You gather evidence to ground decisions in real human behavior, providing the context and proof needed to move in a truly human-centered direction.
- **Collaboration path:** Your team strengthens its vision by blending diverse expertise, balancing aspirational goals with practical considerations to ensure inclusive and comprehensive decision-making.
- **Design path:** You translate research insights and collective ideas into concepts and potential solutions, seeking creative approaches that feel natural and effectively meet user needs.
- **Innovation path:** You venture into uncharted territory to explore new markets, pressure-test core assumptions about the problem space, and spark entirely new directions for the business.

These paths aren't necessarily sequential, and changing priorities can cause you to jump between them rapidly. But when you know which path you are on in the project journey, you can navigate with intention and better see how gestures connect and guide your team's progress.

Know Your Goals

Product organizations are guided by an overarching goal, their North Star. For many of you, this is creating a human-centered product that meets the real needs of people. In the rush of daily decision-making, you can sometimes lose sight of what you're moving toward. The compass for navigating the many pathways in the product journey is comprised of knowing your goals. And knowing your goals has the added benefit of helping you see how gestures steer your progress.

An outgrowth of knowing which path in the product journey you're on is that it helps you frame how to make use of gestures along the way. Not every gesture is meaningful for every moment. A sharpened focus allows you to filter out the noise and recognize the ones that support your immediate objective, while still keeping you oriented toward the destination ahead.

NOTE STAY OPEN TO NEW DIRECTIONS

Find a balance between being attuned to what may support your goal, while staying open enough to see the unexpected.

Attend to Gestures That Matter

Not all gestures are created equal. Some hold a lot of meaning, others very little, and some none at all. Some can be large yet empty; others are small but densely packed with information. Some simply echo what's already conveyed in speech, while others add depth and detail you can't get from words alone.

No need to track every flick of the wrist or twist of the torso. The gestures that matter are the ones that help move your product work forward. In meetings, stand-ups, design reviews, workshops, and user sessions, look at the gestures that surface insight, clarify meaning, and spark new direction. These are the gestures that are more than background. They are tools. Use these to make ideas tangible, build team creativity, foster safety, and anchor design in real human experiences.

You'll learn how to spot and use these gestures throughout the chapters to come. For now, remember this: gestures that matter are the ones that appear in the flow of product work and do something. They add nuance, surface insight, and spark collaboration, helping you move further on the journey toward products that truly resonate.

Don't Worry, You've Got This!

Humans are inherently expressive, kinetic beings who are constantly engaged in a silent choreography of movement and words. Infants gesture with intent before they can speak. Parents use gestures to gently chide a child at the dinner table, colleagues gesture to emphasize a point, and you gesture to illustrate concepts. It's as fundamental to human behavior as laughing, crying, eating, or sleeping. Everyone gestures, and everyone gestures a lot! It's simply what humans do.

People are also instinctively adept at composing their gestures and effortlessly skilled at interpreting those of others. You know a head shake in the Western world means "no" without thinking about it, and you understand that a tap to the wrist, with or without a watch, signals time. This fluency is automatic, it's intuitive, and it's largely subconscious. But when you raise your awareness and step beyond instinct, the value of gestures amplifies. Using gestures to enhance your work isn't about mastering something new; it's about refining what you already do. The more you practice, the more natural it becomes.

Don't worry. You've got this.

Prepare for Your Journey

Going deeper with gestures unlocks a new level of understanding—one that sharpens how you build products for and with people.

No matter what path you're on, gestures help you do more. They can drive you toward deeper user insights, more inclusive and effective collaboration, more user-centered design, and more innovative products. They can help you navigate the curves and crossroads of product development. Watch them. Use them. Let them guide the way.

Grab your field notebook. Unfold your map. Open your eyes. And let the journey begin!

Takeaways

- **You need to go deeper than what users say.** Product development tools are often biased toward language, causing teams to miss critical insights. To truly understand user needs, you must look beyond words to what the body does.
- **Gestures are functional tools for doing work.** More than just "hand waving," gestures actively support the product journey.

They are tools that can be used to support thinking, enhance communication with layers of meaning that words lack, and coordinate action among people and teams.

- **Know your goal to focus on the gestures that matter.** You don't need to track every twitch and shrug. By understanding which path of the product journey you are on—be it research, collaboration, design, or innovation—you can intentionally focus on the specific gestures that will provide actionable insight and help move your work forward.
- **This is not a new skill to learn, but an innate ability to refine.** You are already an expert at instinctively interpreting and using gestures. The goal is to bring this subconscious, fluent ability into your conscious professional practice. This reframes the challenge from learning a complex new discipline to simply sharpening a natural human skill you already possess.

FIELD NOTES FROM DANE

As part of my job, I regularly have access to the recordings from various product leadership meetings. These gatherings are often long, jargon-laden, and at a business level that is beyond what I might think about day-to-day. When I'm busy, which, let's be frank, is all the time, I am often tempted to just use a redux of these meetings, like the transcript or even an AI-generated summary.

But I often reflect on what I might be missing. Was there some unspoken gap in how members of the team were discussing the roadmap? Did someone subtly signal their authority, perhaps by raising a hand to quiet the room during a heated debate, revealing who the ultimate decision-maker really is? Would I have taken notice of the PM leaning back in their chair, disengaged while the engineers hash out technical details, a subtle signal suggesting this discussion may not be crucial for product direction and more about backend architecture.

So much of the knowledge that I rely on to make adept and strategic decisions in the product world simply is not captured in the transcript of a meeting. When I only pay attention to language, I miss out on the important aspects of team dynamics that are not possible to capture in language alone. Maybe you've noticed similar dynamics in the meetings you attend as well. It doesn't take formal training; it takes practice. When you rely on your intuitive and innate ability to interpret gestures, you can do it, too.

FIELD NOTES FROM STEPHANIE

As a former professional dancer (see Figure 1.5), I learned quickly that running choreography full out every time was inefficient. It takes stamina. So, instead of rehearsing with the entire body, dancers often let their hands do the dancing. We call this *marking*.

Marking is a dancer's shorthand: a reduced version of the movement performed through the hands. Standing in place, a dancer can replay an entire sequence with small gestures. A curved hand traces the larger pathway of the arms. A quick swirl of the finger signals a turn. A pause holds the timing of a phrase. The full dance is still there, but just compressed into the hands.

FIGURE 1.5
Stephanie performing at the Joyce Theater in NYC.

Dancers use marking to recall sequence, check timing, and work through transitions without expending the energy of a full performance. But marking is not simply a private cognitive aid. It is also a social and communicative act.

As a teacher, I often use my hands to mark combinations for dancers. Without moving across the floor, I can show where the body travels, how timing unfolds, and how one movement connects to the next. The hands communicate the structure of the dance. They enact its direction, rhythm, form, and sequence.

This is what makes marking so effective. It reduces the effort required to think through, remember, and communicate complex movements while preserving the essential features of the idea.

Espresso Yourself? Oh I know exactly where that is.
So you go straight past the thing...and then you curve around where the other thing was and go past that. You know the one!
...and then honestly? You just feel your way from there. You'll know it when you see it. Can't miss it.
That is so helpful, thank you so much.
It's that way.
Yeah, his directions were great!
Dane. He said "past the thing" twice...
Did you watch his hands at all?
I was focused on what he was saying.
His words were saying one thing, his hands another!
Hey, don't you study this stuff? Why didn't you watch his hands?
...I was just really lost in his smile.
Get your head out of the clouds. Pay attention. Some of those gestures matter!

CHAPTER 2

How the Body Talks

Gestures are *not* filler. They're not flourishes of personality or idle movement. They're part of how work gets done together. Just as a button affords pressing or a handle affords pulling, the body has affordances, too. Gestures are the body's affordances for thinking, communicating, and coordinating.

For decades, researchers in cognitive science, linguistics, and anthropology have shown that the movements of our hands, posture, and gaze aren't background noise. They're functional. A single circling motion can mean very different things depending on context. It could reveal how a user understands "continuous" updates. It could help a designer think through a refresh step in a user flow for themselves. It could wrangle a team's focus during a brainstorm. Same movement, different job.

When you tune into these affordances, you stop seeing gestures as decoration and start seeing them as tools. Tools that reveal fragile ideas before they vanish, sharpen meaning when words fall short, and organize attention so that teams move together. In product work, that's your magic ingredient and may very well mean the difference between missing the signal and building the right thing.

The Many Ways the Body Talks

The best way to understand how gestures work is to see them in action. Forget about product roadmaps and user flows for a moment and picture a more universal challenge: being lost. The simple act of giving and receiving directions is a masterclass in how humans use their bodies to think, communicate, and coordinate. It reveals how people build shared understanding when words alone aren't enough.

Imagine you are searching for a local coffee shop that a colleague raves about. It's not showing up on your phone's map. So, you wander around fruitlessly and decide to ask someone for directions. You then approach a friendly stranger standing on the sidewalk in front of you.

You ask the stranger if they know where the coffee shop is that you can't seem to locate. Luckily, they nod and seem to know. "You're going to turn right," he says as he extends his hand outward in an arcing motion. (Here, the gesture adds crucial detail.) But you miss it.

"Okay, so I keep going this way . . . " You ask, seeking confirmation, as you align your gaze and look beyond the tip of your extended arm and finger. " . . . And then I take a right?" as your hand cuts a sharp angle. (Your gesture reveals a misunderstanding.)

He noticed your sharp gesture to the right that did not match what he meant. "No, the first turn is actually a curve to the right, not a sharp turn." He repeats the arc gesture, this time larger and directly in your sight line. (His gesture corrects the misunderstanding.)

But then there is a pause in the conversation. The direction-giver's gaze drops, seeming uncertain. He pulls his hands closer to his body. His torso twists slightly left, right, then left again. Quietly, almost to himself, he says, " . . . a left? Yes, a left." He shifts his hand into your view and, leading with his fingertips, carves a precise 90-degree angle from the curved road. With confidence, he says, "Then you take a left." (His gestures aid his own recall and memory.)

You want to make sure that you understand: "So, I go straight," as you point in front of you, "then right," as you make a curve, and "then left," as you make a sharp angle. (Your gestures request confirmation and lock in the thinking.) You both nod to signal that the understanding is reached. (The final gesture signals completion.)

Thanks to gestures, within a few minutes, you are sipping a delicious latte.

This exchange accomplished something that words alone could not. The gestures and talk worked together to create a shared understanding that led you to the coffee shop. This is the work of building products in miniature. Every day, you collaborate to understand user needs and work with your team to make ideas real. Gestures are an essential, often underappreciated, part of how you get that work done.

Think, Communicate, Coordinate

Written and spoken language are made up of words. The body talks through movement. Like words, gestures transmit information, invite response, and spark action. A pointing hand signals direction, an arc sketches the shape of the road, and a nod seals agreement. Each movement adds another channel to what words alone leave unfinished.

THE AFFORDANCES OF GESTURES

An *affordance* is what something makes possible. A door handle affords pulling. A button affords pressing. Designers use the term to describe how products or interfaces invite action. When a product's affordances don't match its intended uses, you'll notice (see Figure 2.1)! The design does not afford what it's supposed to do.

FIGURE 2.1

The Carelman coffee pot shows the (misaligned) affordances of the design for use with the body.

Gestures are affordances, too. They are actions that help make thinking, communicating, and coordinating the world around you possible. You want to make use of all their affordances. And a gesture doesn't just do one thing. It can draw on multiple affordances at once—supporting thought, shaping meaning, and aligning attention.

Gestures are more than hand waving. They get work done! 👏

Gestures are physical actions that partner with talk to help people accomplish something together. To make full use of the utility of gestures, it helps to see the body through three overlapping lenses, each with its own set of affordances:

- **The thinking body:** Gestures bring ideas out of the head and into the world, making thought visible and workable.
- **The communicating body:** Gestures sharpen, extend, or even correct what words alone leave vague.
- **The coordinating body:** Gestures organize people, things, and actions so that everyone can act together.

When you see them this way, you appreciate how essential gestures are. Treat them as tools, not flourishes, and you'll see how they drive progress, whether that means surfacing hidden needs in research, reaching clarity in design discussions, or keeping teams aligned in collaboration.

Simply put, they are part of how human beings get things done.

A SHORT HISTORY OF GESTURES

Some of the first direct attention to gestures came from early rhetorical traditions. Gestures were framed within the broader view of effective persuasion and public speaking (Aristotle, Cicero, and Quintilian). Skilled orators mastered the use of words in partnership with the artful coordination of the body (see Figure 2.2). Gestures were used to reinforce words and emphasize spoken ideas. Choreographed use of gestures also aimed to heighten, but not to hijack, emotional responses that added power to the message delivered in language. But moderation was key! Excessive and unruly gestures were seen as needing to be tamed and intelligently mastered. Orators, politicians, and religious leaders, for example, were trained to employ gestures with precision, neither too excessive nor too sparse, as the proper use of gestures reflected character, authority, and discipline.

In Eastern traditions, gestures were valued not just alongside words but often in their absence. In South Asian traditions, mudras, or specific hand shapes paired with gaze and movement, carried shared meanings that conveyed emotions, actions, and entire stories. In Chinese philosophy, bodily expression was also tied to character and moral conduct. Confucius linked moderate gesturing with self-control and virtue, while excess signaled disorder.

continues

A SHORT HISTORY OF GESTURES (continued)

FIGURE 2.2
Statue of Marcus Tullius Cicero in front of the Palace of Justice in Rome.

By the Middle Ages, gestures lost much of their value. They were associated with indulgence, lack of refinement, and even deceptiveness. People were advised to "keep their hands to themselves." Only minimal, trained gestures were deemed acceptable. By the late 19th century, a use for unruly gestures reemerged. They could function, most particularly, as a window into the subconscious. Psychoanalysts spotted the value in this!

And by the mid-20th century, gestures came back into full favor. No longer seen as outbursts or moral slips, they were recognized as constructive. Today, they are understood as tools for communication, thinking, and coordinating, enhancing rather than detracting from human advancement.

And here's the takeaway: gestures are evergreen. They've outlasted centuries of shifting reputations because they're woven into the fabric of humanness. A hand shaping an idea in the air. A circling finger that sparks shared understanding. A gaze that directs attention. These embodied nuances can't be replicated with the same depth in language alone.

The Thinking Body

The *thinking body* is thought in motion. Gestures quietly sketch ideas in the air. They help people work through problems and make sense of complex information. They also often explain what words leave unsaid. Importantly, thinking gestures support everyday reasoning and recollection, like doing mental math to tip a server or visualizing where you parked your car by turning invisible ideas into visible form.

While thinking gestures primarily serve the speaker and help them to organize, structure, and test out ideas in real time, they are visible to you, the hearer. This visibility makes them valuable. The thinking body externalizes thought and, through this action, surfaces aspects of people's mental models and sensory traces of cognition. These gestures reveal how people imagine, reason, and decide. Attending to these gestures lets you go deeper by observing thinking in action and uncovering information that can expand your understanding of others.

The gestures of the thinking body afford three things:

- **Support problem-solving.** They help a person work through their own challenges and test out ideas in real time.
- **Surface tacit knowledge.** They bring forward a person's prior experiences and expectations that may be clear to the speaker but not to the listener, and they are never spoken aloud.
- **Reveal thinking.** They make visible your and others' abstract ideas, reasoning, and features of mental models.

By paying attention to thinking gestures, you can gather insights into people's needs, assumptions, and expectations that language alone may not reveal. That's what it means to go deeper. Ultimately, the thinking body offers you a rich and valuable track of insight that refines your understanding of others and enhances your product journey.

NOTE **GESTURES AS THINKING**

Gestures are integral to how people think and learn. As David McNeill put it, "Gestures are a window into thought." They present a picture of thought in motion and make visible aspects of thinking that are not expressed in words. Foundational research in the field has shown that:

- **Gestures and speech form a single system.** Together they reveal aspects of thought that words alone can't capture.[1]
- **Gestures offload cognitive effort.** Moving the hands helps people solve problems and reason through complexity.[2]
- **Gesturing strengthens memory.** Producing gestures while learning boosts recall and understanding.[3]
- **Gesture–speech mismatches reveal when knowledge is still developing.** When hands and words diverge, it often signals new ideas are forming.[4]

Gestures Support Your Problem-Solving

Thinking gestures help people work through problems in real time. Imagine how to fold a paper airplane that can glide far. With no paper nearby, you start miming the folds in the air. You fold, pause, restart, gesturing your way through a few iterations until the process clicks. You just thought with your hands.

---

1 McNeill (1992) and Kendon (2004) showed that gesture and speech form a single system, emerging together from the same underlying processes of thought and expression.

2 Goldin-Meadow (2011) reviewed dual-task studies showing that people remember more on a concurrent memory task when they gesture while explaining problems than when they do not, indicating that gesture can reduce cognitive load and free working-memory resources during reasoning. Similar effects have been found in spatial reasoning tasks such as mental rotation and spatial visualization (Chu & Kita, 2011), problem-solving with physical or mechanical systems (Garber & Goldin-Meadow, 2002; Perry & Elder, 1997) and scientific models (Stieff, Scopelitis, Lira & DeSutter, 2016), and explanations of dynamic or continuous change (Alibali & Goldin-Meadow, 1993).

3 Experiments show that producing gestures during learning enhances memory and retention relative to speech alone by engaging sensorimotor processes that support memory formation (Cook et al., 2008, 2012; Goldin-Meadow & Beilock, 2010), and recent frameworks link these effects to attention-memory mechanisms (Guo et al., 2025).

4 Gestures often show ideas that haven't yet made it into words. When hands express something different from what they say, it's a strong sign that knowledge is in transition (Church & Goldin-Meadow, 1986; Goldin-Meadow & Alibali, 1993). Making certain gestures can also help lock in new understanding (Goldin-Meadow, 2003; Novack & Goldin-Meadow, 2015).

This kind of gestured problem-solving is both common and useful. Gestures let people test ideas, hold alternatives in play, and discover solutions through action. For example, a packaging designer trying to fit a new phone and a bulkier charger into an existing box design might sketch the arrangement in midair (see Figure 2.3). One balled hand becomes the power brick while the other flattens to represent the phone. By rotating and repositioning, they explore how the components could fit before ever prototyping the plastic mold that will hold them.

FIGURE 2.3
A designer explores ways to fit a new charger and phone into an existing box design.

Thinking gestures help people work out problems, identify glitches, and in the process, become sparks of innovation. When you see someone solving a problem through gestures, it reveals their steps and offers an in-the-moment view of their thinking and whether it's on the right or wrong track.

Gestures Surface Your Tacit Knowledge

Gestures also often act as anchors of prior knowledge. They help people recall personal experience by engaging the body's motor systems. In these moments, the body supports memory retrieval and allows people to "re-experience" something they've done before.

Imagine your parents or grandparents call you because they can't remember how to use the remote on the new TV you got them (see Figure 2.4). You remember using the remote to navigate the channel guide. But what buttons did you press to get there? Your thumb hovers midair and then presses invisible buttons in sequence. You squint a little and think to yourself, that doesn't feel right. You try again, tapping out a different sequence until it clicks. Now you're confident you know what to say!

FIGURE 2.4
People frequently access everyday knowledge, like remembering the buttons on a remote control by replaying prior experiences through the body.

Replaying steps in the body helped you remember critical information before communicating something that might have caused more confusion. Gestures here tapped into the embodied memory of what worked last time. And now everyone can get back to binging their favorite shows.

Gestures don't just recall the past; they surface tacit knowledge and memories, bringing them forward into the current moment. When you see tacit knowledge surface through gesture, you're seeing a direct link between past experience and present needs. This is your cue to dig deeper, as that embodied memory is often the key to understanding someone's current expectations.

Gestures Reveal Others' Thinking

Gestures are not just thinking tools for the speaker; they can also reveal the internal mental processes of others.

There's a common assumption that thinking is hidden, locked away in the mind. But gestures show that's not true, it's actually visible. When you attend to thinking gestures, you also gain a glimpse into someone's cognition. In this way, *gestures are a window into the mind.* They make thought tangible, turning internal deliberation into something you can observe and interpret.

And you can make use of this to go deeper. By strategically observing thinking gestures, you gain more than just a look at someone's problem-solving skills or past experiences. It gives you a front row seat to the underlying architecture of their thoughts: their mental models.

WHAT ARE MENTAL MODELS?

In cognitive science, a mental model is an internal representation of how the world works. It's a small-scale story that people build in their minds to reason, predict, and act without starting from scratch each time. Think of it as a cognitive shortcut for navigating reality.

A critical insight that has emerged from research across disciplines is that mental models are not composed of abstract structures, like lists or flowcharts in your head. Rather, they often contain sensory impressions accreted over years of experience perceiving and acting on the world. This includes visual and motor imagery, touch, smell, and sound. In this more expansive view, a mental model becomes useful when people encounter novel problems and settings because they can replay their prior experiences through mental simulation and seek out similarities to guide their actions. Gestures are a frequent feature of mental simulation, as replaying mental imagery primes movement and produces visible action.

How do you see these mental models in action? You look at the relationship between what a person says and what their hands do.

Sometimes, you'll see moments when gestures and speech match, where they convey the same information. For example, a user might say, "I turn the knob to the right," while making a decisive right-turning motion. This alignment is a strong signal that their mental model is stable.

But often, the most valuable insights come when gesture and speech do not match. When a person's body tells a different story than their words, you get a lot more (see Figure 2.5). For example, a user might say, "You just turn it," while their hand wavers left and right, which reveals that their mental model is unstable or that they are navigating a moment of uncertainty. Or a stakeholder might say, "The AI is working," while circling a finger at their temple, exposing a flawed mental model of the AI "thinking" in the same way a person does. In both situations, gestures become a signal that someone else's understanding is either stable, fragile, or incorrect.

FIGURE 2.5
Brittle knowledge, uncertainty, and other facets of mental models often emerge when speech and gesture convey different information.

For product teams, this observation gives you a measure of how malleable their thinking is and highlights exactly where you might need to probe deeper or refine a concept.

Why the Thinking Body Matters

Paying attention to the thinking body affords you a channel into cognition that words may only partially reveal. Thinking gestures let you see people's problem-solving in real time, their unspoken assumptions, and their hidden mental models, often braided together into a single action.

When you tune into this stream of information, you enable a kind of cognitive empathy that strengthens human-centeredness. Understanding how people think pays off in two key ways: Within your team, you can surface a wider array of ideas during collaboration; with your users, you can pinpoint where an experience truly clicks and where it creates friction. This allows you to create products that are effective not just because they look good, but also because they are designed to complement how people actually think. Gestures help you move beyond designing for what users say and start designing for how they reason.

The Communicating Body

The *communicating body* is meaning in exchange. These gestures are relational, taking place between and among people. Unlike the thinking body, which primarily serves the speaker, the communicating body is often intended for others. Gestures here are about creating shared understanding.

Whether conscious or not, these movements help messages land. By attending to the communicating body, you go deeper by enriching what is said and how it is understood. This helps you get to what another person truly means, and it supports a deeper, more evolved mutual clarity.

The gestures of the communicating body afford three things:

- **Reinforce meaning.** They underline or emphasize what's already been said.
- **Add new meaning.** They supply details or dimensions that speech leaves vague.
- **Fill in for words.** They substitute for talk entirely, fast-tracking alignment or action.

The communicating body offers a dynamic and visible channel that runs alongside words but carries its own weight. For product organizations, tuning into this channel can mean spotting misunderstandings as they emerge, catching details that speech alone leaves unsaid, and reaching the kind of shared clarity that turns scattered talk into full alignment.

NOTE GESTURES FOR COMMUNICATION

Communicative gestures are how people convey nuance, build clarity, and ensure that their message lands. As Adam Kendon observed: "Visible bodily action, including gesture, can play a crucial role in the process of interaction and communication." Research has shown that:

- **Gestures are part of the utterance.** They work with words to shape meaning, not as afterthoughts.[5]
- **Gestures signal pragmatic functions.** They mark transitions, highlight importance, and manage conversational flow.[6]
- **Gestures reveal and reinforce meaning.** They make visible what the speaker wants understood, adding layers that words alone may not capture.[7]
- **Gestures enrich expression.** They emphasize, clarify, and provide nuance, much like intonation in speech.[8]

Gestures Reinforce Meaning

In everyday interactions, gestures often underline and reinforce what words already say. When used in this way, they don't add new content, but they show intensity, priority, and commitment. These are signals that are easy to miss if you only listen to talk or just read a transcript.

5 Kendon (2004) showed that gestures align with the timing and semantic structure of spoken clauses, revealing that speakers plan gesture and speech as a single communicative act.

6 Clark (1996) and Goodwin (2000) documented how subtle bodily movements like hand lifts or gaze shifts serve as pragmatic markers that regulate turn-taking, signal emphasis, and guide how conversations progress.

7 McNeill (1992) demonstrated that gestures often express imagistic details of a speaker's meaning, such as motion, shape, or spatial relationships that remain unspoken but are essential to understanding the thought behind the words.

8 Fricke (2013, 2014) argues that gesture and speech form a unified grammatical system: gestures supply deictic cues, emphasis, and embodied nuance that spoken prosody alone cannot carry, enriching how meaning is packaged and interpreted.

Imagine a strategic planning meeting just after leadership has passed down an urgent new business target, reconfiguring the quarterly roadmap. The engineering lead needs his team to understand how this changes their priorities for tackling technical debt. He says, "This means we have to refactor the authentication service before we touch the database indexing." As he speaks, he uses the tips of his fingers to slice the air, enacting a sharp, downward chop, separating the first task from the second (see Figure 2.6).

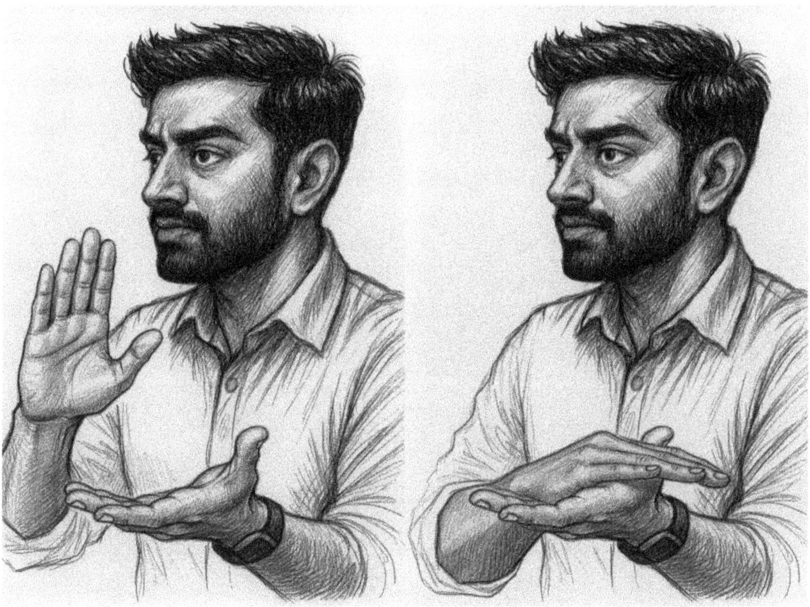

FIGURE 2.6
An engineering manager emphasizes the priority of addressing a particular backlog item, reinforced by his gesture.

The words alone communicate the sequence. The gesture, however, communicates the finality. It adds no new information but reinforces the message with unmistakable intensity. The hand movement visually severs any other possibility, signaling that this order is a hard constraint, not a suggestion.

Reinforcing gestures are priority markers. They show where emphasis lies, what matters most, and how committed someone is to their point. Noticing them keeps people aligned on what really counts.

SHARED MEANING IS NOT UNIVERSAL

There are cultural variations in gestures that are important to be aware of. Many of you likely did not take offense to the 👍 thumbs-up emoji. But some may have. A simple thumbs-up almost ubiquitously signifies approval in many Western cultures. However, in parts of the Middle East and Greece, it was once construed as obscene. These vestiges may still linger. If a very talented member of your team is from the Middle East, a thumbs-up may be interpreted as "up yours." Similarly, the "OK" sign, positive in the U.S., may earn you a dirty look in Brazil for its vulgarity.

Some cultures invite more gesturing while others play it down. When in Japan or Northern Europe, you may experience a more reserved approach to gesture use than you will in Italy or Spain, where highly expressive hands, faces, and bodies are embedded in the cultural repertoire. (These expressive cultural gestures have a name, often called *Italianate gestures*.) Awareness of these cultural nuances is essential for establishing respect and building rapport. Understanding how gestures shift in meaning across cultures prevents misunderstandings and fosters respectful interactions. Pay attention to those hand signals. They often speak volumes!

Keep an eye on those cultural gestures and use them appropriately. Not being aware could be the end of a potentially valuable exchange. 👌

Gestures Add New Information

Gestures can do more than reinforce words; they can expand them. The gestures you most want to catch are the ones that add something new. These complementary movements supply critical details you'd miss if you only listened to words alone.

Imagine two designers are reviewing the assembly for a new flat-pack bookshelf. One designer expresses a concern about a key joint. "I'm worried this joint will fail over time," she says. "A simple screw won't be enough here." As she speaks, she holds her hands perpendicular to each other, wobbling them back and forth to show the side-to-side racking stress the shelf will endure. Then her colleague mimes a different solution. He balls up his right hand in a tight fist and stacks a cup-shaped left hand to cradle the fist. He then rotates his hand until it abruptly stops and locks in. The first designer asks, "Do you mean a cam lock?" (See Figure 2.7.) He nods, and the two continue discussing how this would help better lock the two planes of the shelf together.

FIGURE 2.7
Two designers discuss the structural issues with a bookcase design, using gestures to align on the need for a sturdier locking mechanism.

Her words stated the problem in general terms: the joint will "fail," but her hands demonstrated the lateral stress. His hands then elaborated on how to address the issue they identified. His gesture demonstrated the specific rotational stress of everyday use and then mimed the "twist-and-lock" action of the cam, showing exactly how it counters that force. The gesture supplied the crucial detail of the locking interaction of the hardware that their words left out.

Gestures that add new meaning are value multipliers. They enrich communication by making complex or abstract ideas concrete. When words fall short, the hands can supply the missing dimensions, clarifying intent and rounding out the message. Catch them and you gain clarity. Miss them and you lose the very nuance that makes a solution work.

Gestures Fill In for Words

Sometimes, gestures do more than complement words. They take over the work of speech altogether. A quick checkmark motion over an open palm can signal a request for the restaurant bill. No words needed. The server brings you the bill.

Imagine a retail chain trying to speed up checkout lines during the holiday rush. A customer hovers their credit card over a new payment terminal, ready to tap. He waits, glances at the screen and at the side, then looks up at the cashier and says, "Could you help with this?" As he speaks, he taps his phone against his palm.

The cashier understands immediately. "Oh, these new systems moved the sensor," she says, rotating the payment terminal toward the man and tapping the air above it (see Figure 2.8).

FIGURE 2.8
A man requests help with using a payment terminal in gesture, communicating to the cashier that he's unsure where to tap without that being clear in his talk.

The words "Could you help with this?" could mean almost anything. But the gesture filled in the object of the customer's plea and showed that they couldn't find where to tap for contactless pay. (Notice the answer came in gestures, too!)

When gestures fill in for words, they communicate wholly, without speaking a word. This can fast-track interactions and speed up an exchange. When a gesture without words goes unseen or gets dismissed, it can send the interaction in the wrong direction and require rounds of clarification, or worse, lead to incorrect assumptions.

NOTE HOW PEOPLE SIGNAL EMOTION AND STANCE

A shrug signals uncertainty or indifference. A pounding fist shows frustration. A sideward glance can project disinterest. Fast tapping fingers reveal impatience. These gestures don't expand content, but they show how someone feels or their emotional stance in the moment.

Why the Communicating Body Matters

Paying attention to the communicating body affords you a channel into the collaborative space where shared understanding is built. Communicating gestures let you see how a vague idea is given precision, how a priority is given emphasis, and how a simple statement is enriched with new detail, all within the live exchange between people. They are the tools you and others use to negotiate meaning together.

When you tune into this stream of information, you improve the speed and quality of understanding and, in turn, collaboration in your product journey. This is because gestures enable a kind of collaborative precision. If you and others are aligned not just on the words but on the rich detail behind them, you prevent the costly rework that comes from building on an incomplete idea. Gestures can help you move beyond capturing what one person says and start building on what your team or users truly mean.

The Coordinating Body

The *coordinating body* is interaction in flow. These are the public, visible gestures that direct attention, manage rhythm, and make collaboration possible. Unlike the thinking or communicating body, these gestures live in the shared space between people, things, and ideas. They are meant to be seen and used to direct action.

By visibly weaving together parts into a whole, coordinating gestures allow you and others to orient to one another and the social-material environment, stay attuned, and build shared understanding as work unfolds. Attending to the coordinating body lets you distribute effort and stay synchronized, as people move work forward fluidly.

The gestures of the coordinating body afford two primary functions:

- **Guide conversations within the social environment.** These gestures help people manage the live rhythm of talk and action. For example, they signal when to continue, clarify, or close a conversation while maintaining flow.

- **Link tools and ideas in the material environment.** These gestures connect people to what matters most in their shared physical space. For example, they bring scattered elements into a shared field by anchoring attention to, for example, screens, prototypes, and sticky notes.

The coordinating body offers a live view of collaboration in motion. It shows how people stitch ideas, artifacts, and actions together across shared spaces. For product teams, tuning into this layer means seeing how understanding actually takes shape—how focus shifts, alignment forms, and work moves forward. When you can see those patterns, you can guide them with intent, deepening comprehension and helping groups reach meaningful progress faster.

NOTE GESTURES FOR COORDINATING

Coordinating gestures are how people manage attention, align actions, and bring shared work into focus:

- **Gestures organize joint action.** They align people's movements, speech, and gaze, enabling shared focus and synchronizing activity.[9]
- **Gestures link talk to tools.** They connect what's said to the physical world and artifacts that ground collaboration.[10]
- **Gestures manage timing and rhythm.** They cue turn-taking, signal shifts, and maintain the flow of conversation and work.[11]
- **Gestures synchronize the social and material surround.** They knit together people, things, and ideas so that understanding and effort move as one.[12]

---

9 Goodwin (2000) showed that in collaborative tasks people use gesture, gaze, and body orientation to assemble a shared field of action, effectively "building" a workspace together.

10 Goodwin (2007) documented how professionals like archaeologists and air-traffic workers use gestures to anchor talk to physical artifacts, turning objects into active participants in reasoning. Streeck (2009) extended this by showing how everyday speakers lean on nearby tools, screens, and surfaces to make their ideas graspable to others.

11 Kendon (2004) traced how gesture and speech form an integrated temporal system, revealing that movements often anticipate or shape upcoming turns in talk.

12 People recruit bodies, objects, and space to coordinate courses of action, allowing groups to "think together" through the integration of talk, movement, and material arrangements (Goodwin, 2013; Streeck, 2013); (Goodwin & LeBaron, 2011). In disciplinary learning, Stieff, Scopelitis, and Lira (2022) show how people's embodied actions align peers, tools, and representations to support shared reasoning.

Gestures Guide Conversations

Conversations are full of unspoken choreography. Coordinating gestures keep people in sync and ideas in flow by managing the live rhythm of talk. Gestures, gaze, and small shifts in posture help everyone see what's happening in real time and adjust to one another without stopping to explain.

Imagine a research readout where a researcher is explaining a participant's reaction during a usability test. She's halfway through her point when the product manager, wanting to add a crucial detail, leans forward slightly and lifts a single finger (see Figure 2.9). It's a quiet, unspoken bid to speak. Catching this signal, the researcher finishes her sentence and gives a slight nod his way, ceding the floor. The PM picks up seamlessly: "Right. And I would add it was hesitation, not frustration." The exchange happens without interruption or awkward overlap. A few subtle movements keep the rhythm intact.

FIGURE 2.9

A raised finger and a nod coordinate a smooth handoff in conversation between a researcher and a product manager.

When you see these signals, the lean, the nod, the hand raise, you see how conversation is not just words exchanged in time. It happens when you actively shape the flow of dialogue with others. By reading and responding to these gestures, you can ensure that discussions are more inclusive, that crucial clarifications happen in the moment, and that the rhythm of team collaboration moves fluidly forward.

Gestures Link Up External Resources

Just as coordinating gestures guide the flow of talk, they also link it to the material world around you. In collaborative work, people don't only talk! They point, trace, tap, and turn toward things. These gestures connect words to the shared environment, pulling attention to what matters most in that moment. A gesture toward a screen, a sketch, or a sticky note can instantly orient everyone to the same idea and ground abstract discussion in something visible and shared.

Picture a user in an interview explaining how she manages photos between her work phone and personal laptop (see Figure 2.10). "It's a mess," she says, spreading her fingers and circling her right hand loosely over the laptop screen to illustrate the clutter. Then she lifts her phone with her left hand, jutting it between herself and the interviewer. "I just need to get these over here," she explains, and holds up the phone again to emphasize "these" and repeats her circle gesture with her right hand while saying "here." The gestures link her words to the visual referents, directing everyone's attention to the external tools in her organization process.

Next, she begins describing how she wants the photos organized once they're synced. "I want my family photos over here," she says, balling her right hand into a loose fist and hovering it over the top-right corner of the computer screen. "And my work photos here," she adds, sliding her right fisted hand toward the left corner to create a second, distinct pile. Her hands give visible form to the abstract categories she's describing, mapping her idea of order into the digital space in front of her.

Coordinating gestures create a shared field for interaction. They make unseen connections visible. They link talk to things and abstract ideas to concrete points in space. Without them, you'd only hear "It's a mess." With them, you see a user's expectations for organizing files and how the current tool does not meet those needs. These gestures align attention and environment and turn vague talk into actionable insight.

FIGURE 2.10
The user explains the challenge of organizing her photos between her laptop and phone and how to effectively separate them into two piles.

Why the Coordinating Body Matters

Paying attention to the coordinating body gives you a channel into how action takes shape. Coordinating gestures regulate attention and align effort so that people and ideas move together. They turn talk into momentum, keeping focus steady and work in flow. A lean can invite a turn in talk, a point grounds a conversation, and a nod signals closure. Each small action helps maintain rhythm and keeps collective progress visible.

When you tune in to this layer, you gain a practical tool for guiding work as it happens. Coordinating gestures help you draw people in, time your responses, and link ideas to the resources that matter most. They let you build alignment without stopping the flow. They reveal how users coordinate with their surroundings, and they keep collaboration fluid and focused. The coordinating body gives you a way to move work forward efficiently while staying connected to meaning as it unfolds. Gestures are the quiet engine of collective momentum.

The Three Bodies Talk Together

The thinking, communicating, and coordinating bodies don't do their work in isolation. The affordances of all three bodies work together to get something done (see Figure 2.11). This matters!

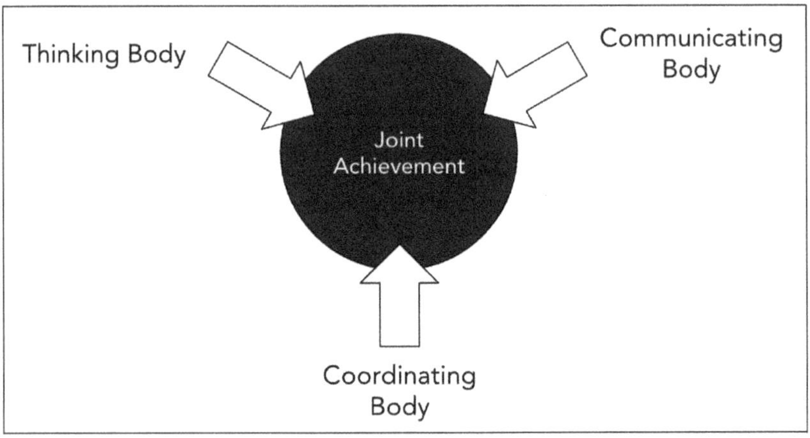

FIGURE 2.11
The three bodies function as an integrated system, working together moment by moment to support joint achievement.

The three bodies and their affordances form an interconnected channel of information that reveals how people think, where meaning takes shape, and how alignment in action emerges.

They often overlap and build on one another, sliding fluidly between roles to move toward joint achievement. A gesture that begins as a tool for thought can, in the same motion, become a communicative cue that redirects attention and reorganizes how people connect. When you treat gestures as tools, you gain access to a resource that's always with you—no extra toolbox required.

Gestures become part of your toolkit on every path in the product journey (see Table 2.1).

TABLE 2.1 THE CONTRIBUTION OF GESTURES ON EACH PATH OF THE PRODUCT JOURNEY

Path	Goal	Contribution of Gesture
Research path	Deepen user understanding.	Gestures reveal genuine user insights and pain points.
Collaboration path	Strengthens teamwork and ensures inclusive decision-making.	Gestures establish belonging and strengthen team inclusivity.
Design path	Translates insights into intuitive, effective experiences.	Gestures surface and explain ideas; test out concepts before you build them; and explore and advance design possibilities.
Innovation path	Explores novel possibilities and challenges assumptions.	Gestures fuel innovation by revealing how people map new ideas onto existing experience, exposing friction and opportunities.

When you learn to see gestures as tools with multiple affordances, you expand your reach as a member of a product organization. You stop overrelying on words and start working with the full range of human expression and action. That shift is what makes ideas clearer, collaboration stronger, and innovations more likely to stick.

NOTE SIMULTANEOUS AFFORDANCES OF A GESTURE

The same gestures can cover more than one affordance simultaneously. A gesture that begins as a tool for thought can instantly become a signal for others. A communicative gesture can redirect attention and, in the same motion, reorganize how a team connects. The affordances overlap, build on each other, and slide between roles, moving work toward joint achievement.

Listen Up, the Body's Talking

The thinking, communicating, and coordinating bodies each do their part. Together, they give you a toolkit for understanding, designing, and collaborating more effectively across every path in the product journey.

In many other disciplines, gestures already play intentional roles. For example, in education, they support teaching and learning. In cognitive science, they are used to explore how people think. In medicine, they serve to communicate intent and coordinate action in a high-stakes environment. In law and politics, gestures are a form of persuasion. They punctuate arguments, command attention, and amplify conviction. (Skilled politicians rehearse gestures as deliberately as their words.)

Yet in product, design, and UX, gestures remain underused. You capture words, clicks, and paths, but the body's work often goes underutilized. The body offers affordances for every stage of the product journey—from research, to design, collaboration, and innovation. Treat gestures as data, as design material, and as collaborative resources. To overlook them is to ignore a range of action already available to you that's ready to make your work sharper, faster, and more human.

Takeaways

- **Gestures are functional tools, not decoration.** Gestures are the body's affordances for getting work done. Whether giving directions, holding a meeting, or designing a product, gestures are used to think through problems, create shared meaning, and coordinate action, making them essential to achieving any shared goal.
- **Thinking is made visible through gestures.** The thinking body makes cognition observable, externalizing thought so it can be worked with. Thinking gestures allow people to problem-solve in real time, access embodied knowledge from past experiences, and reveal the structure of their mental models. Thinking gestures become especially revealing when they mismatch the words people utter.
- **Communication is incomplete without the body.** The communicating body creates shared understanding where words alone fall short. Communicating gestures are used to reinforce the priority of a message, add critical details that speech leaves out, or substitute for language entirely. Paying attention to them is key to ensuring that a complete and precise message is both sent and received.
- **Joint action is orchestrated by the body.** The coordinating body organizes how people work together by managing attention and flow. Coordinating gestures direct the rhythm of interaction without interruption and ground abstract talk by physically linking it to the shared environment. They are the visible engine of alignment and momentum in any collaborative setting.
- **Treat gestures as levers, not just background behavior.** You are already innately skilled at reading the body's signals in everyday interaction. The challenge is to elevate this skill to a conscious practice by using gestures as something to see and use to push your product work forward.

FIELD NOTES FROM STEPHANIE

I was working with a team of curriculum designers to develop a biology lesson on fish for elementary students. My first task was to understand the concept well enough to design a simulation app. Mara, a research biologist, began explaining how fish gills function. "So, you have the fish, right?" she said, opening her hand with her thumb tucked toward her palm and her fingers loosely spread.

In that moment, I watched the communicating body at work. Mara's gesture filled in for words, giving form to an idea introduced verbally. The shape of her hand showed me the spatial structure of the gill with its openings. Her movement didn't replace speech; it extended it. Mara then pushed her hand into the space between us. "This," she continued, "is the gill." As her hand stayed suspended between us, I recognized that the coordinating body was in play. She wanted me to see her hand, so I shifted my gaze to it. In that instant, her movement organized my attention, coordinating a common frame of reference to a handmade representation that communicated the shape of the gills.

Then, with a small forward thrust of the gestured hand, she asked, "What does this get you?" The movement marked a shift in turn-taking, opening the floor for me to respond. Her question was both verbal and embodied. The gesture itself not only invited my participation, but it also signaled to me to make use of it. Here, the coordinating body signaled to me to pick up the gesture and continue the exploration.

I mirrored her hand shape, adding a soft flutter of my fingers to imagine how the gills might move across water (see Figure 2.12). The affordance of my gesture was different from hers. It wasn't working to communicate or coordinate anymore. It was intended to be used for problem-solving. Here, the thinking body took over. I drew the gesture closer to me, into my own space, where I could experiment and reason through the idea taking shape.

FIGURE 2.12
Mara presses the gesture into the shared interaction space for Stephanie to see (left); Stephanie uses her hands to think through a concept (right).

My left hand became the fish; my right hand, the water. The fluttering fingers of my right hand traced my mental model of how water might flow through the gills. My **thinking body** was active, helping me reason through the relationship before the words fully arrived. Softly, I said, "The way the water moves must have something to do with bringing in oxygen." Mara watched my hands, seeing my reasoning unfold. The gesture I made for myself, my **thinking gesture**, was also visible to her. It became a bridge, simultaneously serving the **communicating body**, making my thoughts available for her to see. Without any need for further explanation, Mara nodded in confirmation. That small movement of her head, a response of the **coordinating body**, let us both know that understanding had been reached.

In this moment, I experienced how the body's affordances intertwine and how gestures partner with talk to help two people arrive at a joint achievement of understanding.

FIELD NOTES FROM DANE

Early in my research career, I studied how students learn to mentally transform molecules in organic chemistry. The task sounds abstract, but it is fundamental: take a molecule drawn one way and redraw it from a different vantage point (see Figure 2.13). Understanding three-dimensional space and its operations is a core competency in the discipline, one that shapes how chemists reason about reactions.

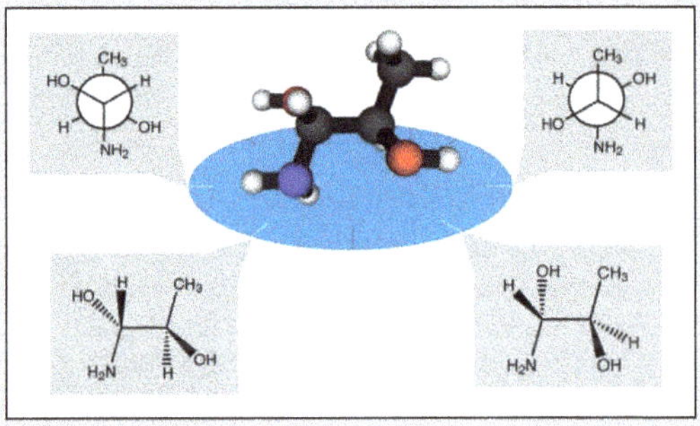

FIGURE 2.13
Equivalent structural diagrams of the organic molecule *(1R,2R)*-1-aminopropane-1,2-diol.

Going in, I had a hypothesis that students would all approach the task largely the way I do: mentally "pick up" the whole molecule and rotate it.

I was wrong. As I watched students work through the task and talk through their reasoning, I paid close attention to their hands. What I saw wasn't a singular strategy but the signature of three distinct approaches.

Some students did what I had predicted. Their hands lifted and turned in space, grabbing the molecule and rotating it around a central axis. You could see the molecule rotating holistically in their gesture. This was the **thinking body** at work, externalizing a complete spatial mental model, making the invisible rotation visible.

But where it got interesting were the students who did something different. For some, rather than imagining the whole molecule moving, they locked onto a single atom, often one that was visually prominent—depicted large, a different color, or projecting into or out of the plane of the diagram. Their gestures traced the trajectory of that one referent atom rather than the whole structure. Their strategy was still spatial, but piecemeal. The thinking body was again doing the work of reasoning but revealing a more nuanced mental model of rotation.

Then there was a third group. These students moved their hands across the diagram itself, pointing to labels and tracing symbol positions on the page. Their gestures stayed flat, in two dimensions. What they described as "rotating" the molecule was, in gesture, nothing more than rearranging labels. The molecular structure never extruded into three-dimensional space.

What struck me was that all three groups used nearly the same words. Rotate. Translate. Move this over here. Reading a transcript alone, you might conclude they understood the task in broadly similar ways. But the gestures told a completely different story. A student could say, "I rotate the molecule," while their hands showed what that actually meant.

Without attending to the gestures, I would have missed that variation entirely. It was the thinking body that gave me access to how each student was actually reasoning, not just how they could describe it. Watching their hands, I could see where understanding was solid, where it was partial, and where the three-dimensional structure of the task had never really taken hold. That is a level of insight that language, on its own, will often struggle to provide.

How are there are seventeen options? I can never remember what I get...
Do you remember how much milk is in a cappuccino versus a latte?
You ask this every time! You always like it more...
...equal. Right!
I'll have a cappuccino... a grande.
Oh, of course. Coming right up!
LA GRANDE
SEASONAL DRINK
132 oz SHARABLE!
One "La Grande" for Dane!
I'm not sure what I ordered. It also cost five times my usual...
I bet he didn't see you point. Go order again and see if you can get us a giant donut, too!

CHAPTER 3

How to "See" Gestures

When you start paying attention to gestures, suddenly they seem to be here, there, and everywhere. A flick of the finger catches your eye. You notice a subtle downward gaze. You're keenly aware of your crossed arms and tilted head. A raised eyebrow, a balled fist, a circling finger, a tap of the toe. All these movements seem to jump out at you.

At first, this heightened awareness is dizzying. The sheer number of gestures, both yours and others', can be overwhelming. But remember that gestures are tools that get work done. The body's affordances to support thinking, communicating, and coordinating drive product work! But in the middle of a fast-paced user interview or a chaotic design session, how do you spot these bodies at work? How do you filter the meaningful movements from those that fade into the background without distraction?

The good news is that you already discern the value of a gesture instinctively. When someone shakes their head in response to a question, your brain instantly registers the side-to-side motion as "no." But discerning the gestures that allow you to go deeper requires cultivating an intentional way of "seeing" the gestures that matter.

Spotting Gestures That Matter

What are gestures that matter? They are the specific movements that surface insight, clarify meaning, and spark new direction. Spotting them involves knowing your goal in the moment and attending to the dimensions of gestures.

Your goal is the outcome you are trying to achieve as you advance on your product journey. Whether you're trying to gain a deeper user insight, clarify an idea in a meeting, or align your team, knowing what you are trying to accomplish will direct your attention to the gestures that are most relevant for advancing your work.

Once a relevant gesture catches your attention, attend to its dimensions to confirm its value and uncover its contribution to the moment. The dimensions you want to attend to are the following:

- **Space:** Look at the physical space where a gesture happens, and you will see its affordances and intent. This will tell you whether the gesture is working to support thinking, enhance communication, or guide the coordination of people, things, and ideas. This space will also clue you into who the gestures are for—the speaker, the hearer, or both.

- **Gesture-speech alignment:** Listen to the speech that accompanies gestures to hear potential meaning. Remember to focus on the mismatches when the words don't align with the gestures (see Chapter 2, "How the Body Talks").
- **The gesture's type and function:** Look at the shape and motion of the gesture to see its particular function in the moment. Look for whether it is representing an object or idea, directing conversation or attention, or revealing an affect.

When you look at gestures both through the lens of your goals and their dimensions, you will filter and sort each gesture and end up with the ones that matter.

NOTE GESTURES THAT MATTER

Gestures that matter are the movements of the body that go beyond words to reveal thoughts, enhance communication, deepen collaboration, and expand thinking and ultimately advance your work along the product journey.

Your Goals Are Your Filter

You can't attend to every gesture. And you certainly do not want to. Some hold value and others do not. To filter to the ones that matter, frame your awareness by the goals that drive your work.

Those goals become clearer when you situate your work within the larger product journey. Your journey toward your product North Star depends on achieving smaller, specific objectives along the way. These objectives often align with one of four key paths in the product journey: research, collaboration, design, or innovation.

Along any of these paths, you'll encounter moments where meaningful gestures emerge—in conversations with users, brainstorming sessions with colleagues, or presentations to stakeholders. Knowing your goals acts as your first-pass filter for recognizing the gestures that matter. Therefore, it's essential to know what path you are on in the product journey. Within that path, ask yourself: *What problem are you trying to solve right now?*

For example, if you want to understand your users' pain points, you are likely on the research path. You will want to prioritize gestures that occur in conversation with your users—thinking gestures that reveal their mental models and tacit expectations, communicating gestures that add specificity to vague descriptions, and coordinating gestures that physically ground their problems.

Table 3.1 provides you with a guide for the gestures to focus on depending on where you are in the product journey.

TABLE 3.1 THE GESTURES THAT MATTER ON EACH PATH OF THE PRODUCT JOURNEY

Path	Goal	Gestures to Notice
Research Path	Deepen user understanding.	• **Thinking gestures** that reveal users' mental models, expectations, or moments of confusion. • **Communicating gestures** that add specificity to vague descriptions or show what users mean. • **Coordinating gestures** that physically ground problems in tools, spaces, or sequences of action.
Collaboration Path	Strengthen teamwork and ensure inclusive decision-making.	• **Thinking gestures** that show emerging ideas or active problem-solving. • **Communicating gestures** that express agreement, disagreement, uncertainty, or requests for clarification. • **Coordinating gestures** that manage turn-taking, link people to artifacts, or organize the flow of the conversation.
Design Path	Translate insights into intuitive, effective experiences and things.	• **Thinking gestures** that work through a design problem or make an abstract idea concrete. • **Communicating gestures** that explain design concepts, interactions, or intended user experiences. • **Coordinating gestures** that link sketches, prototypes, and other artifacts to shared understanding.
Innovation Path	Explore novel possibilities and challenge assumptions.	• **Thinking gestures** that reveal the stable ways people make sense of the world, including the embodied patterns that persist even as their environments change. • **Communicating gestures** that reveal whether an innovation fits people's social expectations, like showing where users feel at ease, and where they resist. • **Coordinating gestures** that show whether an innovation works with the body, like whether interactions feel physically sustainable, intuitive to navigate, and integrated into how people already organize their actions.

Another important mechanism for filtering the gestures that matter is to note that everyone has habitual gestures. Some may look meaningful at first, but after extended observation, you may realize that a thumb-and-finger tap or oft-repeated shrug is simply part of someone's personal repertoire rather than a gesture with specific intent. Recognizing and setting aside these stylistic gestures helps you focus on those that truly carry meaning.

Grab your field notebook. Open your eyes. And let the search begin!

Watch the Space

Where a gesture happens tells you who it is for and what it affords. And this, in turn, helps you determine who it is serving and how—whether it is serving to help someone think, communicate, or coordinate.

Gestures typically appear in three primary spaces (see Figure 3.1), each space signaling its potential affordance.

- **Space of the person:** Gestures that occur close to the body act as a thinking tool for the speaker. These gestures support problem-solving and surface tacit knowledge. These gestures are for the speaker but are visible. If you look at them, you will see other people thinking in motion.
- **Space between people:** Gestures that occur in the space between speakers act as a communication tool. These gestures reinforce meaning, add new information, and fill in for words. If you look at them, you'll see resources for building ideas together, regulating conversation, and maintaining connection.
- **Space among things:** Gestures that occur in the space among things act as a coordinating tool. These gestures guide conversations and link up external resources. If you look at them, you will see how people link others, objects, and the surrounding environment.

When you pay attention to the space where a gesture happens, you recognize what affordances are at play. This helps you understand how a gesture is serving your goals.

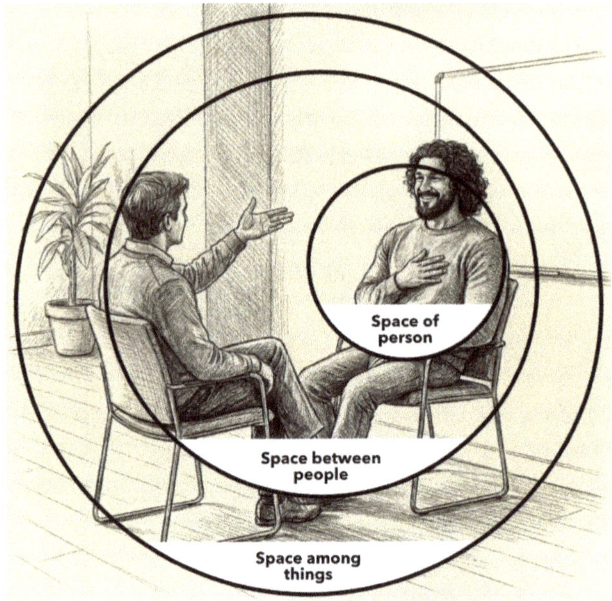

FIGURE 3.1
Gesture space is defined around an individual speaker, between individuals, and in the broader social and material environment.

PRACTICE TIME

SURVEYING THE SPACE

Let's practice identifying the space of gestures! Imagine that you've walked into Espresso Yourself with your copy of *Body Talk*, and you notice Dane and Stephanie walk in. (You can't believe you've bumped into them out in the wild! 🤩) You take the opportunity to sharpen your observation skills by practicing how to see gestures that matter. You settle into a corner with a coffee cup full, your field notebook in hand, and the dimensions fresh in mind. Your goal right now is to identify the space of gestures produced by the thinking, communicating, and coordinating body. You begin to watch.

Dane glances at Stephanie and then at his hands, "Do you remember how much milk is in a cappuccino versus a latte?" Then he stacks his hands to show the milk's height. Stephanie rolls her eyes as she balances her own palms as if weighing two cups. "You always like it more...," she says. Dane finishes her sentence, "...equal. Right!" (see Figure 3.2). Assured, Dane turns to the barista: "I'll have a cappuccino...grande," pointing toward the cup on display.

FIGURE 3.2

Dane and Steph clarify their order by using gestures.

You look at your field notebook full of scattered words and half-drawn images. You noticed that both speakers used gestures throughout that fell into the three spaces: the space of the speaker, the space between speakers, and the space among things. Now test yourself! Identify the space and role of each gesture (see Figure 3.3). (Bonus if you can identify who the gesture is for!)

***#1:** Dane thinks about milk ratio.* ***#2:** Stephanie discusses balance.* ***#3:** Dane points to display cup.*

FIGURE 3.3

Key gestures from Dane and Stephanie's interaction.

Answers: (1) Space of speaker → This is a thinking gesture for Dane to recall his favorite drink, and Stephanie sees it. (2) Space between people → This is a communicating gesture for Stephanie and Dane to land on the right milk/espresso ratio. (3) Space among things → This is a coordinating gesture for Dane and the barista to direct his attention.

Simple enough, right? Well done! 👏

Track the Speech

Valuable gestures often emerge alongside language. On their own, gestures can be ambiguous, but speech provides the context that makes them interpretable. When you look at whether speech and gesture match or mismatch, you can begin to decide if a gestural moment is worth digging into for deeper meaning.

When gestures align with speech, the words anchor the movement, reinforcing their meaning. Imagine someone saying, "The ball is rolling down the hill," while enacting a rolling motion with their hand. Here, the gesture and speech work together to make the message clearer and more vivid. This pairing is called a *match*. Although worth noticing, they aren't telling you more than what you know from words. So, toss them! Keep your attention on mismatches.

When gestures and speech don't align, this pairing is called a *mismatch*. A mismatch is a strong clue that a gesture worth capturing has just emerged. When the words say one thing and the gestures "say" another, something more is being revealed. For example, if someone says, "You separate the two parts," as their hands perform a rotating motion. The gesture adds new information, revealing that separating the parts requires twisting them against each other.

Often, you will see a mismatch when someone is confused. For example, they might say, "I'm going left," while their hand points to the right. The contradiction itself is a clue worth exploring and noting.

Mismatches are a potential gold mine. They reveal unspoken thoughts, cognitive processes, and mental models that words alone leave hidden. You'll notice them across all three bodies of gesture: in thinking as people work through ideas, in communication as meaning is negotiated between speakers, and in coordination as those meanings are grounded in the surrounding environment. These moments where gesture and speech mismatch will signal opportunity to clarify ambiguity, expose underlying assumptions, and move toward deeper understanding. Keep these mismatches! Put them in your field notes and remember that *words + mismatched gestures = deeper meaning.*

Spotting Mismatches

In the space between the words people speak and the gestures they perform lies a deeper layer of meaning. When you notice a mismatch between the two, it's often a clue that something is worth looking at more closely. These mismatches can uncover deeper meaning.

Here are some examples of what gesture-speech mismatches can do (see Figure 3.4).

FIGURE 3.4

A gesture-speech mismatch can surface across a wide range of human experience, from unspoken emotions and tacit conceptions to spatial reasoning and active problem-solving.

In all these examples, the gesture-speech mismatch signals something unfinished—information that deserves to be explored because it can make, break, enrich, or expand understanding. When someone expresses one conception in their words and another in their hands, their idea isn't yet fully aligned or articulated. The mismatch reveals this gap and invites you to look closer to uncover what's still forming beneath the surface. Unlike the gestures you tossed, you want to keep these!

PRACTICE TIME

TRACKING GESTURE AND SPEECH

Let's return to your field notebook and the scene of Dane, Stephanie, and the barista. Now review the same gestures you collected and further inspect them for clues in the words that were exchanged alongside them (see Figure 3.5). With what you've learned, you're ready to go deeper. Was there a match or a mismatch in what Dane and Stephanie said and what their gestures depicted? What deeper meaning, if any, do they hint at?

***#1:** "How much milk is in each of these?"*

***#2:** "You always prefer it more [equal]."*

***#3:** "I'll have a large."*

FIGURE 3.5

Key gestures from Dane and Stephanie's interaction aligned to the concurrent speech.

Answers: (1) Mismatch → This is a gesture that makes "how much milk" more specific by showing height in cup, adding deeper meaning by revealing the source of Dane's confusion. (2) Mismatch → This is a gesture that makes "equal" a matter of balance between coffee and milk, adding deeper meaning by clarifying Steph's tacit conception about Dane's drink preference. (3) Match → This is a gesture that points to the cup that Dane mentioned, no deeper meaning added.

The relationship of talk and gesture contributes to fuller meaning than if attending to words individually. Good job! 🙌

Determine the Gesture Type and Function

Now that you've mined both space and speech, you can begin narrowing in on a single gesture's function in the moment. Start by determining its type and then look more closely at what it is doing in context. This will confirm that this is a gesture that matters and further refine your understanding of its contribution.

As you know, gestures afford thinking, communicating, and coordinating. A gesture's affordances are what it *can do*. A gesture's function is what it specifically *is doing* in a moment. Because people use the body's affordances in regular, patterned ways, distinct gesture types have emerged to capture those common functions.

Gestures can be slotted into three functional types:

- Representational gestures
- Pragmatic gestures
- Affective gestures

By determining the immediate function, you move from a vague sense that a gesture is important to a precise understanding of what it is doing in that moment and how it functions in the achievement of the current and long-term goals.

You want to keep in mind that different gestures come forward in different settings. In user interviews, for example, representational gestures often dominate as people describe ideas or processes. On the other hand, in collaborative sessions, pragmatic gestures like pointing, hand offs, or rhythmic beats help manage flow and attention. Staying aware of the context helps you interpret what the gesture is doing.

Representational Gestures

When you see gestures that depict a thing, an action, or an idea, you're spotting a movement drawing on the affordances of the body to think and communicate, known as a *representational gesture.* The two flavors of representational gestures that you encounter are the following:

- **Concrete representational gestures function to depict specific, tangible objects or actions.** They align closely with the physical features of what they represent. For instance, a rounded fist becomes a ball, or a finger tracing a square outlines a window.

- **Abstract representational gestures function to convey conceptual or metaphorical ideas.** They lack a direct physical counterpart. For instance, palms pressed together can suggest finality, or pedaling hands can infer motion or ongoing effort.

Representational gestures are movements that can make the invisible visible. They transform unseen or unavailable objects, actions, and ideas into visible form and give shape to thoughts. These often occur in the space of the speaker and the space between people and are easily seen by others. Here are some examples of what representational gestures can depict (see Figure 3.6).

FIGURE 3.6

Representational gestures bring the unseen into view by giving physical form to imagined objects, actions, and abstract ideas.

Pragmatic Gestures

When you see gestures that appear to manage conversation, guide attention, or organize how people work together, you're spotting a pragmatic gesture. Pragmatic gestures are task-oriented movements that draw on the affordances of the communicating and coordinating body. They let you see how people regulate interaction and maintain flow. And they often appear in the space between people and among things. The common variants of pragmatic gestures you will encounter are the following:

- **Gestures that regulate interactions** function to guide the flow of conversation and organize thinking.
- **Gestures that support mutual understanding** function to align perspectives and get everyone on the same page.
- **Gestures that link up people, things, and actions** function to connect resources in the social and material environment, helping coordinate what comes next.

Pragmatic gestures are the body's task-oriented tools for managing the flow and clarity of an interaction. They function to regulate the conversation, support mutual understanding, and organize the surrounding environment. When you see these gestures, you see how people organize interaction without words. Here are some examples of what pragmatic gestures can do (see Figure 3.7).

In all these examples, pragmatic gestures reveal the work of collaboration itself. They are the signals that determine whether an interaction flows smoothly, stalls out, or finds a new direction. When people use these gestures, they are actively negotiating the rules of their shared process in real time. These movements reveal the invisible scaffolding that supports joint action, making the otherwise hidden dynamics of how people engage with each other visible.

FIGURE 3.7

Pragmatic gestures can manage the flow and clarity of an interaction.

Affective Gestures

When you see gestures that reveal emotion, like an eye roll, fingers drumming on the table, or a hand pressed to the chest, you're spotting an affective gesture. Affective gestures are movements that externalize feelings, moods, and attitudes, showing both their kind and intensity. They draw on the affordances of the thinking and communicating body to make emotions visible in real-time. This helps others see what someone is feeling, often without the need to exchange words. Here are some examples of affective gestures you might notice and what they reveal (see Figure 3.8).

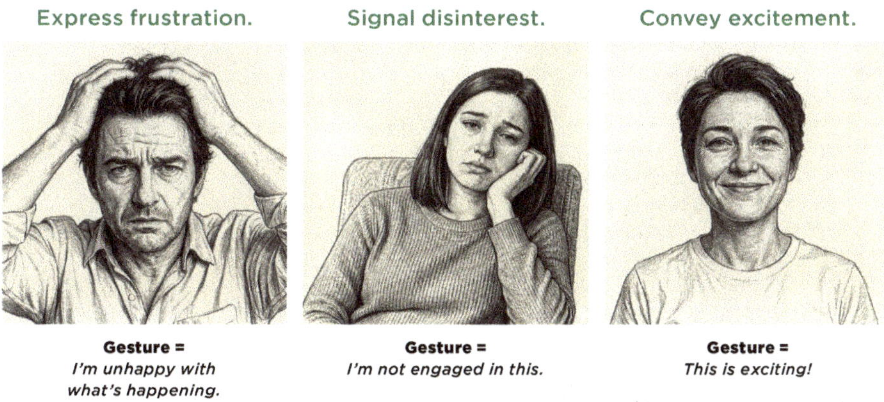

FIGURE 3.8
Affective gestures convey emotional information.

In social interactions, affective gestures become valuable because they can also influence the dynamics of the group. For example, they can help create empathy, signal frustration, and even diffuse tension.

Keep in mind that changes in posture, clenched hands, or eye rolls signal affective cues that reveal how someone feels in the moment. You'll want to notice shifts in tempo or tension. For instance, when movements grow rapid, tight, or fluid, these qualities can offer valuable clues about confidence, frustration, and engagement.

PRACTICE TIME

INSPECTING THE GESTURE TO DETERMINE TYPE AND FUNCTION

Time to revisit your field notes to identify the type and function of the gestures you collected from spotting Dane and Stephanie in the coffee shop. Review each of these gestures to identify whether you're seeing a representational, pragmatic, or affective gesture (see Figure 3.9).

#1: "How much milk is in each of these?"

#2: "You always prefer it more [equal]."

#3: "I'll have a large."

FIGURE 3.9
Key gestures can now be mapped to their type and function.

Answers: (1) Representational gesture → This is a concrete representational gesture that depicts Dane's understanding of milk levels, (2) Affective & pragmatic → There are actually two gestures in this example! The eye roll is an affective gesture that conveys Stephanie's exasperation with Dane's indecision. Stephanie's hands serve a pragmatic function by encouraging Dane to order the cappuccino by restating his preference of balance between espresso and milk. (3) Pragmatic → Dane indexes the coffee drink size that he wants the barista to make.

The gesture itself, like specific words, has a specific function that moves an interaction toward an achievement. Way to go! 🤙

Pulling It All Together

Now you have the full field guide for seeing the gestures that matter. You've practiced a two-step process for identifying them. First, let your goals guide you. When you know what path you're on in the product journey, you know where to look for gestures in the settings where that work happens. Second, use the dimensions of space, speech, and type and function to refine how a gesture contributes to your immediate goal and your journey toward the product North Star. When you put these lenses together, patterns will snap into focus.

Together, your goals and the dimensions help you sort a crowded field of movement and let you determine which gestures to set aside and which to keep. Practicing the process of identifying and interpreting the gestures that matter is essential in product development, because missed gestures can mean missed opportunities for deeper understanding at every stage of the journey. Every gesture has the potential to nudge your product work forward; this guide helps you know which ones to notice so you don't veer off course.

Let's revisit Dane and Stephanie at Espresso Yourself as their ordering process comes to a close. Dane nods to the barista and says, "I'll have a cappuccino... grande," pointing toward the 16-ounce cup on the display behind the counter. Barry doesn't notice Dane's gesture. He only hears the word "grande." At Espresso Yourself, there's a new seasonal drink called the "La Grande" that is 132 oz. of coffee to share. Dane pays.

When Barry sets the drink on the counter, Dane can't help but notice it's gigantic. "That explains the extra cost," he thinks to himself. "Oh, I meant that one," he gestures again toward the large 16-oz. cup on the display. Barry notices and realizes the mistake, "Hey, I'm sorry about that, let me get you a donut on the house."

Dane is satisfied, but will Barry's manager be?

There is a lesson here. When gestures go unnoticed, there can be consequences. Small mistakes can add up, and those costs eventually land on the business. After all, Barry gave the customer something extra to balance out the mistake and keep them happy.

In product development, the stakes of missing the key information that gestures offer can be much higher. When those signals go unnoticed, the result may be revenue loss, dissatisfied customers, or design glitches that surface only after the product reaches the market. Learning to notice gestures helps prevent these costly misunderstandings.

With practice, you'll get better at spotting gestures that matter. And once you can see them—truly see them—you'll be able to understand others more clearly, drive more innovative ideas, and create products and experiences that don't just work, but work for the humans who use them.

YOUR BODY "SEES" TOO

As you collect gestures that matter, notice not only with your eyes but with your body. What a gesture stirs in you can signal that something important is happening. Your body naturally detects tension, curiosity, or confusion before your mind names it. Treat those sensations as an invitation to investigate why a gesture caught your attention and what work it's doing in the moment.

In practice, these *felt* cues help you sense which gestures might be important. A gesture that makes you pause, lean in, or ask a clarifying question often hints at value. Seeing gestures that matter isn't just passive observation; it's an embodied practice of noticing when your own response points to meaning. When you can feel the pull of a gesture to respond, resist, or realign, you've likely found a moment worth examining.

Notice your body's reaction. It can tell you just as much as your eyes! 👀

Hone Your Skills in the Wild

Start practicing your ability to spot gestures that matter as you move through everyday life. Watch for them at your local coffee shop, around the dinner table, or in a favorite movie scene. The more you notice them, the easier they become to recognize.

Keep in mind that certain signals often precede meaningful gestures. Hesitations, pauses, backtracking, or shifts in gaze and posture can indicate that a meaningful gesture is about to appear. Also, notice verbal cues such as "like this" or "something like that." This talk frequently indicates the need to pay attention to the gestures that accompany it. By tuning into these combinations of speech and behaviors, you can begin to catch gestures that matter.

You also want to pay attention to gestures that repeat or persist across moments, speakers, or contexts. Recurring gestures are often significant. Their repetition suggests they play a role in how someone is organizing their thinking or communicating an idea. When you notice one, mark it as worth further attention.

Practicing this kind of observation in everyday settings will make gestures easier to spot when you are on your product journey.

As you observe, keep your goal in mind. Ask yourself, What am I trying to understand right now? The answer might be simple, like confirming the details of a coffee order, or more complex, like noticing a user's mental model not fully expressed in words.

Perk up. Tune in. Take note of what you see when you truly look closely. Ask yourself:

- Where did that gesture happen?
- How does it align with language?
- How is it functioning in the interaction?

Then put together all the tidbits of insight you have gained by attending keenly and see what was contributed by the gesture. Sometimes your attention to gestures won't get you much more than an uptick in the vibrancy of human interaction. But you will find many instances when it will gain you a morsel of new insight and maybe even an entire journey of unanticipated understanding.

Takeaways

- **Gestures add depth.** Gestures often reveal insights that go beyond words, adding layers of meaning to interactions. Focus on gestures that bring something new, unexpected, or clarifying to the conversation.
- **Context shapes meaning.** To understand a gesture, consider its context—space: Is it near the body, shared between speakers, or extending outward to the environment? Speech: Does it align with spoken words, or does it add new information? Type and function: Is it representational, pragmatic, or affective? How does it contribute in the moment?
- **Mismatches are clues.** When gestures and words don't align, pay attention. These mismatches often highlight unspoken priorities, emerging understanding, or moments of confusion.
- **Be selective.** Not every gesture matters. Hone your ability to focus on those that carry meaning relevant to your product goals.
- **Practice "seeing."** Developing the skill to observe and interpret gestures takes practice. Start by noticing gestures in daily interactions, asking how they contribute to communication and collaboration.
- **Path matters.** Your path toward product goals guides where and how to look for meaningful gestures. Use your role and team dynamics as a lens to identify key interactions and moments.

FIELD NOTES FROM DANE

I recently worked with a team of engineers to build a scalable containerized microservice for a new analytics feature. Our goal was to create a resilient system that could calculate user time-on-task with high-fidelity log data. The product goal was clear: get the engineering challenges solved so we could test-launch a proof-of-concept service.

But before we could start writing the code, the other engineers and I needed to understand the quirks of container architecture. I love working with engineers. We share a nerdy kinship and are problem-solvers at heart. But what I don't tell them is that their gestures are my favorite thing to watch. Systems and algorithms live mostly in the abstract, so engineers—perhaps more than anyone—use gestures to communicate and think all the time.

During a meeting, we discussed a video we had watched as home-work. The narrator in the video (see Figure 3.10) presented a diagram of container architectures. He explained how containers and their libraries, application code, and runtimes are layered efficiently to share resources like network and processing power.

The engineers represented components with abstract representational gestures by tracing rectangles in the air to depict memory, networks, and secrets. They then connected the discussion from these abstract depictions to blocks of code: the injected runtime config, secrets folder, and script. Gestures added layers of meaning and helped connect the abstract concepts to the code that needed to be written.

For me, the gestures that mattered were those that helped me to understand the concepts I needed to know about container architecture from my peers and look for how they translate those concepts into tangible work in their code editors.

FIGURE 3.10

Still from the video showing the diagram that the engineers represented in gestures.

FIELD NOTES FROM STEPHANIE

When I stepped off the stage and into the classroom, I took choreography with me. I do not mean choreography as performance. No jazz hands. No triple pirouettes. I mean choreography as the careful arrangement of movement, space, timing, and attention to support explanation.

Years of dancing had trained me to think through the body. When I began teaching, I found myself using that same training in the lecture hall. My hands became part of the lecture. One hand could hold an idea. The space between my hands could show a relationship. A turn of the wrist could animate change.

One project brought me into collaboration with a chemistry professor who taught stereochemistry, a topic that asks students to imagine molecules in three dimensions. We wanted to give students more than one way into the concept. So, we choreographed the lecture.

I watched his teaching the way I might watch a rehearsal. His hands were already working. They shaped bonds, marked transformations, and held relationships in the air. The movement was there, but it needed definition. So, we made adjustments. He learned to hold a gesture a little longer, make it large enough for students to see, slow a motion when the concept needed time, and let the gesture arrive with the words (see Figure 3.11). At times, he invited students to "Watch my hands here," letting them know that part of the explanation was happening in his body.

Those intentional adjustments changed the lecture. The gestures no longer floated around the explanation. They carried part of it. Words, hands, timing, pauses, and space worked together to give students more points of entry into the knowledge. The lecture became more than words and diagrams. It became an embodied explanation.

We studied the difference. Students who experienced the choreographed lecture understood the concept better than students who received the same explanation without the planned gestures.

FIGURE 3.11

The body becomes part of an explanation. Here, the professor uses his arms, hands, and gaze to help students see spatial relationships between molecules that are difficult to represent in flat diagrams.

Excuse me! Would you have a moment to chat about your experience today?
I've recorded your experience, but did you have any additional feedback?
Well, it wasn't what I ordered...
When I was in Vienna, the Kellner always remembered what you ordered. It was great!
I don't think he understood what I wanted.
Let me review the footage.
Experience ordering today
Barista did not understand customer
Possible cause: Difficult for baristas to remember customer orders?
LA GRANDE
Yeah, she never saw that you were pointing!
She heard my words, but didn't understand me.
Thanks! I've got a great recording to use.

CHAPTER 4

Understand Users' Gestures

You now have the tools to spot the gestures that matter. It's time to put them to work to navigate the research path of the product journey, where the goal is to deepen your understanding of users. You'll use this skill to notice the thinking, communicating, and coordinating gestures that emerge in common product research settings like user interviews and observations. Talking to people about their experiences and watching them in their natural environments are foundational practices for any team working to define and refine the problem their product will solve.

That said, the challenge is that what people say is often vague or incomplete. Maybe you've seen this in a transcript where a user says something ambiguous like a new product "looks fine." On the page, those words seem clear enough. But what if you also observed them make a small pinch-and-pull gesture, drawing a thin line in the air? That movement suggests that it may actually mean the product feels "fine," as in thin or brittle. Suddenly, the whole interpretation changes entirely!

Gestures in interviews and observations give you an additional input for building practical empathy by letting you see beyond the surface of what people say to the beliefs and experiences underneath. They also create openings in the moment to advance the conversation toward greater depth. In short, gestures both signal how someone is thinking and invite you to respond, clarify, and continue pushing the conversation toward greater depth in real time.

Seeing how the body talks in addition to the words people share brings you closer to a richer understanding of users. Words tell one part of the story, while gestures reveal another as they surface glimpses of mental models and unmet needs. When you attend to words and gestures, you get a more complete picture.

The Goals of Interviews and Observations

Remember that your goals are your first-pass filter for noticing the gestures that matter (see Chapter 3, "How to 'See' Gestures"). Now, on the research path of the product journey, your goal is to understand people well enough to make sense of their lived experience and zero in on problems that your product might address.

To do this, take stock of the rhythms of their everyday life: their habits, routines, friction points, and the tools they rely on. Look for the nuances of their past experiences and the details of how they approach problems and tasks in their work or personal life. Pay attention to what frustrates them, what delights them, and the deeper motivations that help explain why they act the way they do.

You might already think of this as building empathy. But gestures take you a step deeper into empathizing. They offer a visceral way to see and inhabit people's frames of reference. The gestures that will help you reach your goal of understanding users are those that let you do the following:

- **Observe traces of prior experience.** Gestures that reenact past events show how memory shapes someone's current expectations.
- **Peer into evolving thinking.** Representational gestures that depict objects, actions, or concepts surface glimpses of a person's mental model in the moment.
- **Document behavior in real time.** Gestures reveal how people physically engage with tasks, tools, and interfaces as they work.
- **Press thinking forward.** Gestures that accompany pauses, hesitations, or incomplete ideas signal opportunities to clarify, probe, and elicit deeper explanation.

On the research path, thinking gestures will give you the richest information about your users because they can surface the content and relationships in people's mental models. But communicating and coordinating gestures deserve your attention as well. They act as helpful side doors that support deeper interpretation. For example, communicating gestures clarify vague descriptions and reveal important interpersonal cues, like whether a participant is aligning with you, hesitating, signaling uncertainty, or expressing confidence. Coordinating gestures show how people physically organize and work within their environments, mapping how they sequence actions, handle tools, or move through a task. Together, these cues help you understand not just what users say they do, but how they actually navigate the systems, spaces, and constraints that shape their experience.

To keep your attention focused on the gestures that matter in interviews and observations, stay clear on your goals and watch for gestures that reveal how people think and how they act, and what underlying problems those actions might indicate. Getting this right is vital because these insights become the raw material your team will use to shape the product roadmap.

NOTE PRODUCTS ARE PART OF SYSTEMS

People do not use payroll software, toasters, or car infotainment systems in isolation. Every product is embedded in physical and social systems that impose design constraints and requirements. This will influence the relative importance of thinking, communicating, and coordinating gestures as well.

Set the Stage

Good preparation is the foundation of every insightful interview or observation. Depending on what input will effectively guide product decisions for your team, you may decide to watch people in their natural environments or sit down with them for one-on-one conversations. In either case, you want to create the conditions where gestures can naturally emerge and be seen.

When you conduct ethnographic observations in, for example, homes, workplaces, or stores, your primary role is that of an observer. Your task is to see the body in context. Gestures in these settings already have meaning because they are part of the natural flow of activity: how people reach for tools, coordinate with coworkers, navigate space, or improvise solutions. To capture that richness, you want to minimize your influence so the behaviors you witness are genuine. Preparing for an observation means identifying the spaces, tasks, and interactions where gestures are most likely to matter, and positioning yourself so you can see them clearly without disrupting the natural flow. When your focus is on embedded observation, you want to blend into the environment enough that people's thinking, communicating, and coordinating gestures unfold as they normally would.

In many product scenarios, however, you want to drive directly at what and how people think. That's why you conduct one-on-one interviews. Here, your role shifts. You're no longer only an observer, but you're also a participant shaping the interaction. Your questions, pacing, presence, and even your own gestures influence the gestures that emerge from others. Because of this, you want to be intentional about how you structure these conversations. To properly set the stage for an interview, you want to do the following:

- Design a protocol with gestures in mind.
- Arrange the physical environment.
- Establish and foster rapport.
- Get users to gesture.

These practices form the backbone of this chapter. The focus is primarily on interviews because the skills you use here also equip you for seeing gestures in your observational research. If you can create the right conditions for spotting gestures that matter in an interview, you will be well prepared to do the same in naturalistic settings.

Taking these preparatory steps ensures that you are not leaving anything to chance. You are building the foundation for interviews and observations that surface a deeper, more embodied understanding of people and their needs.

Design a Protocol with Gestures in Mind

Most interview guides are written for the ear. Design yours for the eyes as well. Think of your interview protocol not just as a list of questions to be answered, but also as a framework that invites movement, expression, and visible thought. Review each question and ask yourself: Would answering this make someone show me something through their body? Would a physical demonstration with hands, arms, and gaze tell me more than words alone?

If the answer is yes, build that into your plan. Add prompts that open space for the body to join the conversation:

- "Can you show me what that looked like?"
- "How do you usually do that?"
- "Walk me through that."

You can also anticipate when gestures are likely to appear. Questions about processes, comparisons, changes over time, or emotional experiences often bring them out. Questions that evoke mental and motor imagery, like what someone saw, spatial information, and how they see something evolving in time, will also strongly evoke gestures (see Figure 4.1).

Mark these moments in your interview guide so you can slow down, give space for expression, and let gestures unfold before you move on.

The same principles apply in observation. Position yourself where you can see the body clearly, note when gestures appear, and jot quick impressions in your field notebook. Later, you can revisit those moments in conversation to clarify meaning.

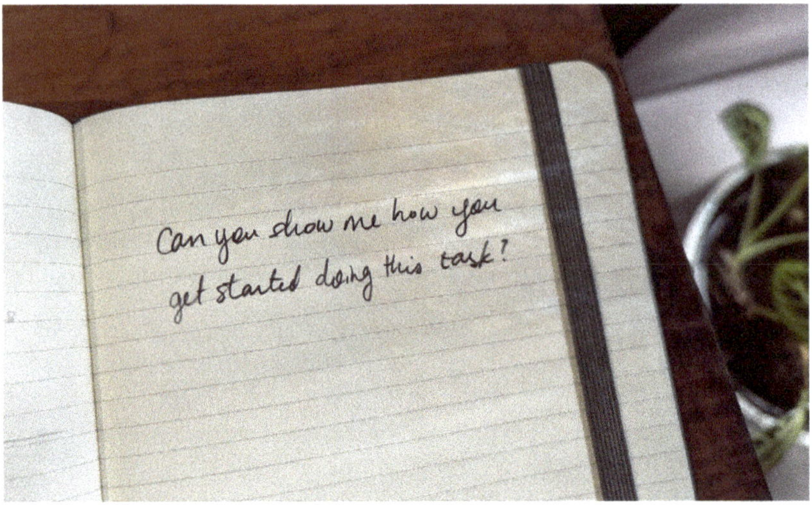

FIGURE 4.1
Questions about processes, spatial information, and how things change over time reliably invite gestures. Mark these moments in your interview guide so you know when to slow down and watch.

Arrange the Physical Environment

If you want to see the body talk, you have to set up the space so it's easy for people to move and easy for you to see what their bodies are saying. Although people naturally "talk" with their hands, gestures can disappear or be inhibited when the environment works against them. Your goal is simple: make gesturing available. Arrange the interaction so that nothing restricts or blocks the movements of the hands and body.

First, make sure the hands are free. Whether in person or on a screen, if people are holding coffee cups, phones, or clipboards, their gestures are weighed down. If their arms are pinned under a table or outside the camera frame, their gestures are hidden. If notes, laptops, or materials clutter the space in front of them, gestures get trapped. Clear the field and keep hands free.

Next, open the space. The way you sit also matters. Leave a few inches between your torso and the edge of the table so the body has room to move. If a table is necessary, shift materials aside to create space. How you situate your own body also sets the tone. When you lean back slightly and keep your hands visible, you signal permission: it's okay to move. Most people will unconsciously follow your lead. See Figure 4.2 for the subtle differences between an environment that inhibits gestures and one that supports them.

FIGURE 4.2
An environment that inhibits gestures (left) and one that promotes gestures (right).

Finally, design the visual frame so gestures remain visible. In both in-person and virtual settings, aim to make the upper body easy to see. If you're recording or meeting on video, frame the camera so that both the interviewer and participant are visible from the waist up—the area where most gestures occur. Small adjustments such as raising the camera, adjusting chair height, or moving back a few inches can make a big difference.

When you design the space so gestures can appear, you make it easier to see how people think through ideas, communicate intentions, and coordinate their actions with the world around them.

Establish and Foster Rapport

Rapport is an essential ingredient of any interview or observation. It builds trust, respect, and a sense of safety that sets the tone for the interaction. When people feel respected and seen, it opens the door for them to share. Use your body to create an inviting environment for the conversation to unfold. Even small movements can set the tone for relational comfort and feelings of alliance in the interaction. First impressions really do matter!

ARRANGE THE SPACE IN VIDEO INTERVIEWS

When running an interview over video conferencing software, setting up the space requires planning. A little preparation at the beginning can make a big difference in capturing visible gestures in video calls. In these settings, the video frame is often limited, so you want to think about how both you and the participant appear on camera.

Invite participants to sit back slightly so their upper body and hands are visible and make sure that your own hands and gestures can be seen as well (see Figure 4.3). This creates a more natural conversational space where both people can use their bodies to explain ideas. If you notice they've gestured off-camera, don't be afraid to ask for clarification. ("I see you've done something with your hands, but I couldn't quite see that.") People are usually happy to repeat gestures again in view of the camera.

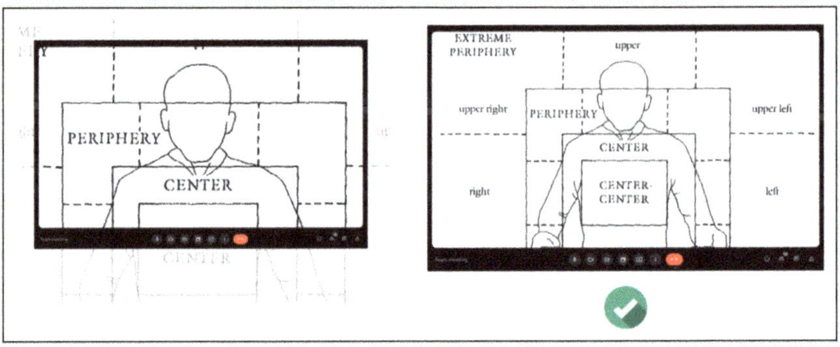

FIGURE 4.3
Have all participants sit back in the frame of the camera during virtual calls for better visibility of the gesture space.

A few minutes at the beginning of the call can set up the rest of your conversation for excellent gesture production and visibility.

Keep your posture open and your gestures responsive. As comfort grows, gestures expand, postures loosen, and the exchange feels collaborative rather than extractive. You don't need to choreograph rapport; you just need to embody it. Try these simple adjustments:

- **Keep your body open.** Uncross arms, soften shoulders, and let your hands rest in visible space between you and the participant.

- **Mirror naturally.** Subtly reflect the form and tempo of the other person's gestures. Mirroring builds unconscious alignment, so use it to signal empathy, not mimicry.
- **Lean in and then ease back.** A gentle forward lean signals interest. Easing back gives space for reflection. The alternation keeps the exchange balanced.
- **Use nods and small-scale movements.** Small affirming gestures ("I'm listening") encourage people to keep going.
- **Convey friendliness.** A slight tilt of the head, a lifted chest, or palms visible, and an inviting expression communicate warmth even before you speak.
- **Keep your gestures responsive.** Match the emotional tone. For example, be slow and measured when the topic is sensitive, lively when energy rises.

When you model openness, people then feel invited to participate fully with their words and their bodies. So, think about how you establish rapport every time you talk to users.

Get Users to Gesture

When people gesture, they think more deeply, communicate more clearly, and can make complex ideas easier to organize and explain. You want to get people gesturing!

There are ways to get people gesturing through various priming prompts. Start with something that invites physical demonstration. Ask them, "Can you show me how you log in to this app?" or say, "Walk me through how you make your morning coffee." These small, familiar actions wake up the body's natural rhythm of movement and make gesturing feel comfortable right from the start.

You can also include a task at the beginning of a think-aloud protocol that evokes mental and motor imagery alongside verbal explanation. For example, you can ask someone to explain how they fold a T-shirt or organize their workspace. These tasks trigger the parts of the brain to visualize and simulate action, the same regions that are involved in planning and moving the body. This priming not only ensures that you get detailed explanations, but it also makes gestures more likely to emerge as the conversation unfolds.

Consider also modeling gestures at the outset. By using your own gestures naturally as you talk, you establish gestures as a valid and accepted part of the discourse. And what's more: movement is contagious! When you gesture, you give permission for others to do the same. Once gestures are flowing, you'll find that people explain their ideas more clearly and reveal their thinking more completely.

NOTE MANAGE YOUR OWN GESTURES

Your gestures matter just as much as your participants'. Use them thoughtfully and artfully. Too many and they can distract, overwhelm, or dilute the meaning of your words. Too few and your exchanges can fall flat, leaving key ideas unattended. Think of your gestures like Goldilocks. You want just the right amount. You want to employ movements that enhance clarity, invite collaboration, and help ideas land without stealing the spotlight. When used with intention, your gestures become a quiet dialogue partner that supports and does not overshadow your words.

See Thinking in the Moment

Now the stage is set and the conversation has begun. When you conduct an interview or an observation, your primary role often begins as a spectator. You want to sit back and listen with your ears *and* your eyes. Remind yourself that it's important to simply let people talk and give their thinking room to emerge and evolve. As people talk, their bodies naturally join the conversation. You get a front-row seat to see what's in their head play out in their gestures.

You want to pay attention to these gestures. As you saw in Chapter 2, the thinking body is a primary source for making thought visible. It reveals problem-solving processes and surfaces tacit knowledge. Thinking gestures are often produced for the speaker, but they are visible to you. Watch them! They are most often representational gestures that depict objects, actions, and features of abstract concepts. These gestures matter because when interpreted with language, they reveal users' mental models.

Mental models are the holy grail in connecting user feedback to product direction. As a member of a product team, you've likely heard or framed decisions in terms of user mental models. If you can understand users' mental models, then you can understand more about their relationship to the product. You will learn what's working, what needs attention, and where the critical gaps lie in their experience.

MENTAL MODELS INFORM PRODUCT DESIGN

Mental models are the internal "rulebooks" people use to make sense of the world. The psychologist Kenneth Craik coined the term in the 1940s to describe how the human mind builds simplified internal representations of reality to help them navigate, make decisions, and predict outcomes.[1] Decades later, Don Norman connected the concept to product development through *The Design of Everyday Things*. His seminal text established a shared understanding that people act according to their internal version of a product, which may differ from a designer's intent. When the conceptual model of a design and how people act misalign, then errors, confusion, or frustration often occur (see Figure 4.4).

FIGURE 4.4
A "Norman door" is a poorly designed door that confuses people, often by featuring a handle that affords pushing or pulling when the opposite is needed; it often necessitates corrective signage.

Norman argued that good design works to bridge that gap, making the conceptual model clear and intuitive so the user's mental model aligns with the designer's intent. Over the past several decades, the mental model has influenced the design of digital interfaces and physical products alike. Mental models serve as a crucial foundation for how to model user behavior and create more intuitive, human-centered experiences.

1 In his 1943 book *The Nature of Explanation*, Craik proposed that the mind builds internal models of the world that people use to reason, predict outcomes, and guide behavior.

Mental Models in a Glimpse

Occasionally, a single gesture reveals an entire mental model in one clear stroke. These rare but valuable moments are easiest to spot when a movement instantly confirms one of several competing explanations you're already weighing, crystallizes a clear pain point into a single vivid action, or is so iconic that its meaning is immediately clear.

A viral video trend provides a perfect, real-world example of a single gesture revealing a mental model (see Figure 4.5). In these videos, a parent and child stand on opposite sides of a physical barrier. An off-screen parent then asks both their spouse and child: "Show how you take a picture."

The father raises his hands to his face, forming a shape as if he's holding a point-and-shoot camera. He squints one eye and mimes pressing a physical shutter button. The child, by contrast, holds one hand out flat like a smartphone and uses her other hand to tap the "screen." In a single movement, their gestures reveal two distinct, generationally-shaped mental models for the exact same action.

FIGURE 4.5
An adult and child respond to the prompt "show how you take a picture" in a viral short video trend.

This example also highlights how mental models rarely disappear. New ones often build on or coexist with older understandings that are still relevant in the present context. Though the father has likely used a smartphone as a camera, his gestures show that the earlier model of framing a shot and pressing a shutter button still is part of how he imagines taking a picture. Gestures let you see this richness of overlapping histories, habits, and interpretations that language alone can flatten.

This kind of instant mental model revelation through a singular gesture is not common, so grab it when you can. Remember that no two people have the same experiences, and those differences shape the mental models that gestures help you see.

Mental Models Over Time

More often, mental models are not revealed in a single moment, but instead through a collection of individual gestures over time. A single gesture contributes a piece of the puzzle as a fragment of someone's thinking. Each gesture represents distinct elements like the shape of an object, the motion of an action, or the structure of an abstract concept that are parts of a greater whole.

If each gesture is a piece of the puzzle, their assembled combination then becomes a coherent picture of their mental model (see Figure 4.6).

FIGURE 4.6
Piecing together mental models is like building a puzzle: each gesture gives you a piece, and only by assembling them do you see the full picture.

To understand how gestures provide pieces of mental models in the moment, imagine you are part of a team working on a cloud storage product. The product manager who is responsible for the roadmap for the company's desktop sync app has flagged that you are getting elevated complaints with users reporting that their files are being deleted without their permission. You decide to set up a few interviews with hands-on users to have them walk through how they sync files between their devices.

You know you want gestures to be visible because you suspect users may have a different mental model than how the sync client was designed, and some nuances might emerge in this mode. So, you set up your protocol to open with a question that is likely to evoke gestures: "Walk me through how your files are saved in the cloud."

The user jumps right in and explains, "Well, I start by saving the document to a specific folder." As they say this, they tap their flat palm downward to the right of their body, keeping their hand close. You recognize that this is likely a thinking gesture depicting setting something aside, in an imagined folder corresponding to the folder being synced. You notice that this is a concrete representational gesture that mismatches what is said in words by offering additional spatial information about the location of the sync folder: close to them on the table in front of them.

In a moment, you've just caught a glimpse into this user's mental model of saving a document in the cloud. The conversation has just begun, so you won't fully understand its importance yet, but jot it down in your field notes and keep your eyes open for additional fragments (see Figure 4.7). You will be able to return to each piece of the puzzle you collected from the interview in your post-interview analysis.

FIGURE 4.7
A user taps a flat palm downward to the right of their body, gesturing as if placing a file into an imagined folder (left); a researcher's field notes capture the gesture as a fragment of the user's mental model (right).

Later in the conversation, the user adds more to their explanation, "I have to wait for it to go there," accompanied by a quick, upward shooting motion of their hand as if launching a small rocket. This gesture adds spatial contrast and separates *"there"* as a distinct location from where they had imagined placing the document in a folder on the table. You are starting to get a little more information and see that this user conceives of the destination for that file as above them (this is in contrast to where it started, which was by their side). You note that this is likely an abstract representational gesture performed close to the body that shows how the user thinks about how and where a file is synced to the cloud from their local client. You know this gesture matters because it is a mismatch to what was said. The language is imprecise, but the gesture establishes a visible action that the destination of the file is distinct from where it was first saved. It also conveys a hint about the user's conception that the transfer process is (or should be) quick and direct.

Aha! You just caught another glimpse into the user's mental model. Importantly, it provides contrast with the previous depiction, indicating where they saved the file in the space next to them. This suggests that there are two spaces that are important: next to and above the user. Again, you may not know the significance of this yet but jot it down (see Figure 4.8).

FIGURE 4.8
The user shoots their hand upward, gesturing to show a file traveling up to "there."

Later, the user adds, "Then I can get it on my machine at home." As they say this, their hands reach upward and mime manually pulling something toward themselves, like taking an item down from a high shelf. This abstract representational gesture, performed in the space of the body, establishes a distinct process of "retrieval." Again, you know this gesture matters because it mismatches the language:

"getting it" on the laptop could mean anything, but the gesture distinctly mimicked grabbing something from a high shelf and pulling it down. Rather than the user thinking about syncing as an automatic process, perhaps they see this as a manual step. A potential explanation is coming into focus—this user might not be aware that their files are automatically updated across all devices when the device is online. Maybe this is why they think the desktop client is deleting their files.

Here again is another piece of the puzzle. Jot this one down, too (see Figure 4.9).

FIGURE 4.9
A user reaches upward and then pulls their hand downward, depicting cloud file retrieval as a manual act (left); field notes capture the gesture as a third fragment of the user's mental model (right).

FROM GESTURES TO PRODUCT DECISIONS

During analysis, you have the opportunity to step back and consider what these gestures and the fragments of mental models they reveal mean when viewed together. Looking back at your field notes from the interview about saving files in the cloud, you identify the placing gesture, the launching-up gesture, and the pulling-down gesture, and a coherent mental model begins to emerge. These fragments are gold once you string them together.

The full picture now shows that this user thinks of cloud storage as a physical warehouse in the sky, one they must interact with manually. As a result, they may not realize that editing a file on one device could overwrite another copy elsewhere. For a team designing a cloud solution, this person would trust that a helpful safeguard might be to display a warning the first time a local file is about to be overwritten, ensuring that the user understands exactly what is happening.

Remember that your task in the moment isn't to solve the puzzle, but to collect the clues. You might not grasp the full picture of a person's mental model as it happens, but you know you can assemble it later in the analysis.

NOTE EMOTIONAL STANCE MATTERS, TOO

Gestures also reveal attitudes like frustration, delight, and confusion. This is where the communicating body frequently steps in. Watch for the emotional range of reactions. Remember, "It's OK" coupled with a dismissive flick of the hand means it's probably not OK! Collect those in your field notes as well.

When you notice gestures that surface mental models, either in a glimpse or over time, it's fodder for design and product ideas! Maybe it sparks new questions, contradicts assumptions you or the team have, or highlights something you hadn't even thought about. Ultimately, what you see in the body gives you a foundation to build on.

Draw Out Additional Thinking

Interviews are dynamic interactions suffused by words and gestures. Your role will shift frequently between listening deeply, observing keenly, and actively participating. As an active participant, you have an opportunity to enrich the quality of information you get from any interview by using gestures to both clarify and push thinking.

There will be moments when a user's thinking gets stuck, becomes fuzzy, feels incomplete, or is just not clearly communicated. These are your opportunities to use gestures to move from a "half-baked" idea to something deeper and more refined. Don't miss these moments to advance the conversation.

Clarify Thinking

Remember that gestures that don't cleanly align with talk often signal that someone's idea is still ambiguous or incomplete. This is your cue to pull on the thread and draw out more clarity. By responding to both a user's words and gestures, you invite them to continue explaining their thinking, bringing you closer to a shared understanding. A simple "tell me more," or a nod that signals "go on," can often do the trick.

When you notice a mismatch or ambiguity between gesture and talk, you have two options: jot it down to analyze later or step in to clarify now. Knowing the difference will affect the depth and quality of your insights. Some misunderstandings can wait, but others, especially those tied to a user's understanding of a key concept they are sharing with you, cannot. If a gestured idea remains unclear and you move on, you risk building your analysis on incomplete data. Clarifying in the moment protects the accuracy of your data and gives participants the chance to refine their own thinking aloud. When you use gestures to cue clarification, you're not only ensuring your understanding—you're helping make their mental model more visible in real time.

Let's return to the cloud-storage interview. Later in the conversation, you realized that the user's earlier explanation of how files were synced may be the source of confusion. You say, "You said something earlier about syncing." As you speak, you place your left hand in the space between yourself and the user and loop your finger in a rewind motion to indicate that you want to backtrack. This is a pragmatic gesture that directs the flow of conversation back to the topic you want to revisit.

The user recognizes the cue and revisits that part of their explanation. "Oh, right! So then when I am back home, I can get it on my laptop." As they say this, their hands again reach upward and mime manually pulling something toward themselves.

When they first explained their understanding, you were the quiet observer. You saw the mismatch between vague language and specific gestures and jotted it down. Now you recognize this as a critical point of ambiguity. The user's mental model is right there, hovering in the air, but it is still fuzzy. You decide to step in for clarification.

You lean forward slightly into the shared space, a pragmatic gesture that signals engagement and interest. Then you mirror the user's earlier motion, performing the same pulling-down gesture as you ask a probing question that connects words and gestures: "That's interesting," you say while completing the motion (see Figure 4.10). "When you say you 'get it' on your laptop, can you walk me through that moment?"

The user explains that they imagine manually syncing their files each time.

FIGURE 4.10
An interviewer leans slightly forward and mirrors the user's pulling-down gesture while asking a follow-up question, using the user's own movement to invite clarification.

By repeating the user's gesture, you do two things at once: confirm that you saw what they did and offer a concrete piece of their own thinking to reach mutual understanding. By stepping in and using their gestures, you carry the concept from ambiguity to clarity. The vagueness becomes an opportunity for deeper detail. You now have a mutual understanding and the chance to explore a misconception in their mental model. The user believes syncing requires manual action to pull data from the cloud.

Pushing Thinking

Sometimes, you will notice that ambiguity in talk and gestures requires more than just additional clarity from a user. It actually represents ideas that are not fully formed and might benefit from being pushed into new territory. You are inviting them to build connections between ideas that they have hinted at, novel scenarios, and edge cases that they may not have fully reasoned through. When you see that a user's thinking is incomplete, you can use a well-timed question and gesture to guide them toward a deeper, more refined understanding.

This isn't about correcting them or leading them to a specific answer. It's about creating the conditions for their own "aha!" moment. You do this by asking a question that encourages them to connect two different parts of their experience. The answer isn't something they already know; it's something they will discover as they respond. By watching their gestures, you can see the thinking happening in real time, even before they find the words.

Let's go back to the cloud storage interview one last time. You have just clarified that the user believes they have to manually "pull down" files to their laptop. Now, you want to see how far that mental model extends. You recall that earlier in the conversation, the user mentioned accessing their files on multiple personal devices, including their phone. You see an opportunity to push their thinking. You ask, "That's really helpful. You mentioned using this on your laptop and your phone to access your files. Does the syncing work the same way across all of those devices?"

The user pauses. The question forces them to reflect on and synthesize across their experiences on the laptop and phone. As they begin to think, you see their hands, which had been resting openly, pull in closer to their torso. This subtle shift of bringing the hands toward the body is a signal that the thinking body is back at work (see Figure 4.11). They are working through ideas in their own space.

FIGURE 4.11

A user's hands draw inward toward their body as they pause, signaling that internal processing is underway in response to the interviewer's question.

After a moment, they look up, a flicker of surprise on their face. "Huh. You know what? No, it's not the same," they say, thinking aloud. "On my phone, the files are just... there. They're automatically updated for me. I never have to get them from the website like I do on my laptop. It just happens."

With this intervention, you've both triangulated your insight that the user sees syncing as a manual process. Importantly, you've also helped them discover an inconsistency in their own mental model. They don't have one model for how cloud storage works; they have at least two, and they are context-dependent. For the laptop, interacting with the cloud is equivalent to pulling files from a manual warehouse. For the phone, it's an automatic, magical sync. It's important to recognize that they may never have noticed the gap in how they understood these two experiences until you prompted them to do so.

NOTE **WATCH FOR BOTTOMING OUT**

People will often reveal that they've hit the boundary of their understanding or ability to further clarify their explanation. When a user shrugs, turns their hands up, and tilts their head to the side, they are indicating that they may not have more to contribute. Watch for this because explanations that seem to originate from these mental models may actually be brittle ideas constructed on the fly and would not come up in a similar conversation on a different day.

Guide the Interaction

As an interviewer, you are a facilitator responsible not only for the topics you cover, but also for the human experience of the conversation itself. Guiding the interaction means not only consciously observing what a user's body tells you but also making use of your body to manage the flow of the conversation and the feeling of trust. You will do this primarily by doing the following:

- Directing the pace and sequence of the conversation
- Checking in regularly

Direct the Pace and Sequence

To manage the flow of the conversation, you will want to use pragmatic gestures to act as the conductor steering the interaction. This ensures that the interview stays on track and feels like a natural dialogue rather than a rigid checklist.

To keep the conversation moving forward without interrupting, use small nods and slight forward leans to signal, "I'm with you, keep going." When you need to switch gears smoothly, use your body to mark the transition. Sometimes, a physical reset like placing your hands flat on the table or shifting your posture can act as a paragraph break, signaling that a new topic is beginning. Like the interview with the cloud product participant, a rewind gesture can also indicate that you want to return to a topic from earlier in the conversation.

When a participant begins speaking at length or drifting from the focus, pragmatic gestures can help you redirect politely. A slight forward lean paired with a small hand lift can signal that you would like to jump in. Briefly summarizing what they said while drawing your hands slightly inward can also signal that you are wrapping up that thread and moving the conversation forward.

Check In Regularly

Beyond keeping the pace of the conversation, you also want to stay in sync with and attuned to your participant. You're aiming to maintain a steady sense of alignment and trust throughout every interview or observation.

Think of people's bodies as a barometer for their internal state. When you see their gestures shrink, slow, or move out of view, it can signal fatigue and hesitation. This is your cue to pause or soften your approach. When their gestures expand and become more energetic, it can signal that engagement is high, and you can explore a topic more deeply.

At the same time, you must manage your own presence. Keep your posture open to communicate collaboration, not authority. You can build rapport by subtly mirroring the rhythm and tone of someone else's gestures but be careful not to lead with your body. A vigorous nod can unintentionally push someone toward agreement, while pointing at a feature you like can bias their response. Your goal is to create a sense of safety and respect, which allows for more honest and insightful answers.

CASE STUDY: UNCOVERING MENTAL MODELS OF AI

This case study brings the principles of making use of gestures to understand users more thoroughly to life. It demonstrates how a product team used gesture analysis in a real-world project to uncover deep user insights and guide the product roadmap.

The Challenge: Designing a Trusted AI Tool

In mid-2023, a product team at an EdTech company began exploring how AI could be positioned within an intelligent grading tool. Before development, they identified several foundational questions they needed to answer to establish a clear North Star for the product roadmap.

The interviews aimed to uncover instructors' and students' mental models of general-purpose AI tools. Recent industry reports showed rapid adoption among students, while instructors lagged behind and often framed AI use as academic dishonesty. Understanding the attitudes of both groups was essential for identifying early risks and constraints on the product.

The team focused especially on gestures that might reveal subtle details of these mental models. This was critical because AI was still new, and many people had limited or uneven prior experience with it. The interviews sought to understand what would drive adoption, how people were actually using AI, and how institutional policies shaped their behavior and perceptions. With these questions in mind, the team conducted a series of foundational interviews to guide the product's direction.

Setting the Stage for a Gestural Conversation

Carmen, a sales professional and early adopter of AI tools, was an ideal participant. She had been a teacher in her previous career. As a sales professional, she was often visiting schools each week and having conversations with instructors about their attitudes and openness to AI. In addition to this, she was an early adopter of general-purpose large language models (LLMs) and regularly experimented with platforms such as ChatGPT and Gemini for productivity, like drafting communication and summarizing meetings.

This interview was conducted in person and video-recorded to capture both speech and gesture. The camera was positioned to frame most of Carmen's body, showing her personal gesture space, the shared space between her and the interviewer, and the surrounding area. To encourage natural movement, the physical setup placed them at a slight angle to one another and created an open, shared space between them.

continues

CASE STUDY: UNCOVERING MENTAL MODELS OF AI

Before beginning the core questions, the interviewer primed Carmen to gesture with a short warm-up task: "Walk me through how you organize your desk at the start of the day." This simple exercise awakened her natural rhythm of movement and established gesture as a normal and valued part of the conversation.

The Discovery: Two Meanings for One Word

The interviewer asked an open-ended question selected to evoke gestures, "How does a machine learn?" which Carmen understood to mean AI. As Carmen began describing her interactions with general-purpose AI tools, she repeatedly used the word "inputting." Right away, this became an important concept in Carmen's mental model that the interviewer wanted to dig into.

Mental Model: The "Machine as Apprentice"

Carmen started by explaining that a machine learns "based on repetitive and over time signals that you input into it." When she said this, she extended her hands out from her chest in an offering gesture, coinciding with her concept of input (see Figure 4.12). This was an abstract representational gesture performed close to the body that was the first of a series of back-and-forth exchanges that Carmen produced to show something being transferred from her to the AI and back again.

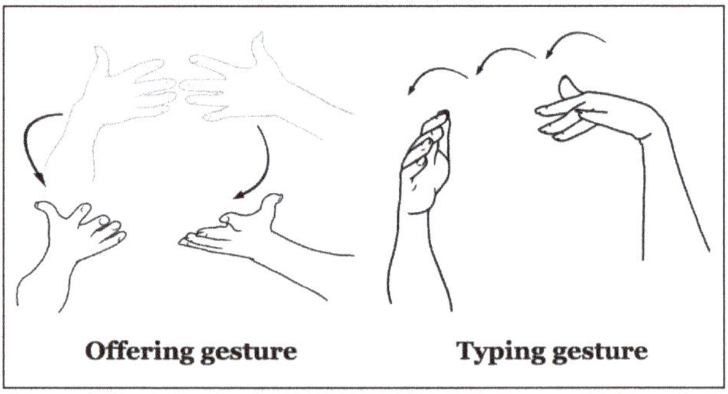

FIGURE 4.12
Carmen gestures to indicate that she is "inputting signals into the machine" (left); she mimics typing action while asking the AI to "make her emails sound friendly" (right).

The interviewer then noticed the ambiguity in Carmen's gesture and made a request for clarification that pushed her thinking further. When prompted to provide an example of what she meant by inputting repetitive signals, Carmen then mimed typing on a keyboard close to her body as she described telling the AI to "make this email sound friendly." This concrete representational gesture gave form to inputting as a specific action of typing in words in exchange with the AI. It also gave further nuance to the offering gesture, defining it as a type of transactional exchange.

At this point in the conversation, the interviewer noted how these gestures were beginning to reveal Carmen's mental model. This first set of clues established a baseline for her broader understanding of machine learning. Taken together, the gestures suggested that Carmen viewed herself as the active agent—training the machine through her inputs and engaging in a two-way process that she initiated and guided, rather than passively received.

Later in the conversation, more clues about her mental model emerged. She explained that the machine learns "over time." As she said this, her hands performed a series of rolling accumulation gestures and step-by-step building gestures in the space close to her body, her left hand making punctuated hops away from the frame of her body (see Figure 4.13). This thinking gesture was far more informative than her words. Recognizing the gesture-speech mismatch, the interviewer leaned forward and asked, "It sounds like you're describing a process of iteration?"

Step-by-step building gesture

FIGURE 4.13
Carmen's step-by-step building gesture qualified "over time" as a sequential series of steps that she controlled.

"Yeah, iteration!" she confirmed. From that point on, Carmen adopted the term "iteration" throughout the interview—a marker that the interaction did, indeed, move her developing thinking along. The active, iterative process she described of teaching the machine through repeated inputs over time suggested that she viewed AI as an apprentice she was responsible for training.

Interestingly for her, the "computer" became a social actor participating in a back-and-forth exchange. At one point, she even took on the computer's role in the conversation, asking, "Do you want to regenerate

continues

that?" This moment of stepping into the computer's voice showed how easily she anthropomorphized the system. By speaking as the AI, she framed it as a quasi-human agent with intentions, questions, and a role in the joint task.

Mental Model: It's "Happening to Me"

An important shift in understanding her mental model occurred when Carmen was asked to describe specific machine learning tools she encountered in her everyday phone use. She quickly focused on Instagram Search as something that learned from her input, based on who she follows and what she searches for in the app. Carmen continued to use the word "inputting" to describe how Instagram learns from her, but her gestures hinted at a shift in her mental model of inputting.

Rather than showing herself directing the exchange of information, she used a sequence of coordinating and representational gestures to map out how multiple services connect and communicate with one another. She lifted her right hand, palm up in a cupping shape, close to her body at shoulder level to perform an abstract representational gesture indicating her Amazon cart. She then flipped her hand over and pointed down toward her phone as she stated, "knows what's in my Amazon cart" (see Figure 4.14). These pragmatic gestures clarified that Instagram knew what was in her cart.

FIGURE 4.14
Carmen uses her phone as a prop, positioning Instagram search as a node in a network of services communicating information that did not involve her.

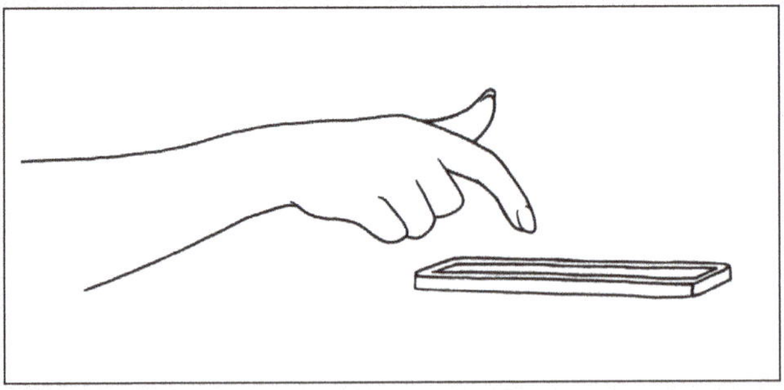

Next, she extended that same hand forward into the space between her body and laptop, pinching her index finger and thumb to frame a small rectangle. This abstract representational gesture referenced the Google Chrome browser open on her computer. Once that reference was established, she then made a pragmatic, coordinating gesture as she pointed to her phone and stated that "Instagram knows what's going on in my Google Chrome." And then in a fluid motion, she extended her arm toward her computer and swirled her pointing finger over her computer where her browser lived. These gestures extended the words to show that these services were connected together and "knowing" was a process of communication between her shopping cart and browser that was mediated by Instagram.

Through these gestures, Carmen illustrated a complex, invisible network of systems communicating across devices and platforms—one that operated independently of her actions. The open-handed offering gesture she once used to show her active role was now gone. This insight was further confirmed when Carmen used the word "inputting," and she used pragmatic air quotes, her fingers flexing to signal distance and irony (see Figure 4.15). "I didn't give any commands to do it," she explained. "It's just happening to me."

Carmen's mental model had distinctly shifted from one marked by agency and control to one where agency had been ceded to machines. She explained how the process of how machines learned was now "happening to me" and was given clear form in gesture.

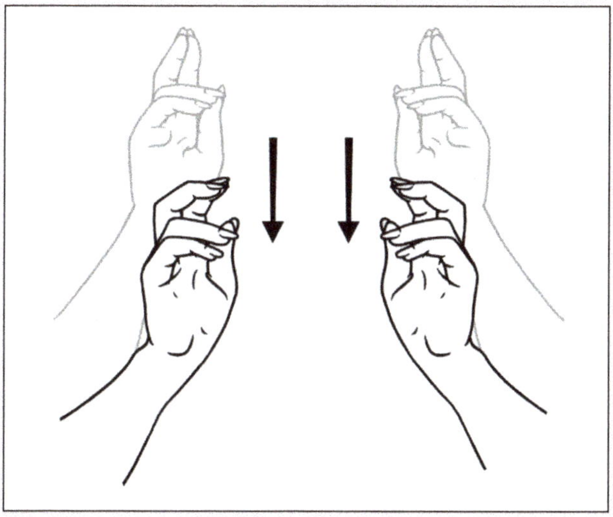

FIGURE 4.15
Inputting becomes an abstract notion in Carmen's gestures, placing air quotes around the term.

The Strategic Impact: AI as a Social Actor

Glimpses of Carmen's mental model were visible in the moment. The interviewer spotted the clues in gestures and used them to prompt further thinking and clarification. It was apparent that Carmen was grappling with two ways of understanding how machines learned: one active and agentive, the other more passive and external.

continues

However, it wasn't until later, during detailed video analysis, that the distinction became fully clear. The team could see that for the same linguistic label of "inputting," Carmen was drawing on two different, contextually shaped mental models. With tools like ChatGPT, where she typed prompts and received responses, her gestures showed a back-and-forth exchange that made her the active instructor, teaching the machine what she needed. With systems like Instagram Search, by contrast, her gestures revealed that machine learning happened outside her control. The machine absorbed her behavior passively, turning her from an agent into an observer.

This was a crucial insight for the EdTech product team considering the roadmap for their AI-powered grader. If people were using new AI technologies that gave them a sense of agency, AI was no longer just a tool but was becoming a social actor that they could personify and train. This revelation was made possible by attending to the gestures.

The product team went beyond just thinking about specific features to also considering how the architecture of the grading system would position AI socially amid the sensitive relationship between an instructor and a student. This pushed the team to ask a new, high-stakes question: in a grading context, *what kind of social actor should AI be?*

This sparked a critical design debate about where to position the AI. Should it be a visible mediator that interacted with the student directly and gave them feedback? Or should it be a background assistant that empowered the instructor while remaining invisible to the student? Ultimately, the team decided to prioritize a path that kept the AI in an assistant role to the instructor, ensuring the primary relationship supported by the design was the human relationship between the instructor and student.

This decision was grounded in a deeper understanding of user mental models that would have been entirely missed by analyzing words alone.

When you learn to see gestures in interviews and observations, you deepen your understanding of users. You are doing more than collecting what people have said. You are gathering visible clues about how they understand the world, where they hesitate, what they assume, and how they move through systems and tasks. When you attend to gestures on the research path and what they naturally reveal about people, you come away with a fuller picture of their experiences that gives you and your team a stronger foundation for defining problems, identifying opportunities, and deciding what to do next.

Takeaways

- **Set the stage before you start.** Creating the right conditions for gestures to emerge should not be left to chance. Design your protocol for the eyes as well as the ears—free the hands, arrange the space, establish rapport through your own body, and prime users to gesture with warm-up tasks that invite physical demonstration.
- **Gestures are windows into mental models.** On the research path, thinking gestures are your richest source of insight. They surface users' understanding of a system, what they expect it to do, and where their model breaks down in ways that words alone may not make clear.
- **Mental models are often revealed over time.** A single gesture gives you a fragment, and a collection of gestures gives you the picture. Your job in the moment isn't to solve the puzzle but to collect the clues, noting each gestured piece so you can assemble the full mental model in your analysis.
- **Gesture-speech mismatches are your cue to dig in.** When what someone says and what their gestures do don't align with one another, something important is forming beneath the surface. These are the moments to slow down, clarify, and press thinking further.
- **Shift between observing and actively drawing out thinking.** Your role in an interview moves fluidly between spectator and participant. When a user's thinking is stuck, incomplete, or fuzzy, use gestures to clarify ambiguity and push toward new connections, helping them arrive at their own "aha" moment.
- **Use your body to guide the interaction.** Your own gestures are a facilitation tool. Use pragmatic movements to manage pace, signal transitions, return to earlier topics, and check in on your participant's engagement—all without interrupting the flow of conversation.

FIELD NOTES FROM STEPHANIE

I have often used gestures in my own teaching to understand students' thinking and help them take that thinking further. In one class discussion, a student was talking about the rights of undocumented people. "There needs to be justice," he said. The words could have meant many things. Deterrence? Fairness? Equal treatment? But as he spoke, his hands told me there was more to the idea. Close to his body, his fingers loosely interwove, palms turned upward, as if he were holding a complex relationship in his hands. When he said "justice," his hands, still holding the gesture, gave a small beat, and then the gesture disappeared.

I copied the gesture back to him, gently pushed it into the shared space between us, and asked him to say more about justice. He picked the gesture back up. This time, as his hands moved, his idea became clearer. "Justice," he explained, "was not retribution." "It was not even simple equality. Justice meant a community working together so everyone had the opportunity to thrive."

His hands had carried an idea his words had not yet fully formed. By noticing the gesture and returning it to him, I not only gave him a way to push his thinking, but I also gained a deeper sense of his idea of justice.

FIELD NOTES FROM DANE

I study data professionals for a living. My current research focuses on how BI (business intelligence) data modelers and report builders are using AI and how it is reshaping their workflows. In practice, my interviews are dense with jargon and systems so particular to each organization that no two are alike.

I structure these interviews deliberately. I begin with open-ended questions about context: how someone came to work with data, what problems keep them up at night. No screens, no tools. Hands are free, and the **thinking body** is at its most expressive. Then comes a hands-on segment where participants show me how they actually work. Gestures collapse as hands move to a mouse or trackpad. After the demonstration, I pull the conversation back to open discussion, and something shifts. People gesture more freely and differently than before. Using the tool has changed how they think about it.

In one interview, I asked a participant to explain how his team had built an agentic tool to answer questions about business reports. As he described what it involved, his language grew dense fast. CRM (customer relationship management), data warehouse, flat files, internal documentation. I was tracking, but it was complex.

Then I watched his hands. He reached out in multiple directions, fingers spread toward different invisible sources. Then both hands gathered slowly inward to a single point in front of him. He had not finished his sentence, but I already understood something his words had not delivered: he was not describing a pipeline, but rather a convergence of different data sources into a single place.

I nodded toward his hands and asked, "So you are bringing all of that context into one place that the agent can access?" He paused, looked at his own hands, and said, "Yes. Exactly."

That moment of clarity did not originate in what the participant said, but what his gestures depicted.

I have to figure out why the barista didn't understand Dane's order...
Barry might just have issues remembering orders. My glasses have a great microphone, so the Gestix Pro can use the transcript to figure out what happened!
Ok, analysis machine! Listen to Barry and Dane's exchange and help me figure this out...
GESTIX PRO
vol. 1
ROOT CAUSE: HUMAN MEMORY SPAN
RECOMMENDATION: REMOVE HUMAN FROM LOOP
CONFIDENCE: HIGH
We need to help baristas better remember customer orders. They need help!

CHAPTER 5

Analyze Your Gesture Data

You've seen how to spot gestures in the moment during interviews and observations as a way to gather the fragments of someone's mental model. Maybe you got enough in the moment to be confident about what your users need. If so, that's great! But more often, momentary breakthroughs give way to additional questions. This is where revisiting your video recordings with a systematic approach will help you reach that deeper level of understanding about your users.

You already possess the skill to interpret gestures in everyday life. But when you join that intuition with a reliable research method, you will get so much more! This is your guide for refining and structuring your interpretation of gestures in interviews and observations efficiently. You will see how you can take the gestures you spotted in the moment and discern what they might mean when stitched together.

Let Your Research Questions Lead You

When you return to your video recordings, you enter a different mode of attention. During interviews and observations, you were filtering a flood of information in real time. In the formal analysis stage, you can slow down and look again with fresh eyes. This second pass creates space to notice subtleties—the small mismatches, fleeting gestures, and moments that slipped by too quickly the first time.

At this stage, you are still on the research path, and your guiding goal remains the same: building a deeper understanding of your users. Thinking gestures will, at this point, often offer the richest clues, while communicative and coordinating gestures help fill in essential context. But more than anything, your research questions should guide what you look for in gestures and how you interpret what they reveal.

Strong research questions give purpose to your analysis. They help remove uncertainty from your product roadmap by surfacing what your team most needs to understand in order to act. In gesture analysis, the movements you observe become evidence that helps answer that question.

Instead of asking a broad question like "What frustrates people?," you might ask more focused questions such as: Why is engagement lower than projected? Where are users creating work-arounds because the tool disrupts their established flow? How is the target persona's home or work context changing, and is the current solution keeping up with their evolving needs?

These kinds of questions shape how you analyze gestures. They help you decide which gestures to examine closely and what they might reveal about how users understand a system, navigate a process, or imagine how something works. When a gesture exposes how someone organizes an idea, anticipates a step, or struggles with a task, it becomes valuable evidence for answering your research questions.

As you move into formal analysis, keep three guiding commitments in mind:

- **Be deliberate.** Build some insight through careful observation, interpretation, and comparison, not just by watching video footage and hoping something interesting appears.
- **Take stock of what you know.** Ground your analysis in the gestures, insights, and prior research you already have so you can build on existing understanding rather than starting from scratch.
- **Right-size your data.** Not every gesture is worth analyzing. The scope of your analysis should reflect your time, your risk, and how much clarity you already have about the problem.

By letting your research questions guide you and by being thoughtful about how much and what you analyze, you'll be better positioned to find the gestures that matter most and turn them into actionable insight.

Be Deliberate

Your research questions provide the direction for your analysis, but your mindset provides the rigor. A formal analysis of video recordings requires you to slow down and work deliberately. You need a clear and curious mind as you review video footage, interpret gestures, compare moments, and group emerging themes. This kind of analysis of gestures is not automatic. It is a skill honed through practice.

There's often a tradeoff between speed and depth in research. It's tempting to move fast, especially when timelines are tight and stakeholders want answers now.

This temptation to prioritize speed is especially potent with the rise of AI-powered tools. Many tools seem like they should be able to deliver insights instantly, seemingly without sacrificing accuracy. But this can be a seductive and dangerous illusion. Remember that most AI analysis operates on text alone—the very medium you know to be incomplete. When you feed AI a transcript, you are necessarily supplying it with a shallow data source.

So, remain skeptical of the outputs of your tools and your own assumptions. Ask yourself: How well do you really understand your users? Are personas and journey maps holding up in the face of actual behavior? Do you need more evidence to reduce uncertainty? This kind of inquiry will help you decide when a deeper dive into gesture analysis is worth it.

BE AWARE OF COGNITIVE BLIND SPOTS

Research on judgment and decision-making showed that people rely on two modes of thinking.[1] System 1 is fast, intuitive, and automatic, and while efficient, it is also prone to systematic errors. These errors come from mental shortcuts, or heuristics, that people use to make quick judgments, such as:

- **Attention bias:** The tendency to give disproportionate weight to information that aligns with what a person is already predisposed to notice, often based on habits, expectations, or emotional relevance.
- **Confirmation bias:** The tendency to seek or interpret evidence in ways that support existing beliefs.
- **Salience bias:** The tendency to give undue importance to information because it is vivid, striking, or stands out perceptually, regardless of its actual relevance.
- **Heuristic substitution:** The tendency to answer a simpler question when a more complex one is asked.
- **Cognitive ease:** The tendency to prefer ideas or interpretations that feel familiar or effortless.

People have the capacity to engage System 2 thinking, which is slower, more deliberate, and less prone to these biases.

1 Kahneman (2011) synthesized decades of research with Tversky into a two-system model of judgment, showing that fast, associative thinking is efficient but structurally biased, producing predictable errors across domains from medical diagnosis to financial forecasting.

Take Stock of What You Know

Before you dive deeper into your recordings, pause and recognize that you are not starting from zero. You already have the gestures you captured in the moment, along with whatever you noted in your field observations. And unless this is your very first time learning about your users, you also carry forward what you have gained from previous research about their needs, pain points, habits, and contexts.

This matters because your analysis does more than just answer today's research questions. It also contributes to a longer arc of understanding that continues to grow across projects and product cycles. Each interview and observation offers a chance to address the immediate problem and to notice patterns in how people think and act that hold beyond any single feature.

When you capture those recurring patterns as design principles, your knowledge begins to accumulate in a way that becomes useful for future work. You move from reacting to isolated issues to anticipating how users are likely to respond in new situations. Over time, this growing body of insight becomes a durable foundation for product decisions, not just a set of findings tied to one moment.

Right-Size Your Data

A single hour of video can feel like a mountain of data. You cannot, and should not, analyze every single movement. You already have tossed the gestures that did not gain you anything in the moment during the interview. There are other valuable filters you can apply to data so that you can narrow the field further.

Another way to zero in on the gestures that matter is to right-size your data. Base this scoping decision on three practical considerations:

- **Value of the data to generate new insights:** Do you already have a solid understanding of your users from prior work? If the data expands that understanding, keep it.
- **Risk of getting it wrong:** How much clarity do you already have about the problem space, and what are the risks of drawing the wrong conclusions? If you suspect risk or you work in a regulated industry, keep it.
- **Time to complete the research:** How much time do you have to complete the research? If you're on a tight timeline, keep the gestures with the potential to contribute the newest information.

Once you have set your scope, remember that a reliable tool for filtering gestures is to examine their relationship to the speech. Keep gesture-speech mismatches, as these moments may increase the value of data to generate new insights. Toss gesture-speech matches, as these are redundant with speech—nothing gained, nothing lost!

YOU CAN SCALE YOUR ANALYSIS

You can always decide how deep to go in your gesture analysis. The more detailed your approach, the richer your insights will be. A useful way to calibrate is to consider two factors: how much clarity you already have about the problem you are researching, and how much risk there is in drawing the wrong conclusions (see Figure 5.1).

When problem clarity is low and the risk of getting it wrong is high, a full gesture analysis is worth the investment. When clarity is low, but risk is also low, you can be more selective, focusing only on the gestures most likely to surface new insight. And when you already have strong problem clarity, gestures can serve a narrower but still valuable purpose: triangulating and validating the interpretation you have already developed from your other data.

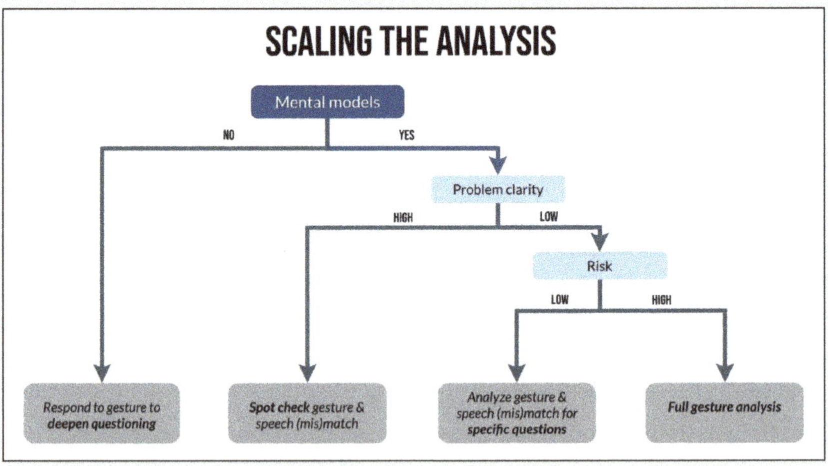

FIGURE 5.1

You can scale your gesture analysis by assessing whether you have high or low clarity about the problem space against the risk of drawing the wrong conclusion.

Calibrate the depth of your analysis to the risk tolerance.

Set Up Your Analysis

Strong analysis doesn't happen by accident. It takes preparation. Meaning can easily slip past you when you're focused on listening and responding in real time. This is where video becomes essential. So, queue up your recordings and let's get started.

If you conducted the interview yourself, you likely already noted a few interesting moments in your field notes. But if you're analyzing video from another researcher or exploring data in a research repository, your first step is a quick scan of the footage to locate gestures.

Skim through the recording and watch for gestures in context. When you spot one that seems relevant to your research question, especially those that add new information through gesture-speech mismatch, note it down in a way that works for you like a timestamp, tag, or even a quick hand-drawn sketch in your field notes. This will make your later analysis much more efficient.

Once you've gathered your gestures, prep your materials for deeper analysis. This involves two key tasks:

- **Demarcate the gestures.** Indicate where each gesture begins and ends.
- **Transcribe gestures and talk.** Create a transcript that pairs the gesture description with the accompanying speech.

Taking the time to get organized now will make your analysis more focused, efficient, and ultimately more insightful.

Demarcate the Gesture

Before you can analyze a gesture, you need to define its boundaries. This means identifying the specific moment of movement you want to study. Researchers often call this the *unit of analysis.*

Each gesture consists of three phases:

1. **Preparatory:** Think of this as the "windup." It's how someone gets ready to make the gesture. Look for them to move a body part, like lifting their hands from their lap.
2. **Stroke:** This is the main part of the gesture, the "pitch." It's where the action happens and where you will find the most important information.

3. **Retraction:** This is the "wind down." The hands and body return to their resting position, completing the gesture.

Figure 5.2 illustrates the phases of the gesture like a baseball pitch.

FIGURE 5.2
A gesture occurs in three stages, like a baseball pitch with its windup, pitch, and wind down.

Sometimes, this sequence is clear and easy to mark. Other times, gestures flow together, overlap, or happen so quickly that it's hard to tell where one ends and another begins. Trust your instincts. Ask yourself: what feels like one meaningful unit of movement? You may not get it perfect, but that's okay. Mark what you see and keep going.

Transcribe Gestures and Talk

Now, it is time to transcribe the gestures alongside the accompanying talk. You will likely have a full transcript readily available from a research platform or videoconferencing tool but be sure to double-check it. Automated transcription software can sometimes misunderstand industry jargon or mishear phrases, so before you align your gestures, make sure that the text you are matching them to is accurate.

Once your transcript is verified, add a layer of detail to describe the gesture. You can do this by snapping a screenshot, writing a short description like a *left-to-right typing motion*, or sketching a loose drawing. Keep it simple and quick; you can always add more detail later.

There are many ways to create a gesture-speech transcript. Use a format that works for you. The goal is to be systematic and explicitly show the overlap of movement and speech. Here are some common and effective options:

Option 1: Transcription with a quick sketch:

If you prefer to work in your field notebook, you can capture gestures as quick sketches alongside talk (see Figure 5.3).

FIGURE 5.3
Example of a quick sketch of a gesture aligned to the transcript.

Option 2: Using a spreadsheet:

Participant	Transcript	Gesture	Time
Carmen	"Make this email sound friendly."	Left-to-right typing motion	00:37:12

Option 3: Inline with the transcript:

> Carmen: [00:37:12] "Make this email <GESTURE> sound friendly </GESTURE> [left-to-right typing motion]."

You should also note moments where there is no talk. This is especially common and valuable during usability testing. When a user is focused on completing a task, they often act in the absence of speech, performing various gestures.

A hesitant mouse movement before a click, a furrowed brow with a lean into the screen, or a frustrated sigh as they lean back are all leading indicators of broader usability challenges. Be sure to capture these instances in your gesture transcript. Just be cautious about over-interpreting their meaning without the context of speech.

Analyze Gestures

Now that you have organized your data, it's time to begin the formal analysis. You have already laid the groundwork by identifying gestures worth a closer look and creating a gesture-speech transcript. This next step is where you formally evaluate what each gesture is doing and how it contributes to a deeper understanding of your users.

How to Evaluate Each Gesture

Although your instinct may give you a hunch about what a gesture means, the only way to know for sure is to evaluate the data systematically. This process involves a clear, four-step loop for each gesture you analyze:

1. **Look at the dimensions.** Reassess the gesture's dimensions—its *space*, its alignment with *speech*, and its *type and function*—to understand its contribution in the moment.
2. **Code it for its meaning.** Move toward formalizing your interpretation by giving the gesture a preliminary code. This is a label that captures your interpretation of the gesture's meaning.
3. **Collect and define your codes.** Assemble all your codes into a central document or a codebook. This allows you to build a running definition for each code alongside examples of when it was applied.
4. **Record your analysis.** Finally, make a record of this entire analysis. Whether you use notecards, a spreadsheet, or a dedicated research tool, document your interpretation so you can return to it when you begin looking for broader connections.

Now, let's apply this process to a critical moment from the cloud storage interview in Chapter 4, "Understand Users' Gestures." From reviewing your video and field notes, you have already identified several gestures like the placing and pulling-down gestures, that revealed the participant's belief in a manual process for syncing files from their computer. You have grouped these under the preliminary code `Manual Retrieval`.

As you re-watch the video, you notice a subtle gesture you missed in the moment. While the participant describes getting a presentation from the cloud onto their laptop for a meeting, they make a quick grabbing and pulling motion in the air to their right, as if plucking an object from a shelf and bringing it close. This reinforces your interpretation, so you add this new instance to your `Manual Retrieval` code.

As you continue watching, you see that following this moment in the recording, in the live session, you asked a question that challenged this one-way mental model: "So, if you change a cloud file on your laptop, what exactly happens on your phone right away?"

The participant starts to answer confidently, "Well, nothing, I'd have to go and . . . " but then stops. After a long pause, they say, "Wait a second . . . I'm confused." As they say this, their right hand, held open with the palm vertical, begins to move back and forth in a slow, wavering motion between their laptop and their phone. You have labeled this the wavering-hand gesture (see Figure 5.4).

FIGURE 5.4
A participant's wavering-hand gesture reveals uncertainty about the direction of cloud sync.

You think this might be another example of `Manual Retrieval` because the user shows something moving from their phone to the laptop, but you decide to rewind and take a more deliberate look. The words "I'm confused" suggest it might mean something else.

First, you look at the dimensions. The gesture occurs in the space between things, the laptop and the phone. It is working to coordinate these resources as the participant thinks through their confusion. This tells you the problem is not located on a single device, but in the uncertain relationship between them. The gesture is a mismatch with their initial, confident words, but a match for their final utterance ("I'm confused"). Crucially, the gesture provides specificity that the words lack, visually identifying the source of their confusion. The gesture is an abstract representational gesture (type) functioning to depict the idea of uncertain directionality (function).

You've convinced yourself this is something new that isn't already in your codebook. You define the new code, `Source of Truth Uncertainty`, and apply it to this wavering-hand gesture. This new code is then collected and defined in your codebook, where it now lives alongside the `Manual Retrieval` code (see Figure 5.5).

By systematically comparing gestures to existing codes and evaluating their breakdown against your running definition, you build up a set of categories that you can slot the gestures into.

Gesture Codebook

Code	Definition	Gesture Example	Speech	Notes
Manual Retrieval	User believes cloud files must be manually moved between devices	Grabbing and pulling motion from the air, as if pulling an object from a shelf	"I'd have to go and get it"	Consistent with one-way mental model of sync
Source of Truth Uncertainty	User is unsure which device holds the authoritative version of a file	Open palm, vertical, wavering slowly back and forth between laptop and phone	"Wait a second... I'm confused"	Gesture-speech mismatch — words initially confident, gesture reveals doubt

FIGURE 5.5

A sample codebook entry showing codes `Manual Retrieval` and `Source of Truth Uncertainty` with definitions and the gesture examples that prompted each one.

Be sure to collect your observations for each participant's gestures that you analyze and show how they accrue to individual codes. Figure 5.6 illustrates how you can do this.

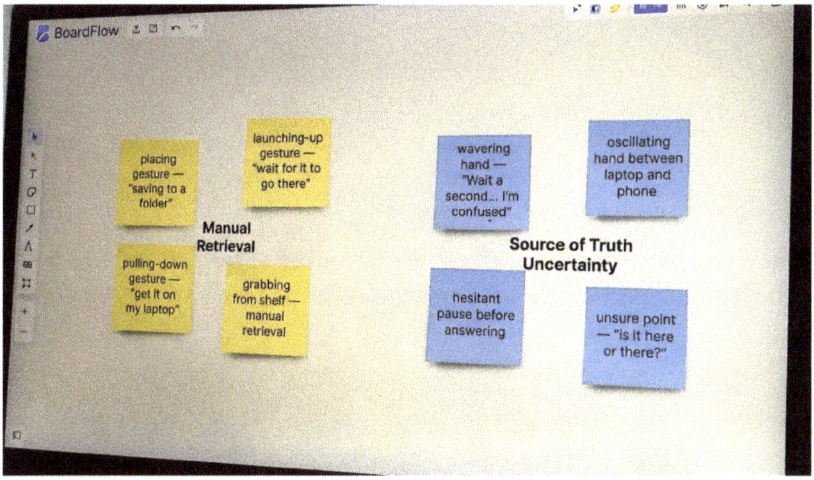

FIGURE 5.6
Individual gesture observations accumulate into discrete codes in the codebook, illustrating how repeated instances of similar movements are grouped into a single, defined category.

COMPARE, COMPARE, COMPARE

Even though the process of analysis is often presented as a sequence of steps, real analysis is rarely linear. Meaning often emerges through constant comparison—looking at one piece of data in light of others that seem similar, then asking: Is this really the same thing? Or is something different happening here? This technique comes from grounded theory, where researchers compare pieces of data continuously to refine their code categories before surfacing themes (see Figure 5.7). The method has you check and recheck your codes, interrogating each new data point for subtle differences, and then refining your interpretations along the way.

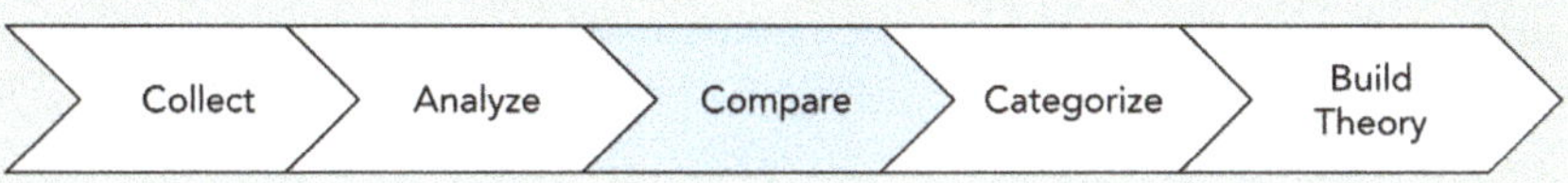

FIGURE 5.7
Stages of grounded theory building that rely on constant comparison.

Look at Gestures Individually and Over Time

A single gesture provides a snapshot, but the full story of your user's experience often unfolds by comparing a collection of gestures over time. Your task is to look for connections and patterns in your codebook.

In the cloud sync participant's case, it now contains several distinct codes, including `Manual Retrieval` and `Source of Truth Uncertainty`. These codes already suggest that the user has an incomplete mental model, but the picture becomes much clearer when you compare them to another moment.

When you review your coded gestures from earlier in the interview, you recall the participant talking about a messaging app. They made

ANALYZING GESTURES WITH SOFTWARE

Modern gesture analysis dates back to the 1970s. Researchers started to incorporate technology into their practice because it added a level of fidelity to their work beyond what they could reconstruct from field notes. These pioneers would carefully watch (and rewatch) a VHS tape of an interview or observation, pause the tape at critical moments, and then use semi-translucent trace paper on a CRT (cathode ray tube) monitor to create the outlines of subjects in those stills at various points in motion.

Luckily for you (and us), software has made this process significantly less painful. Any tool can work but consider a few core features when setting up your tooling. Whatever your software choice, we recommend that it have a few key video manipulation and annotation capabilities. If you work for a company that has multiple software licenses for specialized research products, then there are also some additional nice-to-haves you should consider (see Table 5.1).

TABLE 5.1 CORE FEATURES TO CONSIDER

Must Haves	Nice to Haves
Load in video file(s).	Create breaks or segments in the video.
Identify timestamps throughout the video.	Append text annotations (especially overlapping).
Append graphical annotations.	Automated transcription.
Export analyses to CSV, spreadsheet, or database.	Integrate with your company's research repository or database.

a simple, confident pointing gesture from their laptop to their phone while saying, "Whatever I type here just appears there." You had coded this moment as `Instant Availability`. Now, when you place that confident point next to their later, wavering-hand gesture in the context of cloud files, the evolution becomes clearer. The gesture's form changed from a straight, decisive line to an unsteady oscillation.

This visible evolution in their hands tells you precisely where and why their mental model broke down. They had a working model for one task (messaging) that did not apply to another (cloud files), and the collision of these two models resulted in confusion. Tracking this change gives you a much deeper insight than analyzing these gestures in isolation.

But don't think this means that you need to fork out money to get started doing gesture analysis. There are free tools already on many computers that can be repurposed for the task. For example, programs like iMovie and a text notepad (see Figure 5.8) meet the core criteria and were part of how we analyzed the data for this book! Just pick a tool and give it a try.

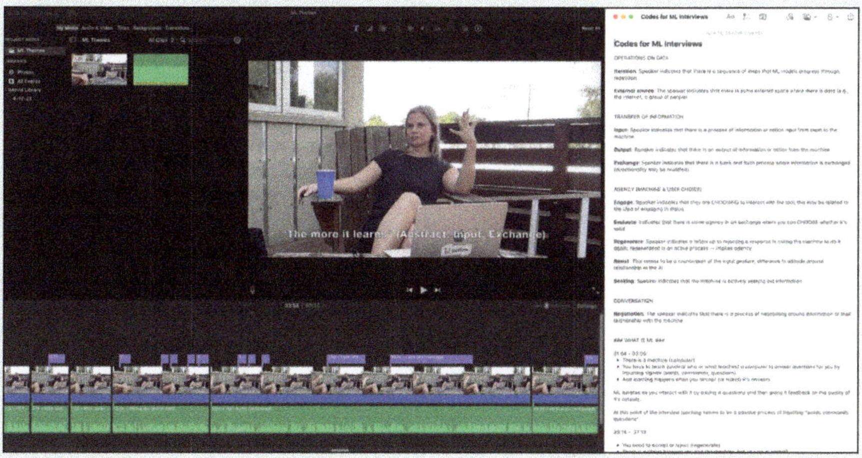

FIGURE 5.8
An analytic setup using preloaded software (iMovie and Notes) in macOS to code gestures and maintain a codebook.

Synthesize

Now that you've coded your gestures and assigned interpretations, it's time to take a higher-altitude look at your data. The goal of synthesis is to move beyond individual codes and find the broader patterns and relationships among them. This is how you build a compelling narrative about your users in aggregate, based on the evidence you have systematically gathered.

How to Draw Conclusions

Begin by reviewing your full set of codes from your codebook. At this stage, you are looking for connections, asking yourself which codes seem to reflect similar ideas or functions. You will start to group these related codes together in inductive clusters. These clusters are the building blocks of your larger themes.

For example, in reviewing your codebook from several interviews about a cloud storage product, you might find a cluster of codes like `Manual Retrieval` (from one participant's pulling-down gesture) and `Step-by-Step Upload` (from another participant's gestures). You could group these under a broader, emergent theme you call *Synchronization as a Manual Process.*

At the same time, you might find another cluster of codes in your data, such as `Instant Availability` (from discussions about messaging apps) and `Instant Update Expectation` (from a calendar context). This second group forms another clear theme, which you call *Synchronization as an Instantaneous State.*

Once you have identified your themes, you can construct a narrative that explains the relationship between them. In this case, the story isn't about one user's momentary confusion. It's a larger narrative about how your users, in aggregate, hold two fundamentally competing mental models for how data synchronization works.

This thematic tension helps explain why you also have a separate cluster of codes in your data, such as `Source of Truth Uncertainty` and `Hesitant Cross-Device Actions`. The user conflict represented by these codes is a direct result of the two larger themes you identified.

Clustering individual codes reveals the core tension between themes *Synchronization as a Manual Process* and *Synchronization as an Instantaneous State*, which gives rise to conflicts in users' mental models (see Figure 5.9).

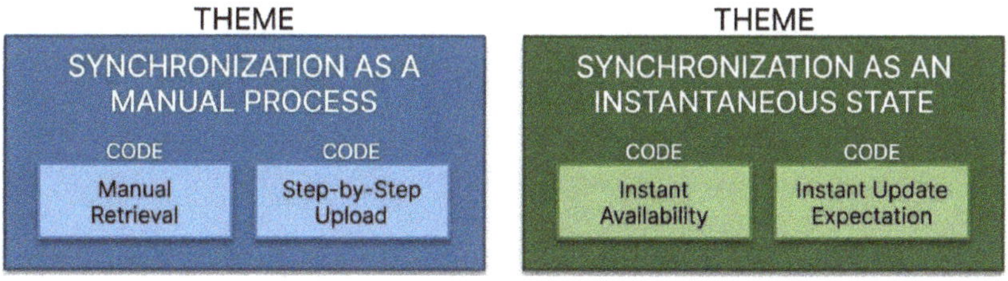

FIGURE 5.9
Individual gesture codes cluster into two competing themes and reveal the core tension in users' mental models.

Distill Design Principles

Congrats, getting this far is no small feat! Now, you want to translate what you've learned about users into actionable advice that your design and product colleagues can run with and make the decisions about what actually will get built.

You've analyzed your data and synthesized it into a compelling narrative. These narratives matter because they allow you to translate your research findings into concrete design directions. The most effective way to do this is by creating a set of evidence-backed design principles.

A design principle is a declarative, falsifiable statement informed by prior research and theory. Unlike a simple best practice or opinion, a strong design principle functions as a reusable hypothesis about how a design will support people's thinking and behavior.

Here, design does not simply mean visual polish or interface details. It refers to the artifact you put in front of people: the software, workflow, interaction, or experience that users engage with. In design-based research, that artifact becomes a vehicle for learning. By observing how people interact with a design, you can test and refine your understanding of how they think, act, and solve problems.

To be effective, a design principle should be testable and refinable as you learn from real-world use. Because designs are placed in front of users and observed in practice, they allow teams to continually evaluate whether their principles hold up. In this way, each design contains multiple opportunities to learn something new about users.

Good principles are also transferable across multiple features, not just a single UI element. For example, the principle "Provide reversible actions" can guide everything from deleting a file to publishing a post.

Finally, strong principles are grounded in theory. They connect to scientific understanding of how people think and behave. This gives your principles explanatory power: they are not arbitrary rules, but guidelines based on how people actually think and act.

A useful way to structure these principles is to think of them as a ladder with four distinct levels, moving from the most abstract idea down to the concrete implementation:

- **Meta-principle:** This is the broad, theory-driven reason why a design works. It often relates to a core psychological or cognitive concept.
- **Design principle:** This is the reusable rule or logic that guides a class of designs. It's actionable but not tied to a specific UI or prototype.
- **Design recommendation:** This is a more concrete guideline that helps operationalize the design principle in terms of what needs to be mocked up or built. It's how you apply the principle in practice.
- **Design instantiation:** This is what actually gets built, like the screen, component, or flow that brings the principle to life.

To see this in action, think about how the team working on the desktop cloud sync client might translate their research findings into design principles.

From the analysis, you learned that some users hold competing mental models. As a meta-principle, grounded in cognitive theory, you might try to address this by stating: "Users need a coherent system model to reduce cognitive load and act confidently." From there, you can derive a design principle: "Make the synchronization status and source of truth visible across all devices." This principle then leads to a design recommendation: "Use clear visual indicators to show whether a file is local, synced, or currently syncing." And finally, this is realized in the design instantiation: a green checkmark icon next to synced files and a persistent "Syncing..." status bar at the bottom of the screen.

When you translate your research into principles this way, you not only guide the design with evidence, but you also set up the next cycle of iteration to directly test your ideas. This creates a virtuous cycle where careful iteration both refines your product and deepens your understanding of human behavior.

NOTE DESIGN-BASED RESEARCH AND DESIGN PRINCIPLES

The approach of using design principles comes from a methodology called *design-based research* (DBR). DBR grew up in the education field but has wide utility for any team-building products for people. Its core philosophy is that designs are not just artifacts delivered to users; they are testable, interactive hypotheses about how people think and act. When a user interacts with a product, you are not only seeing whether the design "works," but also gaining insight into their cognition. In this tradition, principles are declarative, falsifiable statements that are informed by prior research and theory. By explicitly testing and refining these principles, you create a cycle: your product improves, and your team's understanding of its users accrues into durable, predictive knowledge.

Validate Your Insights

Now that you've constructed your story and defined your design principles, how do you know you got it right? Sometimes, the interpretation is straightforward, but other times you may have doubts you want to clear up. Validation is the process of checking your conclusions against different sources. This step ensures that your insights can hold up to scrutiny.

There are several ways to validate your gesture analysis:

- **Proof with a colleague.** Having another person review your analysis reduces the risk of individual biases coloring how you see the data. A fresh set of eyes is one of the best ways to pressure-test your interpretation.
- **Run by an expert.** If you are working with a technical product or in a specialized industry, engaging with a subject matter expert (SME) can help you decode jargon and sharpen your interpretation of gestures.
- **Check with participants.** You can also use member checking to validate your findings by sharing your insights back directly with the people you interviewed or observed.

NOTE CONSIDERATIONS FOR MEMBER CHECKING

Member checking with gestures requires a specific approach. Gestures often occur below conscious awareness, so participants may not recall making them or why they did so. Instead of asking, "Why did you make this gesture?" which they likely won't remember, you should validate the meaning you have inferred from the moment.

Communicate for Impact

Your analysis isn't finished until you have communicated it. If you cannot convince stakeholders of your insights, you have only done half the job. This is where you translate your analysis into a persuasive story that inspires your team to act. Use your gestures as critical tools to make your case.

You can do this with four complementary techniques:

- **Make the abstract concrete.** Use your hands and body to make data and processes tangible.
- **Structure your story in space.** Use the area around you to visually organize your narrative.
- **Convey the user's experience.** Embody the user's actions and emotions to build empathy.
- **Gauge your audience's understanding.** Watch your audience for feedback to ensure that your message is landing.

Your goal when using these techniques is to achieve mutual understanding. The gestures you make are intended for people to see, so make sure that your communicating and coordinating gestures are performed in the shared space, clearly visible to your stakeholders, and crisply employed.

People grasp concepts more deeply when they both hear them and see them in motion. Your insights are often abstract, so use your gestures to make them tangible. For example, to explain the concept of a "broken information flow," you can first use a smooth, sweeping gesture to represent the ideal state. Then follow it with a short, jagged, interrupted movement to show the reality of the user's experience. This makes the abstract idea of the friction visible and felt.

Coordinating gestures create coherence and help your audience follow your logic. Use the physical space around you to create a mental map for them. If you were presenting your insights from the cloud sync interview, you could create spatial zones for your key themes by consistently placing the *Synchronization as a Manual Process* to your left and the *Synchronization as an Instantaneous State* to your right. Then, use clear pointing gestures to guide your audience's attention to those zones as you speak.

The most direct way to bridge the empathy gap is to convey the user's experience. You have two effective options to do this. The first is to let the user speak for themself. A short, well-chosen video clip of a user sighing in frustration or fumbling with a prototype can be a persuasive addition to the presentation or explanation that you could give. But if you don't have a clip, you can also become the user. Instead of just saying that the user in the cloud storage interview was confused, you can re-enact their behavior. Pause, furrow your brow, and perform their slow, wavering-hand gesture between two points in space. This makes the user's experience immediate and visceral.

A presentation is a conversation, so you must constantly gauge if you are achieving mutual understanding. Watch your audience. Are they leaning in, nodding, or are their eyes glazing over? Their bodies provide a constant stream of feedback on whether your message is clear. If you see looks of confusion, you can course-correct and actively seek alignment before moving on.

Finally, be intentional in your delivery. If your hands are constantly moving with meaningless filler gestures, your audience will stop watching them. Rehearse ahead of time and choose the moments where a gesture will have the most impact. Also know that stillness right before you make an important gestural explanation creates anticipation and signals that what comes next is important.

CASE STUDY: DECODING CARE IN PHYSICAL THERAPY

This case study follows a software design team as they partner with a group of medical researchers developing a new physical therapy device. It walks through the full process of gesture analysis, showing how insights emerge as gestures are examined systematically across time rather than in isolated moments.

By revisiting the video repeatedly and tracking gestures as they appear, reappear, and evolve during the interaction, the team begins to see patterns that would otherwise remain hidden. This process demonstrates how systematic gesture analysis in a clinical environment can uncover insights that go far beyond a product's user interface.

Through deliberate analysis of gestures over time, the team surfaces design principles that reshape their understanding of the entire ecosystem surrounding the tool, from the hardware and software to the clinical workflow in which they are meant to operate.

The Challenge: Standardizing Physical Therapy

The medical research team at a large research hospital had been developing a promising new physical therapy device. They had prototyped and manufactured a set of "smart paddles" with built-in pressure sensors that reliably captured force measurements during soft-tissue manipulation. Alongside the hardware, they created a basic visualization interface. Nothing flashy, but enough to show that the paddles could transmit and display force data graphically.

When the software design consultancy joined the project, the initial ask was to improve this visualization interface so that clinicians could use it more effectively. To get clarity on how the interface could be improved, the design team conducted a video-recorded contextual inquiry session with Dr. Stacy, the physical therapist and professor of physical therapy on the research team.

To make sense of their site visit, the designers worked with gesture experts who helped them analyze the video and identify pain points that could translate into design opportunities for the medical research team.

The Discovery: Gap Between Practice and Mental Model

The contextual inquiry session unfolded in a series of clear segments. Dr. Stacy began by articulating her goals for the project. She then moved into a live therapy session, assessing and treating a volunteer patient while the design team observed. Afterward, she walked the team through what she had done during the treatment, explaining the reasoning behind her choices. She followed this with a brief review of the raw force measurement data displayed on the prototype interface. The session ended with a post-therapy interview, where she reflected on the tool's potential and where she believed the work should go next.

From there, the gesture experts focused their analysis on three core parts of the session: Dr. Stacy's goals, the live therapy interaction, and the post-therapy interview. By examining these moments closely, they aimed to document in detail how care actually unfolded in this setting as revealed through gestures and the body.

Dr. Stacy Shares Her Goals

When the session began, Dr. Stacy explained that one of her central aims was to bring more objectivity into physical therapy. Therapists, she shared, rely heavily on their hands to gauge pressure and tissue response. She saw the paddles as a way to anchor those judgments in measurable data.

At the same time, Dr. Stacy emphasized that any new medical device must support, not disrupt, the therapist-patient relationship. As she talked about this, she traced a slow circular motion over the massage table (see Figure 5.10), a gesture suggesting the ongoing, relational nature of the work. This moment was coded as `Goal: Connection`, which later contributed to the broader theme of *Doctor-Patient Connection*.

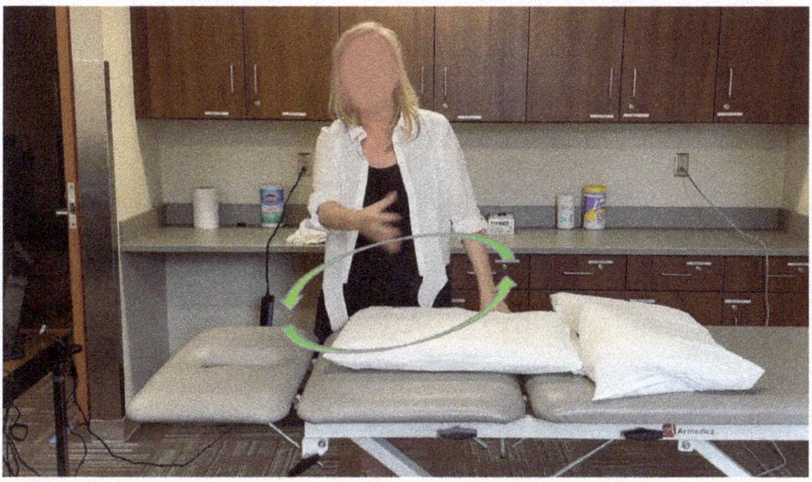

FIGURE 5.10

Dr. Stacy uses a swirling gesture over the massage table while saying "not interfering with that dynamic" to indicate the space of the doctor-patient interaction.

continues

Part of how she imagined the device strengthening this relationship was for it to be "quick and easy" to use. For example, she pointed to the computer screen when mentioning that the interface needed to be more user-friendly. She also spoke about portability, although the meaning of this wasn't fully clear at this early stage. She swept her arm from left to right and back again with the palm facing downward to convey the ease with which something should move through the clinical space.

Taken together, her comments and gestures revealed a vision for a care environment that could make therapy more objective and more reproducible while still preserving the fluid connection between the therapist and their patient.

Clinician as Expert Information Gatherer

As the therapy session began, it quickly became clear that Dr. Stacy's practice involved gathering multisensory information from her patient. She started by placing both hands directly on the patient's back, moving slowly along the muscles while narrating what she felt. "There's some turgidity here," she said. She stepped away from the patient to explain what she had sensed through her touch to the designers in the room. Extending her left hand into their field of view, she held her palm up with her fingers mimicking the shape of holding a ball. She then squeezed her hand in a soft, rhythmic pulse—a concrete representational gesture that conveyed a sense of expansion and contraction (see Figure 5.11).

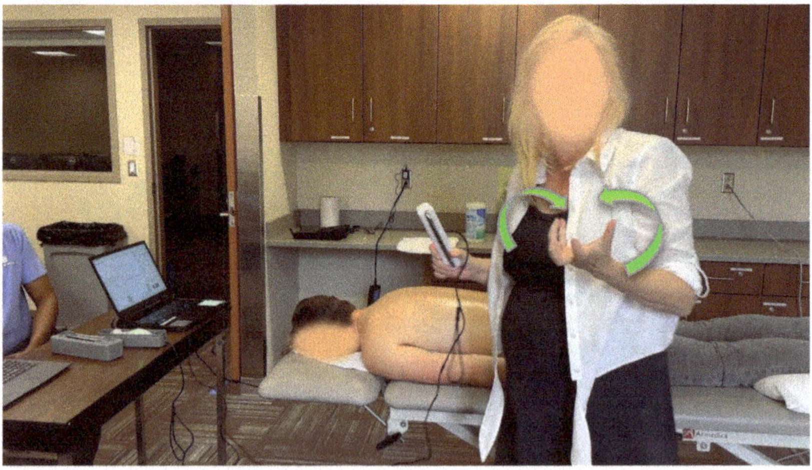

FIGURE 5.11

Dr. Stacy uses a pulsating open-and-close gesture to depict the dynamic quality of "turgidity."

This created a classic gesture-speech mismatch. The static word "turgidity" conflicted with her dynamic gesture, which was coded as `Tactile Feedback`. This mismatch revealed that she was sensing a living, rhythmic quality in the tissue that the current tool could not capture.

Having identified the specific muscle fibers causing the patient pain, Dr. Stacy then switched to the paddles. She moved them back and forth over the spot on the patient's back with increasing pressure. She checked in with the patient, "Is that tender right there?" and then the patient confirmed. This was coded as `Patient Feedback`. She then turned her gaze to the force measurement plot on the laptop. This was coded as `Tool Feedback`.

In this moment, Dr. Stacy was coordinating information across multiple channels: tactile, verbal, and quantitative (see Figure 5.12). She began by sensing the problem area through her hands, then she confirmed that with the patient's feedback, and then triangulated that information into a quantitative measure of force. When considered together, these gesture codes gave rise to the theme *Information Gathering*. This theme showed how in Dr. Stacy's clinical practice, the numerical measurement was only the final step in a richer sequence of sensemaking.

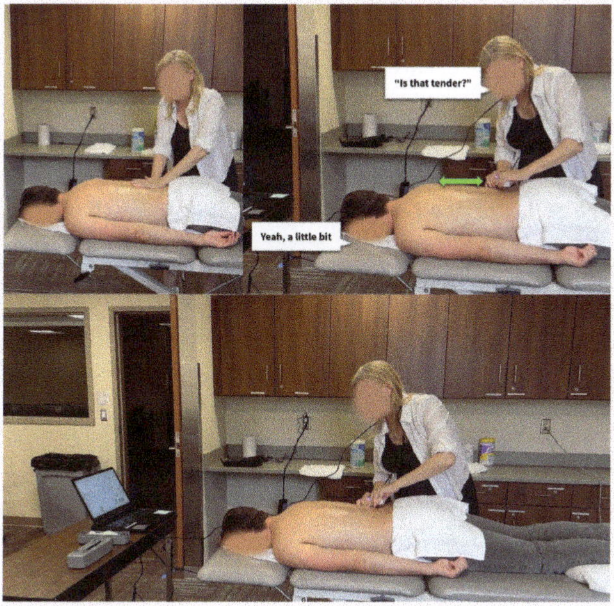

FIGURE 5.12
Dr. Stacy integrates tactile (top left), verbal (top right), and quantitative (bottom) data to identify the "rope" in the patient's muscles.

continues

Through the actions of her body and gestures, Dr. Stacy demonstrated how she constantly and expertly integrated multiple channels of information in order to arrive at a clinical assessment to positively identify the "rope" in the patient's back muscles.

Across these moments, her body showed the real nature of clinical reasoning: it is multisensory and integrative. Dr. Stacy wasn't relying on any single input. Rather, she was synthesizing across modalities of touch, sight, patient response, and device data in a seamless rhythm. Her gestures revealed the clinician not as a passive recipient of numbers, but as an expert information gatherer working across multiple channels of perception.

Seeing the Doctor-Patient Connection

Throughout the therapy session, Dr. Stacy often maintained contact with her patient. On one level, she checked in regularly to confirm she had found the correct problem area on his back. But analyzing her physical actions showed that this connection was also literal. She used her hands, and later the therapeutic paddle, to stay in continuous physical contact with the patient, even as she moved around the table.

At times, she anchored her fingertips as a pivot point while she repositioned herself (see Figure 5.13). She maintained this contact so she could keep track of the exact spot she was treating and quickly return to it without losing her place. We coded this steady anchoring behavior as `Physical Connection`. This code also further contributed to the broader theme of *Doctor-Patient Connection*.

However, the paddles sometimes disrupted this connection. As she walked around the table, Dr. Stacy repeatedly had to manage the paddle's cords, shifting the way they draped over her neck. Because the massage paddles were expensive and her ointment-covered hands were slippery, she took care not to drop them and used the cord over her neck as an emergency catch. In doing so, the tension between the paddle's physical design and her need for uninterrupted patient connection became plainly visible. At one point, she had to stop mid-treatment, lift her anchored hand from the patient, and fumble with the tangled cord (see Figure 5.13). At that moment, the literal connection was broken. This moment was coded as `Interrupted Connection` and became a core exemplar in the theme *Flow of Information*.

When looking at these themes that emerged from a set of coded gestures, a story began to emerge: in clinical practices like physical therapy, information gathering is a process of integrating data from multimodal sources. That information flow is important, and the design of the tools and clinical environment can disrupt that flow of information. These moments are important to notice because they have the consequence of disrupting the doctor-patient connection, a key goal of physicians like Dr. Stacy.

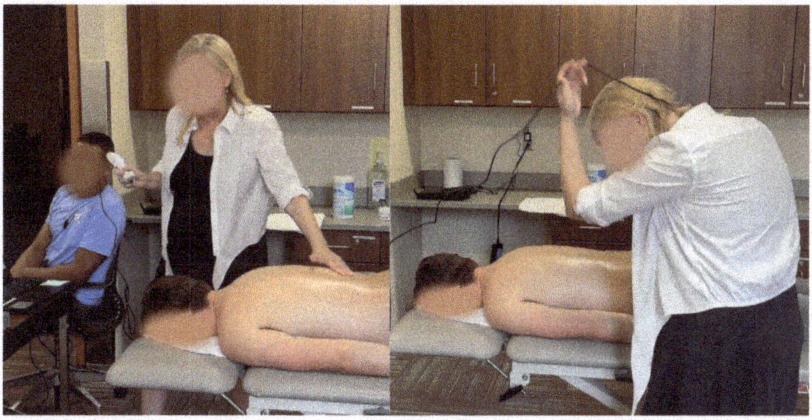

FIGURE 5.13

Dr. Stacy's connection to her patient is broken as she fumbles with the cords on the paddles.

The analysis lets you see this moment in a new way and underscores a key design challenge: the corded tool made it difficult for the clinician to achieve her goals of both increasing objectivity while also preserving the relationship with her patient.

The Sticky Bias Toward Data

In the post-therapy interview, Dr. Stacy settled back into a discussion with the design team about her vision for the therapy paddle system and how it could augment clinical practice. She spoke at length about the value of having objective measurements and what this data could offer her and other therapists. For her, quantification was a way to separate the clinicians who use data from those who don't when caring for their patients. She reiterated that quantifiable feedback was an important step toward standardizing and advancing care.

When comparing Dr. Stacy's gestures across time, her mental model sharpened into view. When she described the traditional therapy method of asking patients whether they preferred "light, medium, or heavy" pressure, she accompanied her explanation with a loose, wavering, sing-songy

continues

gesture. Her posture rocked side to side in an unsteady balance, mirroring the imprecision she associated with these verbal categories. We coded this abstract representational gesture as `Imprecise Data`.

Moments later, when she described the future she imagined through quantification, her movements became decisive (see Figure 5.14). She closed her hand into a fist and drove it downward to a firm stopping point, an abstract representational gesture that conveyed certainty and precision. This gesture was coded as `Parameters` because it evoked a single, definitive value—a number you can know.

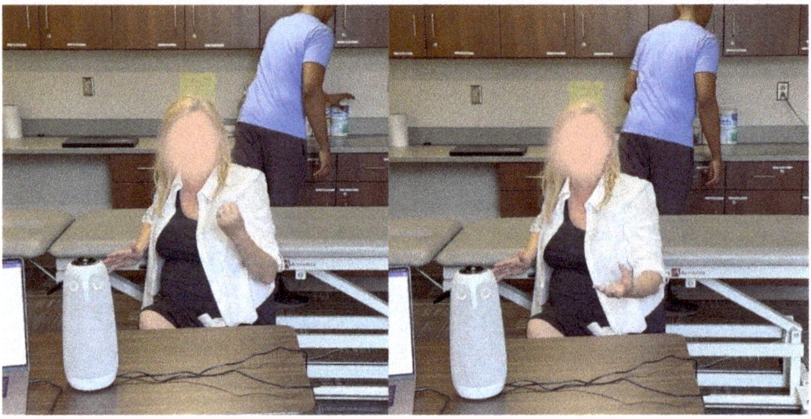

FIGURE 5.14
Dr. Stacy's decisive gesture coincided with her statement that "they would actually know my number."

The contrast between these two gestures made her preferences unmistakable. Subjectivity was unstable and uncertain. Quantification was firm and authoritative. Comparing these gestures revealed a pattern in her thinking. Although her practice involved integrating tactile cues, patient feedback, and quantitative readings, her language and some of her gestures elevated the numerical value above every other source of information. When looked at over time, her body showed a contradiction to this privileging of objective information.

The Strategic Impact: Real Clinical Design Principles

Gesture analysis allowed the design team to move beyond Dr. Stacy's stated preferences and toward a deeper understanding of how she actually worked. Her words highlighted a desire for quantitative certainty, but her movements revealed the fuller mix of cues she relied on. This is the value of analyzing gestures: it helps you see the assumptions and processes that remain unspoken, even for experts. That deeper understanding prevents teams from building only what is asked for and instead supports what users truly need.

By examining her gestures across the session and grouping them into the meaningful broad themes, *Information Gathering*, *Flow of Information*, and *Doctor-Patient Connection*, the team derived several design principles that more accurately reflected the realities of clinical care. Those design principles were:

1. **Keep the clinician at the center of expertise.** Dr. Stacy's gestures across the session showed that she regularly coordinated information across tactile cues, patient feedback, and quantitative readings. These multimodal practices, captured in the theme *Information Gathering*, revealed a clinician constantly gathering, comparing, and synthesizing multiple channels of information. Any design solution needed to preserve and support this role rather than overshadow it with a single stream of numeric data.
2. **Enable seamless patient feedback during the visit.** Her-in-the-moment check-ins with the patient demonstrated how essential real-time feedback was to her clinical reasoning. This behavior appeared repeatedly in the coding and contributed to the broader theme of *Information Gathering*. A design that matches the pace and texture of clinical work would need to make this feedback easy to capture, interpret, and incorporate into the record without slowing the visit or shifting attention away from the patient.
3. **Capture objective and subjective data in the moment.** Throughout the therapy session, Dr. Stacy treated quantitative values from the paddles as only one input in a larger diagnostic picture. Her hands, her eyes, the patient's reactions, and her own impressions all contributed data that shaped her treatment decisions. The gesture-speech mismatch coded as `Tactile Feedback` when Dr. Stacy sensed the turgid muscle in the patient's back as part of the theme *Information Gathering* underscored that the system was missing essential subjective and sensory data. This pointed to the need for the system to incorporate a broader range of data types, including patient feedback and the clinician's own verbal or observational notes.
4. **Avoid disrupting the clinician-patient flow.** The cords that tangled during the session made clear how easily the device could interrupt care. The moment that was coded as `Interrupted Connection` as part of the theme *Flow of Information* and *Doctor-Patient Connection*

continues

demonstrated how fragile the clinical rhythmic could be. Hardware and software alike needed to support uninterrupted movement, continuous contact, and a natural rhythm.

Taken together, these principles highlighted something that was not obvious from Dr. Stacy's words alone. If the design team had focused strictly on her verbal emphasis on objectivity, they might have treated the visualization interface as the central design opportunity. For example, they might have invested in more refined charts and smoother UI elements. They might even have doubled down on the idea that the most important part of this system was the quantitative value the paddles produced.

The gesture analysis pointed in a different direction. It showed that the most meaningful improvements were not limited to the screen. The team began to see the importance of capturing subjective feedback from the patient in real time, such as the precise moment when pressure shifted from comfortable to tender. With this point of view, design ideas focused on making the paddles wireless and secured by a simple hand strap so the clinician could move freely without worrying about dropping the device or managing cords. They also saw the value in allowing clinicians to record quick verbal notes that could be stored alongside the force data, giving future clinicians a richer understanding of what happened during treatment.

What this analysis exposed was an imbalance in what was being captured and archived. Only the quantitative data from the paddles were being reliably stored in the patient record, despite the fact that Dr. Stacy drew on a much wider set of information sources during the visit. Gesture analysis helped the design team see this gap clearly. It reframed the design problem from polishing a UI to asking a larger question: How might we design a smarter, frictionless ecosystem that reflects the full complexity of clinical care?

You do not need to become a different kind of researcher to do this well. You already read bodies every day. With more intention, that innate human skill becomes a stronger analytic resource. Returning to your video recordings with an extended attention to the body as well as the speech lets you catch what was too subtle, too fleeting, or too layered to fully grasp in the moment. It helps you move from quick impressions to durable insights about how people think, act, and what they truly need. This is part of what it means to do genuinely human-centered work: to let people's full expression, not just their words, deepen your understanding and set you up for what is to come next.

Takeaways

- **Let your research questions lead you to the gestures that matter.** A focused, actionable set of research questions helps your team get unstuck and clarify the product roadmap, and it tells you which gestures to prioritize and which to set aside. Be deliberate in your approach, build on what you already know, and right-size your data to calibrate for the risk of drawing the wrong conclusions.
- **Set up your analysis so that gestures can be rigorously examined.** Strong analysis requires preparation. Demarcate each gesture's boundaries (preparation, stroke, retraction) to isolate your unit of analysis and create a transcript that explicitly pairs each gesture description with its accompanying speech so you can evaluate them together.
- **Analyze gestures with a systematic loop.** Turn raw movement into structured evidence by evaluating each gesture's dimensions, assigning it a preliminary code, and collecting your codes in a codebook. Use constant comparison to refine your interpretations and track how a user's gestures evolve over time, because the story often lives in that evolution, not in any single movement.
- **Synthesize gesture codes into a compelling narrative.** Cluster related gesture codes into broader themes and then look for the tensions between them. This higher-altitude view lets you construct a story that explains the core conflicts in your users' experience, grounded in what their bodies revealed and not just what they said.
- **Distill your gesture-based narrative into actionable design principles.** Translate the insights your gesture analysis uncovered into durable, testable guidance that your team can act on. This crucial step transforms embodied user evidence into concrete design decisions and prevents teams from building only what users ask for in words.
- **Communicate insights with your own body.** Bring your gesture analysis to life for stakeholders by using your body to make your findings tangible. Re-enact a user's hesitation, map competing mental models in the space around you, or replay a key mismatch. When your audience can see what the user's body reveals, the insight lands in a way that slides alone never can.

FIELD NOTES FROM STEPHANIE

When I first started doing gesture analysis, I thought "rigor" meant looking closely at everything. Every hand movement. Every shift in posture. Every flick of the wrist. If the body moved, I assumed there might be meaning there. This led me to spend more time than I want to admit analyzing one tiny flick of a participant's hand. I watched it again and again. I slowed it down. I looked at the timing. I compared it to what she was saying. I wondered if it signaled hesitation, dismissal, uncertainty, or some small shift in attention. Eventually, I realized what had happened. She was flicking away a fly.

That moment taught me something important about gesture analysis. Looking closely matters, but looking closely at everything is not the same as doing good analysis. You can burn a lot of time chasing movement that has nothing to do with your research questions. So, I learned to begin with what I now call a "generous pass" through the video. I keep the research question in mind. I watch the whole interaction at a slightly quicker pace, listening to the talk and watching the body together. I jot down timestamps where something potentially meaningful happens: a gesture that adds information, a movement that contradicts the words, a repeated action, a hesitation, a moment where the body seems to be doing part of the thinking.

Only then do I zoom in.

Gesture analysis does not mean treating every movement as a secret code. It is about finding the ones that matter!

FIELD NOTES FROM DANE

Technology has dramatically changed how research is done even in my career. My grad school friends and I still lament having to use a foot pedal as we manually transcribed hours of interview video. Now transcription is something most video conferencing platforms handle automatically.

In just the past few years, AI tools have become the newest frontier for research. They promise to process large volumes of qualitative data: hours of interview footage scanned, moments flagged, patterns identified. I have found genuinely useful capabilities there. But I have learned to be careful about where they end and where interpretation must begin.

This is true for any data generated from human activity, but it matters especially for gesture analysis. Consider something as simple as a point. Index finger extended, arm directed toward something. An automated tool would log these the same way: pointing gesture, pointing gesture, pointing gesture. But the form tells me almost nothing. What I need to know is what the gesture did.

A participant jabs a finger at the table when she says "Right here. This is the issue," the **communicating body** driving emphasis into the point she needs me to take seriously. Another traces a path through the air as he thinks aloud about how data moves from ingestion to reporting, the **thinking body** externalizing a mental model of the pipeline that his words are still catching up to. A third taps the screen and then gestures back toward his notes, the **coordinating body** stitching two threads of the conversation into a single shared reference.

Superficially the same gesture. Three distinct functions.

Without attending to what each gesture accomplished, I would have had three data points labeled pointing gesture and no real understanding of what any of them meant. Gestures are not just forms. They are actions embedded in human interactions, and their meaning lives in what they do: what came before, what followed, and how the gesture moved the interaction forward. That is something I have not yet seen a machine reliably do.

ESPRESSO YOURSELF
COMMUNITY MEETING ROOM
Hope you're enjoying the site visit so far. We need to improve the cafe experience.
We have a broad portfolio across durables, cyclicals, squareables, and robotics. Coffee will be our easiest turnaround!
I think we're going to lose the room.
I'll make us part of the decor. They won't even notice we're here.
The barista misunderstood the customer.
That's what my GESTIX PRO concluded.
The solution is obvious. Fewer humans in the process!
Just a moment...
that's not—
but the video...
They keep missing her...
That does seem to be the theme today.
I tried to tell them they had it wrong, but the big boss was here.
I know. I saw...
8 letters for "major mishap." Starts with "D."

CHAPTER 6

Build Strong Teams That Belong

A team gathers around a table or joins a conference call. Some people lean in. Others hover just outside the circle or have their cameras off. One person's hands move freely as they speak, sketching ideas in the air. Another's stay folded in their lap. No one has said much yet, but the tone of the meeting is already taking shape.

These small movements matter. They shape who feels comfortable speaking, who hesitates, and how safe it feels to offer an unfinished idea. Long before decisions are made or you're trying to ensure alignment, bodies are already signaling who feels like they belong inside the exchange and who may stay on the edge of it.

You've probably seen this before. Nothing overt is happening. The meeting is polite. The work appears to be moving forward. And yet, some people settle in while others quietly pull back, already deciding whether this is a space where their thinking will resonate.

Up to now, paying attention to gestures has helped you understand users more deeply. You've learned to notice how the body supports thinking and how movement helps people reason, explain, and explore ideas. In collaborative settings, that same sensitivity becomes more consequential. You're no longer only observing gestures. You're participating in the network of cues that shape who feels respected and able to enter the conversation, take risks, and stay engaged.

As teams move to translate research insights into design ideas, the success of the work depends on more than meeting logistics or expertise. It also depends on whether people experience the meeting as a place where they belong as the work unfolds.

Bring Everyone to the Table

Getting everyone to the table is more than making sure people are present. It is also about making sure people feel like they belong. Belonging is the felt experience of having real access to participation, influence, and recognition in a group without having to manage or second-guess yourself in order to stay included. The simple reality is that when people feel they belong, they don't spend their energy assessing whether it's safe to speak or whether their contribution will be welcomed. They channel that energy into the work itself.

When people feel like they belong, participation opens up. A wider range of ideas surfaces earlier. Half-formed thoughts enter the conversation instead of staying folded away. Assumptions get articulated and explored before they can narrow the space for collective creativity. The work improves because more of the talent already in the room feels empowered to contribute.

Belonging also lowers the cost of engagement. When people speak more freely, they question and disagree with less hesitation. They don't have to constantly monitor when to jump in or whether they're overstepping. Disagreement becomes more productive, and people stay engaged even when ideas collide or pressure rises.

Beyond this, belonging also signals respect. When people feel recognized as thinking contributors, not just sources of output, they tend to give more—more care, more effort, more commitment to what the team is building together. By contrast, when belonging feels thin or performative, participation narrows. Blind spots grow. Some voices carry the work forward while others recede. What gets lost is not only potentially great ideas, but people's confidence to fully show up.

Teams often try to create belonging intentionally. You set norms for participation. You use inclusive language like "everyone is welcome" and "all voices are heard." You share credit and distribute airtime. These efforts matter and signal team values, but experience doesn't always follow intention. For people closer to the margins because of role, seniority, identity, expertise, or past interactions, rhetoric about inclusion doesn't always change how the team environment *feels*.

This is where teams often stall. You can use the right language and espouse the right values and still find participation uneven. Some people speak easily and often while others hold back or quietly disengage. Nothing is overtly wrong, yet belonging remains elusive.

This is where the body comes in. Gestures and the body naturally regulate who feels able to enter the exchange, who is attended to, and whose participation carries weight. A directed gaze invites someone in. A shift in posture makes room. Attentive timing, like a pause when lifting a hand, signals, "go ahead." These cues register immediately and hold strongly.

When gestures support belonging, participation becomes easier, not because people are told to engage, but because the interaction itself is easier to join. People feel acknowledged and respected, and their presence carries weight. As a result, they offer unfinished ideas, build on one another's thinking, and remain in the work even when uncertainty or disagreement appears.

When gestures exclude people, the opposite happens. They push people to the edge, reinforce hierarchy, and concentrate influence in the hands of the few. An unreturned glance. A contribution that receives no acknowledgment. A body orientation that repeatedly closes the circle. None of these moments is dramatic on its own, but over time, they chip away at belonging and quietly communicate the same message: *You're not quite part of this.*

Bringing everyone to the table is about more than getting people to show up. It is about ensuring equity and participation as the work unfolds. Because belonging is felt in the body before it is articulated in words, gestures are often the earliest signal that belonging is taking hold or beginning to slip. For that reason, gestures cannot be treated as incidental. They function as a facilitation tool that helps belonging become real in interaction. Strong teams take belonging seriously, and that means taking the gestures you create and the ones you observe seriously as well.

Build the Foundation for Belonging

Belonging is fundamental, yet fragile. Teams can create moments that feel inclusive, but without a sturdy foundation to build on, those moments don't hold. The first time that ideas collide, hierarchy shows up, or pressure rises, that sense of connection pulls back and the strength of the team wanes. If belonging is going to last, it needs the stable ground of psychological safety.

Psychological safety is a stable, shared sense that your team is a place where people can bring rough drafts of their thinking, ask difficult questions, and take interpersonal risks without fear of embarrassment or dismissal. Psychological safety is not a "nice-to-have." It is a prerequisite for advancement, constructive disagreement, and creative risk.

Importantly, you cannot establish psychological safety in a single moment. You need to commit to the long haul. It grows when you are consistent and maintain that consistency. People come to feel safe not because they are told they are, but because they repeatedly experience the same response: curiosity instead of judgment, engagement instead of dismissal. Over time, your commitment to maintaining those consistent signals creates a base that people can rely on.

When this consistency is present, safety is not only steadied, but something else begins to form—trust. Trust is the belief that psychological safety is real, reliable, and will continue over time. When trust is in place, people stop testing the environment and begin to invest in it. If psychological safety is the ground, trust is what holds it together, and belonging is what grows from that foundation (see Figure 6.1).

FIGURE 6.1
Belonging is established on a base of psychological safety and held together with trust.

The gestures that matter most for building strong teams are the ones that establish and maintain the foundation for belonging. While thinking gestures still matter, communicating and coordinating gestures do the work here. These pragmatic movements do the work of softening dominance, redistributing attention, and welcoming people in because it communicates that they belong. To establish belonging, you want to make use of gestures that do the following:

- **Signal inclusion.** Small communicating gestures like nods, sustained gaze, open posture, and brief acknowledgments confirm that someone is with the group.
- **Make space.** These are gestures that adjust posture, orientation, or positioning to physically and interactionally open the group to others.
- **Regulate participation.** Look for coordinating gestures that manage timing and turn-taking so voices at the margins are not consistently passed over.

- **Repair exclusion.** Pragmatic gestures respond when someone is pushed aside, overlooked, or interrupted, quietly bringing them back into the exchange.

Understanding how belonging is built changes how you read social interactions, and it changes what you're responsible for. You begin to see which moments open participation and which ones quietly shut it down. Once you understand that belonging is something people enact through their bodies, you need to take accountability for communicating and coordinating gestures responsibly.

Taking responsibility for how gestures shape belonging isn't an extra skill layered onto collaboration. It's part of shared leadership. Belonging is the lived, felt experience that you are creating moment by moment that communicates that trust and safety will hold. Everyone in the room is responsible! Yours and others' gesture awareness is a primary way that your team orchestrates and manages the conditions that support belonging.

Seeing this clearly is what allows you to move from hoping people feel included to actively shaping meetings where participation is possible, equitable, and sustained.

NOTE **PSYCHOLOGICAL SAFETY IN THE WORKPLACE**

Organizational scholar Amy Edmondson, building on earlier work by Edgar Schein, developed the concept of psychological safety to explain why some teams outperform others despite similar talent and resources.[1] Her research showed that teams do better work when people can speak up, question assumptions, surface concerns, and share unfinished ideas without fear of embarrassment or punishment.[2] Teams with strong psychological safety—where trust and belonging can develop—generate more innovative ideas and work through complex problems more effectively.

1 Edmondson (1999) found that higher-performing hospital teams actually reported more errors. She argued this was not because they made more mistakes, but because psychological safety made it safer to admit and discuss them.

2 Schein (1993) argued that learning and change are inhibited by what he called *learning anxiety*—the fear of looking incompetent, losing status, or threatening one's identity. Psychological safety reduces this anxiety, making it possible for people to engage in the behaviors that learning requires.

Set the Stage

Belonging starts taking shape long before anyone speaks. The moments before a meeting begins, how you orient yourself, how the physical or digital space is arranged, and what people encounter when they arrive, quietly shape whether participation feels possible.

These early cues determine whether the room feels open enough to enter, steady enough to relax into, and ready for people to contribute. Creating the conditions for belonging in participation is as much about infrastructure as it is about atmosphere.

It requires two kinds of preparation: an internal shift in how you pay attention and an external shift in how you shape the environment. Together, these moves set up everything that follows. To set the stage for belonging, you want to do the following:

- **Dial in a gesture-conscious mindset.** This is an internal shift in attention. It is about tuning into subtle body cues that signal comfort, hesitation, or exclusion so you can respond in real time.
- **Arrange the meeting space.** This is an external shaping of the environment. It is about designing the physical or virtual setup so that gestures can be seen, responded to, and used to coordinate participation.

These moves don't guarantee belonging, but they make the conditions possible. They determine whether the "room" can hold uncertainty and disagreement once the work begins.

Dial In a Gesture-Conscious Mindset

Before you turn to the agenda, shift your mindset. Research shows that people read one another's bodies automatically and incredibly quickly, often in a fraction of a second. Long before words register, people form impressions of warmth, openness, or approachability from movements alone. These impressions strongly influence whether a space feels available to them.

The same is true of your own body. Even when you are not aware of it, others are picking up on your movements and using them as signals of how welcome or included they are in the moment.

Dialing in a gesture-conscious mindset means making this process intentional. It sharpens your ability to read others' cues like the small movements that reveal comfort, hesitation, confusion, or exclusion before anyone names what they are feeling. It also lets you manage your own signals so you can use gestures that project steadiness, openness, and invitation, while holding back movements that might overpower the room or close it down. Gesture consciousness keeps you attuned to the interactional climate while also actively shaping it.

Keep in mind: this is not about performing scripted gestures. That comes off as inauthentic. Rather, it is about recognizing that the body is always talking. Dialing in a gesture-conscious mindset helps you create conditions where belonging can take root rather than leaving the social tone of the meeting to chance.

Arrange the Meeting Space

Every meeting, retro, full-stack review, or weekly sync lives inside a physical or virtual setup. That setup shapes how safe people feel to contribute and how easily gestures can do their work. So, you need to create the environment to make gestures visible.

When gestures are visible, strong teams make use of them to support belonging by opening the space, regulating pacing, and pulling someone back in from the edges. But when sight lines are blocked, a conference room gets too crowded, or cameras reduce bodies to floating heads (or are never switched on in the first place), you need to rethink the design of the meeting space so that everyone feels they can participate without reserve.

Designing the environment is a conscious choice you're responsible for making. Your aim should be to make gestures visible and usable. When sight lines are open and bodies have room to move, teams can read and respond to one another in real time, helping you stabilize conditions for belonging.

Virtual spaces require even more care. Video grids compress the body, and subtle cues can disappear easily. Camera height, framing, lighting, and grid visibility all shape whether gestures register at all. A teammate who would gesture naturally in person may appear still or disengaged simply because their hands fall outside the frame. In some cases, smaller breakout rooms make gestures easier to see and respond to.

The specifics will vary by format, but the principle stays the same: create a space where bodies are visible, readable, and able to respond to one another. Table 6.1 offers practical considerations for arranging both in-person and virtual meetings.

TABLE 6.1 HOW TO MAKE GESTURES VISIBLE IN MEETINGS

In Person	Virtual
Set up seating. Use arrangements to organize meeting attendees so they can face one another, such as circular or semi-circular. Being eye-to-eye not only encourages more gesturing, but it also helps you spot everyone's contributions.	**Maximize visible grid.** Make sure that attendees turn on their cameras and open up the grid to see everyone. If it's not possible to see everyone in a single view, scroll through the grid. Look directly into the camera to simulate eye contact.
Provide room to move. Avoid crowding. When people can't lift their arms, they're less likely to contribute. Physical constraints equal conversational constraints. Let the body talk!	**Use breakout rooms.** If grids are too crowded, consider using breakout rooms to provide opportunities for your team to use and see gestures more readily.
Provide sufficient lighting. People can't respond to what they can't see! If you lower the lights for a presentation, be sure to raise them back up during the discussion.	**Avoid harsh lighting.** Harsh lighting, whether from front or behind, can easily wash out meeting attendees. Find a balance so you can be easily seen by your team.
Maximize lines of sight. Give everyone a line of sight to hands and faces, not just the loudest voice or most visible leader. Be prepared to shift often to manage this.	**Encourage wider framing.** Encourage camera setups that show arms, face, and torso—not just a floating head in a box.
Gesture in the shared space. Don't hide your gestures and body movements from view. Make them visible to others as often as possible.	**Gesture in the field of the camera.** Beyond wider framing, lift your hands for the attendees to see when you are speaking.

To see the importance of how you design a meeting space and its impact on authentic belonging, consider a routine design review in progress. The team is gathered around shared screens and documents. Rosa, a junior designer, joins the meeting at a visual disadvantage. She is half hidden behind a monitor, slightly outside the group's line of sight. Her first attempt to gesture into the conversation goes unnoticed (see Figure 6.2). The team keeps moving. By the halfway point, Rosa's posture has collapsed inward. She stops gesturing, concluding her contributions aren't wanted.

FIGURE 6.2
A designer's contributions go unnoticed when the meeting space leaves her out of sight.

What looks like low participation is really low belonging, created by an environment where she cannot be seen. A small visibility issue quietly chips away at belonging long before it's called out.

A gesture-visible space allows belonging to become a felt and trusted experience. When people can be seen, their gestures can be acknowledged, responded to, and built on. This makes participation a whole team experience and enriches your meetings. When you set the stage this way it doesn't guarantee belonging, but it makes it possible for teams to build it together once the work begins.

Read the Room

You've arranged the space so that gestures can be seen. Now you shift to noticing what those gestures reveal and who seems confident in the interaction, who seems tentative about whether it's safe to participate, and whether a small adjustment could help establish a steadier and more inclusive atmosphere before the meeting moves forward.

Once people arrive, take a moment before jumping into the agenda. Reading the physical or virtual room tells you a great deal before anyone speaks. A teammate leaning in, elbows anchored and eyes engaged, signals readiness to be part of the team. Someone sitting back with arms crossed, or drifting out of the shared space, may be carrying hesitation or uncertainty.

In virtual meetings, the cues shift, but they don't disappear. A person who stays half off-camera, whose hands never enter the frame, or who suddenly goes still or looks away from the screen may be offering the online equivalent of stepping back from the table. Even small actions, such as how quickly someone unmutes, can gauge belonging. Make use of these small movements because they do a lot! They are the difference between a strong team and one that is disjointed.

Reading the room isn't about diagnosing people or their intent. It's about using your gesture-conscious mindset to tune into the group's rhythm. That awareness helps you notice when participation is restrained or uneven, so you can make it easier for others to enter, soften rising dominance, or acknowledge someone who hasn't yet had a clear chance to enter the conversation. No detailed analysis is required. A broad, attentive scan is enough!

Figure 6.3 highlights some of the gestures to watch for and what they might signal.

Reading the room gives you an early warning system for whether belonging is taking shape. It shows you whether the conditions that allow people to participate are holding or starting to break down. When bodies grow tense, still, or pulled back, those conditions are under strain. This first read is a valuable baseline because it lets you take the temperature of the group and gauge how much work lies ahead as you shift from observation to active intervention.

NOTE READING IS FUNDAMENTAL

Belonging is a continuous commitment, and it requires you to stop and take stock throughout a meeting. It isn't something you do once and move on from. Everyone in the room shares responsibility for noticing when conditions shift and course-correcting is needed. That ongoing effort helps keep the team working at a high level.

FIGURE 6.3

Gestures to look for during a body scan and what they might signal.

Get People Moving

Once you've read the room and get a baseline for whether people "feel like I can belong," you can stabilize this felt sense further and lock it in by inviting a little movement. Nothing dramatic, just enough to help people reset in their bodies and reenter the interaction.

Small, ordinary motions do the work just fine. A brief walk through the room, shifting in a chair, or even reaching for a cup of water activates the same neural and muscular pathways used for gesturing. Those tiny movements can lower the threshold for participation and make it easier to join in.

Larger but still simple movements, like a quick stretch or a 20-second shake-out, extend the same benefits. Even modest movement can boost attention and generative thinking, while reducing inhibition. When you get people moving, you often get fuller participation. And because gesturing is contagious, as more people move, more gestures tend to emerge. That's good for belonging!

Some ways you can get people moving are shown in Table 6.2.

TABLE 6.2 WAYS TO GET PEOPLE MOVING

Activity	Description
Stretch and Breathe	A brief posture reset. Have everyone stand or sit upright, take one slow breath, and stretch arms overhead, out, and down. This releases tension and opens the torso so gesturing and speaking feel easier.
Stand and Shift	A one-minute grounding reset. Standing (if possible), gently shift weight from foot to foot. This boosts circulation, settles restless energy, and helps people re-enter the space.
Mirroring Warm-Up	In pairs or small groups, one person moves slowly while the other mirrors and then switches. This builds shared attention and coordination, making turn-taking and alignment smoother.
"This Is Not a Pen"	Pick up a nearby object and mime what else it could be. This loosens rigid thinking, encourages expressive gesture, and lowers the social cost of offering ideas and stimulating a creative mindset.
Gesture-to-Name	Each person says their name paired with a simple gesture that reflects how they're showing up today. This makes their presence visible and helps quieter participants enter the interaction early. Keep it light and let people play.

WHY SMALL MOVEMENTS MATTER

Research across neuroscience and psychology shows that even brief, low-effort movement, such as standing up, stretching, or shifting posture, can improve attention, reduce stress, and support creative thinking. Light movement increases blood flow to the brain and helps regulate the nervous system, making it easier to focus and engage.[3]

Studies also show that movement lowers social inhibition, which makes people more likely to speak, gesture, and participate.[4] Embodied contemplative practices show that even subtle, intentional movements can regulate emotion and attention through bottom-up sensory and interoceptive (sense of the internal state of the body) pathways, without requiring exertion or intensity.[5]

---

3 Ratey (2008) reviewed clinical, educational, and neurobiological evidence showing that aerobic movement enhances mood, learning, and emotional regulation by altering neurotransmitters, neurotrophic factors, and stress physiology.

4 Beilock (2010) demonstrated that anxiety disrupts performance by hijacking working memory and conscious control, revealing why bodily states and attentional focus play a decisive role in high-pressure situations.

5 Schmalzl, Powers, & Henje Blom (2015) synthesized neuroscience, contemplative science, and embodied cognition to argue that structured movement practices, such as yoga, uniquely regulate attention and anxiety through bottom-up sensory-motor integration that cannot be explained by either exercise or seated mindfulness alone.

NOTE **CONTEXT AND MOVEMENT**

Gesture norms vary across cultures, identities, neurotypes, and bodies. Someone with limited mobility, arthritis, or chronic pain may gesture differently than you expect with their eyes, posture, or a shift of weight. A movement that feels open in one setting may feel intrusive in another. Stay observant. Don't assume. When you're unsure, ask—and share your own preferences too!

Participate and Move Together

The space is arranged, you've read the room, and bodies are ready to engage. As the meeting gets underway, your job is to help establish a tone that supports belonging and equitable participation. Your gestures do this work quietly and steadily by signaling that everyone is welcome, attention is available, and contributions will be received and responded to.

HOW MOVEMENT AND OPENNESS SHAPE BELONGING

Small body cues play an outsized role in how inclusive, connected, and ready to participate people feel. These cues operate beneath awareness, but they shape whether a meeting feels open and available to everyone.

- **Openness sets the tone.** Open, relaxed postures like visible hands, uncrossed arms, and softened shoulders lower social inhibition and signal approachability. People feel more willing to join in when they sense openness in the bodies around them.
- **Synchrony builds cooperation.** When people move in subtle rhythm by matching pace, timing, or small gestures, they trust each other more and collaborate more effectively. Even light synchrony increases willingness to contribute.
- **Attunement strengthens connection.** Mirroring and nonverbal attunement help people feel seen and acknowledged. Small echoes of posture or gesture keep people engaged and inside the conversational flow.

Now you will put your gesture-conscious mindset to work to do the following:

- Sustain the tone.
- Include everyone.

Sustain the Tone

Belonging doesn't lock in once a meeting begins. Even after you've set the tone, you remain responsible for whether belonging is felt moment by moment as the interaction unfolds. Small gestural shifts can change how safe it feels to participate, and those signals register very quickly. An inviting glance can pull someone in, while an eye roll can push them out just as fast.

That means you have real leverage here. Your small, intentional moves can shift the social temperature of the room and carry more power than you might expect. They can make a meeting smoother and more equitable or quietly undermine belonging. So, use that leverage well. When you do, people settle in faster and participate more readily. When you don't, belonging can fall apart. Ideas collide, pressure rises, and dynamics shift. Like a tower of cards, belonging is built slowly, action by action, but can come crashing down in an instant (see Figure 6.4).

FIGURE 6.4
There are no neutral moves. Every gesture either steadies the structure of belonging or risks the collapse.

Midway through a product review, a senior architect responds to a tentative suggestion from a product manager with a quick eye roll before speaking (see Figure 6.5). It's small and almost automatic. No one comments on it. But the room shifts. The PM who offered the idea trails off, thinking to themselves, *"Forget about it, I'm not going to add any more."* The discussion tightens, with fewer interruptions and longer pauses between turns. What changed wasn't the agenda or the feedback itself. It was the signal sent in a fraction of a second: this idea wasn't worth taking seriously. In that moment, belonging cracked, and engagement followed it.

FIGURE 6.5
A quick eye roll from an engineer disrupts the sense that it's safe to participate.

With a small movement, the lead engineer shuts down what could have been an inclusive meeting. To sustain belonging takes work, and what sustains it is consistency: steady, human cues that communicate attention, availability, and respect over time.

Maintaining belonging is a form of collaborative leadership, and it doesn't belong to a single role. Everyone in the room contributes, through their gestures, communicating that "there is room for you here." That responsibility comes with guardrails. This is not about claiming authority or using gestures to dominate, dismiss, or control the room. And it can't be treated as a performance. This can't be faked—when signals don't match intent, people notice.

This is how you build strong teams. You do it by sustaining belonging through repeated, embodied signals that make it safe to participate and worth staying in the work together. And because those signals are updated moment by moment, maintaining a sense of belonging becomes part of how you collaborate effectively.

Keep Everyone Included

Participation naturally rises and falls as ideas move, questions surface, or energy dips. You want to notice whether these fluctuations are natural parts of a meeting's rhythm or whether you need to step in and redirect to help the group stay connected.

Gestures are often the most efficient tool. They let you guide the interaction without overtly singling someone out and without interrupting the flow of work.

There are many ways that you can guide interactions with gestures and keep people in sync. One useful technique is mirroring.

When someone leans in, and you lean in, too, or when you slow your gestures to keep tempo with theirs, you are mirroring (see Figure 6.6). These subtle reflections help people feel in step with one another. This makes it easier for someone to subtly and securely believe that they're part of the group.

FIGURE 6.6
Lucille Ball in a famous mirror gag in the *I Love Lucy* show.

In addition to mirroring, some other adjustments you can use to keep everyone feeling included are the following:

- **Offer an open hand.** Extend a light, palm-up gesture to signal "keep going" or "the floor is yours."
- **Nod gently.** When a teammate nods, gently nod *with* them to encourage that they are valued. (But do not nod too vigorously or often, as this suggests insincerity.)
- **Extend gestures.** When someone sketches an idea in the air, pick it up again later to keep their contribution active and valued.
- **Turn toward the margins.** Shift in slight orientation toward someone quieter to invite them back in without interrupting the flow.
- **Soften tension.** Unclench your hands or release your shoulders to help reset the room when energy tightens.
- **Alignment shifts.** Slightly shift your torso toward someone to show attention and respect.
- **Lean back subtly.** Lean gently away to signal that the floor belongs to someone else. (This reduces perceived competition for turn-taking.)

There are moments when stepping in and subtly redirecting can make a difference. Consider a routine morning stand-up. Four teammates form a tight semicircle, bodies angled toward one another, hands juggling coffee, markers, and phones as they skim their morning updates. Tim, a researcher, stands just outside the arc. No one turns toward him. When he leans in to offer an update, the group keeps talking. He tries again a few minutes later, but the lead never shifts his posture to include him, and the others follow his cue.

By the midpoint of the stand-up, Tim has gone quiet. His posture pulls back. The conversation starts looping, with the same voices filling the space. The energy narrows, and the team wraps without the clarity they expected. And Tim no longer feels solidly part of the team.

Nothing overtly went wrong. But a few small gestures could have changed the outcome. A slight turn toward Tim, an open hand inviting him in, and a moment of mirroring could signal that there was room for his contribution. In their absence, only the most assertive voices shaped the discussion. What Tim was ready to share never entered the room, and the team missed out. A simple gesture could have changed this!

These moves keep the group coordinated rather than defaulting to hierarchy. They help people feel that they are in the mix and not slipping outside it. When your body stays attuned in this way, people feel it. The group holds together. Ideas circulate more freely. And the meeting becomes a place where everyone can participate fully from beginning to end. The upshot is cohesive, stronger teams that are prepared to drive better, more innovative outcomes.

Spot and Repair Disconnects

No team stays in sync the whole time. You may notice small disconnects: an idea goes unacknowledged, someone who was animated goes still, or a teammate quietly retreats. These moments are subtle, but they matter. They are often the first signs that the conditions for belonging are under strain.

But resist the urge to see disconnects as failures. They are a natural part of collaborative work. What matters is what happens next. When the energy shifts or participation narrows, you have a chance to bring the group back together. This does not require calling anyone out or pausing the meeting. Most of the time, a few small, embodied adjustments are enough to reset the rhythm and restore team momentum.

Think of this as midstream maintenance: watching for early signs of drift and using your gestures to help the team reconnect, rebalance attention, and stay engaged. You can spot and repair disconnects by doing the following:

- Restoring the flow in real time
- Leveling the playing field
- Revealing and confronting bias

These moves ensure that people are not sidelined and their ideas are not lost, preserving the psychological safety and trust that belonging depends on.

Restore the Flow in Real Time

When a contribution is met with silence or an idea gets cut off, your team's momentum stalls and belonging slips a bit. These moments do not need a big intervention, but you do need to mend them. Your body is one of the fastest, most unobtrusive tools you have to restore the flow in real time.

Some of the same gestures you use to set the tone or invite participation reappear here, just with a different job. In repair mode, a turn, a pause, or a hand sweep isn't about opening space; it is about mending a rupture and bringing the group back together.

For instance, you might notice the whole space tighten: people talk over each other, the pace runs too fast, or the tone sharpens. In these cases, you can reset the group with a small physical slowdown. A deliberately slower gesture, a brief pause before your next movement, or a visible softening of your shoulders helps de-escalate the moment and gives everyone a beat to reorient. You can also rebuild alignment by mirroring, such as matching someone's pace for a moment or nodding along.

Other situations call for more precision. When you see someone drift to the edges, use a slight turn of your torso or a small hand sweep as an embodied invitation back into the exchange. When an interruption threatens to take over, use a holding gesture, such as a gentle open palm toward the dominant speaker, to protect the conversational space and restore balance. If an idea gets lost, you can physically re-anchor the group by stepping toward the whiteboard and pointing back to a shared reference, which pulls attention toward the collective focus.

You can see this kind of repair happen in ordinary meetings. During a feature review, Toby, a product designer, begins sketching an idea in the air. His hand traces a looping path that shows how user frustration ebbs and flows through a user journey. Midway through the explanation, another teammate jumps in with a loud, "No, no. Not like that...," and the group's attention snaps toward the interruption.

Instead of letting the interruption take over, the design manager steps in quietly. She lifts a softly open palm toward the interrupter, just enough to pause him, then turns her torso back toward Toby and makes a small, inviting hand sweep (see Figure 6.7). His hand returns to the same looping gesture, and he finishes the explanation he had started.

FIGURE 6.7

A small embodied repair gives Toby the confidence to re-enter the meeting and share his thoughts with the team.

The room's pace slows for a beat. Then the conversation resumes. This time, people point back to the motion Toby traced in the air. The idea stays alive. A small, embodied repair protected the flow of the conversation and signaled that Toby's contribution still belonged at the center of the discussion.

These small adjustments recover momentum and salvage ideas that would otherwise disappear. By quietly signaling that contributions are valued, these moves help preserve the psychological safety and trust that keep full participation steady.

NOTE GESTURES THAT LEAVE A TRACE

Some gestures aren't resolved in the moment. They leave a trace long after the meeting wraps up. A repeated eye roll or dismissive posture can create ongoing feelings of exclusion. When these patterns persist, it's worth raising it one-on-one with the person and working together to reset the team's dynamic.

Level the Playing Field

Power shows up in the body long before it appears in words. Who leans in, who takes up space, and who the group subtly angles toward are some cues that can shape who participates without anyone intending them to. When power tilts the room, the conditions for belonging become uneven.

Leveling the playing field is not about diminishing influence. It is about making space for more people to step in.

You can begin by adjusting your own physical presence. If you are standing while others are seated, you are already visually dominant; sit down to meet people on the same plane. If you notice yourself leaning far into the table, especially if you hold authority, recognize that this posture can crowd others out. By softening your shoulders or leaning back slightly, you create room and signal, "You do not have to fight for space here." In virtual calls, you can achieve the same effect by stepping out of the spotlight: stop screen-sharing when it's time for discussion, widen your frame, and sit back so the floor feels more available to others.

In addition to managing your own presence, you can also use gestures to shift participation and redistribute who is included. A hand sweep toward someone quieter acts as a gentle invitation. Turning your torso toward a teammate who has been waiting to speak gives them a clear opening. When you prompt someone for input and then physically step back, even half a step, it creates literal and psychological space for others to move into.

When you make these embodied shifts, you flatten hierarchy in real time. These actions lower the social cost of speaking and strengthen trust, which helps ensure that the feeling of belonging is not reserved for only the loudest voices.

WHEN YOU NEED TO CLAIM SPACE

While power is often wielded unconsciously in hierarchical organizations, it can also be misused to silence dissent or to push forward a specific agenda. Sometimes, you may feel like you're being pushed around, cut off, dismissed, or overshadowed. The unfortunate reality is that some people are just bad actors. You don't need to fight back with words alone. Your body can quietly signal confidence and reclaim space (see Figure 6.8). When that happens:

- **Sit or stand tall.** Adopt an upright posture with open shoulders to signal confidence.
- **Take visible space.** Place your hands on the table or in your lap with palms open to show presence.
- **Use a steeple gesture.** Lightly touch your fingertips together to project calm control.
- **Hold steady eye contact.** Maintain eye contact without staring to anchor your presence in the conversation.
- **Lean in with purpose.** Lean forward slightly when making a point to signal, "I'm here; stay with me."
- **Mirror the group.** Match the posture or tempo of others to help re-sync yourself with the room.

These moves won't stop every form of overpowering behavior. But these actions can shift how you're perceived and help you stay inside the exchange. Projecting strength through your body reminds the room that you deserve to be heard.

FIGURE 6.8
The *Fearless Girl* statue on Wall Street in New York City shows how the body can project power.

Small physical shifts can do what long explanations can't: make participation feel possible. ✊

Gestures Reveal and Confront Bias

Bias often appears in your body before it shows up in your words. Your automatic habits, shaped by familiarity, preference, and implicit attitudes, can function as subtle acts of exclusion, even when you don't intend it. When you lean toward one person but not another, or nod more warmly toward a favored colleague, you send a clear message. The signal is that the person is being judged on something other than the merit of their ideas.

This is precisely why embodied bias is so damaging! It immediately tells some people, "You don't quite belong here," which erodes psychological safety and dissolves trust, and belonging is ruptured.

Gaze is one of the clearest places to see this. Eye-tracking studies show that people unconsciously offer more gaze and for longer durations to those they feel comfortable with or perceive as high-status. Because gaze guides attention, people who receive more eye contact tend to gesture more, speak more, and stay engaged. By contrast, people who receive less often shrink, hesitate, or stop contributing, not because they lack ideas, but because they are accurately reading the room.

The good news is that your gaze habits are changeable, and you can use your eyes as an inclusive tool. Resist the reflex to focus on the same people, sweep your attention across the full group, and make brief eye contact with teammates at the margins. This conscious redistribution of your gaze signals that each person's presence counts.

Building this awareness is ongoing work, and you can start by noticing your own patterns:

- Who do you naturally face?
- Whose comments get your immediate attention?
- Whose gestures do you mirror without thinking?

To see the impact of these unconscious patterns, consider a weekly product strategy meeting where the team is tasked with finding a breakthrough innovation. Priya, an engineering lead, is eager to tap into the fresh perspectives of two recently hired engineers. As the new grads sketch out a radical new direction, Priya's gaze locks onto them. She leans in, nods frequently, and her attention follows them. She is visibly excited by their thinking.

Across the table, David, a seasoned senior engineer with over two decades of experience on this product, leans forward to offer a caution. He starts to raise a hand, but Priya's eyes sweep past him, returning immediately to the younger engineers. His attempt to enter the conversation goes unacknowledged. David slowly leans back, feeling he's being discounted for his age.

But imagine this happened another way. As the new grads finish their point, Priya notices David lean forward. Practicing her gesture-conscious mindset, she deliberately shifts her gaze from the new engineers to David and gives a slight nod, signaling an invitation to speak (see Figure 6.9). By consciously redirecting her gaze, Priya acknowledges that David's perspective is just as valued as those of the rambunctious new hires.

FIGURE 6.9

Priya's gaze reveals bias, but when she's aware of it, she can confront it directly with her body.

Bias lives in reflexes, but the conditions for belonging are built through intentional habits. When you become conscious of these subtle signals, you can counteract them. Your goal is to create a consistent environment where psychological safety is protected, allowing everyone to contribute with confidence, not caution.

THE BODY, POWER, AND BIAS

Research consistently shows that nonverbal behavior reveals social dynamics like bias and power often before they appear in words.

- **Implicit bias manifests physically.** Even when language is inclusive, people often show less eye contact, more closed posture, and fewer affirming gestures toward marginalized or unfamiliar colleagues.
- **Favoritism leaves a trace.** People lean in, nod, and gesture more toward those they unconsciously favor, while pulling back or freezing toward others.
- **Gesture style signals status.** Expansive gesturing is often read as confidence or dominance, while restricted movement is read as caution or lower status—accurately or not.
- **Overgesturing can backfire.** Very large or sweeping gestures can be perceived as dominating the floor and may undermine credibility.

These patterns matter because people don't only respond to what you mean. They respond to what your body signals. Becoming conscious of those signals helps you build a space where trust can grow and where belonging is genuinely shared.

Wrap It Up

How a meeting ends deserves just as much care as how it begins. These final moments are your last chance to keep belonging steady, reinforce the safety you've built, and steady the trust that's forming, which allows people to leave with a felt sense of belonging they carry with them into the rest of their day.

These impressions matter. They determine whether teammates walk away feeling aligned and connected or quietly unsure and out of sync. To wrap up well, you want to do the following:

- Close the meeting with the body.
- Assess and support team strength.

When you close your meetings and people leave feeling a sense of belonging, you improve the odds that this feeling persists outside the meeting itself. It carries over into informal conversations and day-to-day messages. As a result, your team returns to the next meeting with a stronger sense of connection already in place, ready to contribute from the start.

Close the Meeting with the Body

Don't end a meeting with a rushed summary and a scramble to the next call. Instead, close with intention. Take a final pause, literally a breath, to scan the space or the video grid. Notice who is still animated, who has gone quiet, whose gestures were echoed, and whose went unnoticed. These cues give you a final read of how included people felt.

Then offer a gestural bookend to bring the group together one last time, using culturally neutral options such as:

- A simple hand raise to signal "I'm aligned."
- A small side-to-side hand wave for "I'm unsure or still thinking."
- A flat palm held low for "I have concerns."

You can also end with a small synchronized action like a shared stretch, a collective exhale, or a "1, 2, 3 . . ." followed by a synchronized clap. Even simple, coordinated movements boost social cohesion and reinforce the sense that the team is leaving the meeting connected.

Assess and Support Team Strength

Just as you scanned the room or screen at the start, take one last look as you close. This final scan tells you whether the foundation you built earlier through tone-setting, inclusive cues, and midstream repair held steady, or whether it needs reinforcement next time.

While you can't measure safety, trust, or belonging directly, the body gives you clues. Use your gesture-conscious mindset to assess them in the final moments before people disperse or click away. Table 6.3 highlights some visible differences between a strong team where belonging is taking root and one where there is still work to do.

A strong team doesn't rush out the door. They leave with shared alignment, visible ease, and gestures that still echo one another's thinking.

Remember, these closing cues don't just reflect how the meeting went; they indicate what the next one will feel like. They show whether your team is leaving with a foundation strong enough to support trust, belonging, and risk-taking as you move forward.

This is where you begin to see the inclusive culture you're building taking shape, gesture by gesture.

TABLE 6.3 TEAM STRENGTH SCORECARD

✓ Signs of Strong Teams	✗ Signs There's Work to Do
Ideas move through hands. When people gesture as they explain, they're thinking with you. You are in sync. That's where you want to be!	**No one gestures at all.** When the room is still and hands stay hidden, ideas stay in heads. This signals discomfort and disengagement. Invite people back in!
Gestures are picked up. When someone repeats another's gesture, it shows they're aligned and tracking together!	**Gestures are isolated.** When someone offers an idea with an expressive motion and no one nods or mirrors, safety is wobbling!
Physical space stays active. When hands point, trace, and outline ideas, the team is building shared motion!	**Movement is guarded.** When arms cross, bodies lean away, or people shrink instead of expanding, the quiet message is: "I'm not with this."
Mirroring across roles. When teammates mirror posture or movement across disciplines, it signals, "I'm with you."	**Certain people dominate.** When one or two people gesture freely while others stay small or still, you can see who's dominating and who's pulling back.
Rhythm is shared. When nods, gestures, and timing fall into the same cadence, the team is moving at a strong clip!	**Pace feels out of rhythm.** When contributions don't build, people talk past each other, and gestures collide, the group has slipped out of connection. Pause, realign, soften your body, and re-invite.
If you see these signals, your team's not just meeting. They're belonging!	**Remember that your team's strength is on display, and it's not just in what is said!**

Gesture as Culture

Building a team culture where people can innovate, push thinking, and take risks depends on belonging. Gestures are an important, yet often overlooked, way you can cultivate this felt sense of belonging. They're small, but mighty! They move faster than words and register immediately, signaling whose contributions are valued and whose are overlooked. Through fluid motions, they communicate openness or withdrawal, invitation or restraint, exclusion or belonging.

In collaborative settings, gestures are not optional tools you can choose to use or to ignore. Whether you notice them or not, they do the work of shaping who steps in or who gets pushed out. Making use of them to shape the culture of the team starts with attuning your gesture consciousness. But this goes beyond just observing how gestures affect your team; it extends to using them intentionally to shape and sustain a culture where everyone can contribute their best work together. That's what makes a strong team.

The deliberate use of gesture does more than just establish belonging. It helps make belonging durable. That sustained sense of *I belong here* is often the bridge to breakthrough ideas. This is the practical payoff of taking belonging seriously as something you build and maintain.

When you use gestures to support this work, teams perform at a higher level. Ideas surface earlier. Assumptions are challenged more openly. Fragile, half-formed thoughts are offered instead of withheld. The work moves forward not because people are tightly managed, but because the conditions you construct, one gesture at a time, allow people to experience a felt sense of belonging that supports full contribution, even under pressure.

This felt sense of belonging, grounded in trust, fuels fuller participation; the kind that opens the door to creative risk, carries your team toward breakthrough ideas, and lands on out-of-the-box innovations that only emerge when all minds are firing together at full capacity. This full cycle of how teams go from a foundation of psychological safety to innovation can be seen in Figure 6.10.

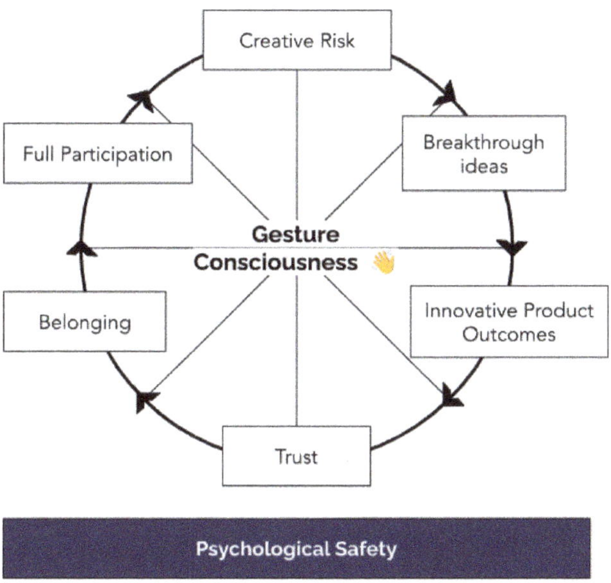

FIGURE 6.10
How gesture consciousness can create a virtuous cycle of innovation in strong teams.

But the responsibility for how you use gestures does not end with better performance or more innovative outcomes. It runs deeper. Gestures are human resources always in circulation in every interaction. The question is not whether gestures are shaping your team's culture. They are. The real responsibility is how you choose to engage them to create a culture that is intentional, inclusive, equitable, and grounded in belonging.

If you lead, facilitate, or participate in collaborative work, your responsibility is also a commitment to being fundamentally human. Gestures are among the most basic ways people extend dignity. Before process or policy, the body signals care, respect, and recognition of difference. When those signals are present, the result is more than strong teams. It is the everyday practice of shared humanity.

Human-centered work includes creating conditions where people can think, contribute, and build together without fear of dismissal or second-guessing themselves. Gesture is one of the most fundamental tools to help with this. Practicing gesture consciousness is a choice to take that responsibility seriously. Gesture by gesture, you decide whether a space invites respect or not and whether people feel they truly belong.

Takeaways

- **Psychological safety lives in the body.** You can state that "all voices are heard," but trust is built or broken through open gestures, attentive posture, and how people are seen and acknowledged in real time. Belonging is felt before it is articulated.
- **Build belonging from the ground up.** Belonging is fragile and cannot be established in a single moment. It grows from a foundation of psychological safety, held together by consistent trust-building signals over time. Without that foundation, belonging collapses the moment pressure rises.
- **Arrange the space so gestures can do their work.** Whether in person or virtual, the physical environment shapes whether people feel able to participate. When sight lines are blocked or bodies are hidden, gestures can't do their work. Designing for visibility is designing for inclusion.

- **Read the room before and throughout.** A quick body scan at the start and regularly throughout gives you an early warning system for whether belonging is taking hold or beginning to slip. Posture, stillness, proximity, and mirroring are all clues to the group's internal state.
- **Use your body to invite, include, and repair.** You don't always need words to fix a dynamic. An open palm, a nod of encouragement, or turning your body toward a quiet person can bring them back into the conversation and rebalance the room without interrupting the flow of work.
- **Level the playing field with your body.** Your posture, gaze, and orientation are powerful tools for managing power dynamics. Sitting down, leaning back, or redirecting your gaze consciously counteracts unconscious bias and ensures that ideas are judged on their merit, not on the status of the person who shared them.
- **Make belonging the bridge to innovation.** The deliberate use of gesture builds a durable sense of belonging, and that sustained feeling of *I belong here* is what gives teams the confidence to take creative risks, challenge assumptions, and co-create truly innovative, human-centered products. Gesturing is not just facilitation; it is culture.

FIELD NOTES FROM STEPHANIE

When I taught in a city school, students chose their seats carefully. Some kept their backs close to the wall. Some watched the room before they joined it. Belonging was never something I could assume. Students entered carrying histories with them: neighborhood loyalties, old conflicts, reputations, and learned ways of staying safe.

For some of them, leaning in, listening, or agreeing with the wrong person carried social risk. So, I worked with the room before I worked with the lesson. I changed the arrangement of the chairs. I moved myself out of the front. We used quick movement activities throughout class: a collective stretch, a rhythm passed around the circle, in-sync claps when someone made a point worth holding onto. These were small things, but they gave students a way to move with each other before they had to risk thinking with each other.

I also watched who had a path into the conversation and who was being shut out before they ever spoke. Then I taught students to notice those things, too: who was turned away, whose idea got dropped, whose hand started to move and then disappeared. For weeks, it seemed like none of it was working. The room stayed guarded.

Then one day, during a discussion of a neighborhood mural, a student who usually stayed guarded began to gesture toward the edge of the image. His hand came forward, then stopped. Across from him, another student, someone from a very different friend group who never spoke to him, noticed. He shifted his chair, opened his body, and said, "Wait. Let him show it."

One body made room for another. That's how belonging gets built. I've carried that lesson into every room I've entered since: classrooms, workshops, design sessions, prison classes—anywhere people have to risk thinking together.

FIELD NOTES FROM DANE

I regularly present research findings and facilitate workshops, often to small or mid-size groups of stakeholders who may not have much context for the work. In every case, I want the same thing: for people to feel like they can participate and contribute to the discussion. Other people's thinking makes my work better, but that only happens if the room feels safe enough to offer it.

I first picked up a simple technique from Lou Rosenfeld, who often opens a session by asking everyone to share what they are drinking. It is small and low stakes by design. People feel invited to turn on their cameras, and suddenly there are bodies in the room where there were only names. I usually have to admit I am on my third cold brew. I have seen people grab their mug and give it a visible shake for the camera, a tiny performance that gets a laugh and breaks something open. Once I had a colleague tell the group they like to mix coffee with orange juice, a combination I had never heard of. The room was buzzing with chatter, and to my surprise, others also loved the combination. (Apparently, if you like a chocolate orange, this is for you!)

Something that small made participation not only easy but fun. Cameras were on. People were leaning in. The room had already decided what kind of space it was.

My presentation may have been about sharing findings, but the real work started well before that. I did not need to declare it; everyone felt it through a simple act of sharing their beverage with the group.

It never forgets a customer or their order, this should help out with the problem in our cafés.
We've been using these GESTIX robots in airports and hospitals. It never forgets anything!
Today I'd like a green tea.
WELCOME ROSA. YOUR LAST ORDER: SMALL LATTE AT 9:12 AM
Nice.
This model is great. It knows what each customer wants.
YOU'VE ORDERED A LATTE 47 TIMES.
...but I want a green tea.
YOU HAVE NEVER ORDERED TEA.
See, this is true data-driven service.
Just a little fine tuning and it's ready to ship.
If you say so.
47 TIMES. NO TEA.
WELCOME TO ESPRESSO YOURSELF. I RECOGNIZE YOU.
Uh huh...

CHAPTER 7

Design Everyday Things Together

Belonging has taken root. The team is connected and energized, ready to take on the creative challenge. Now the work is to build up the best idea and transform it into a tangible prototype of your feature or product.

You're on the design path of the product journey, equipped with a clear understanding of the user's problem. But moving from a shared understanding of users' problems to a solution that meets those needs and *can be built* is the hard work of design.

Design can be conflated with the polished output of a well-crafted interface or product. But really it is an iterative creative process long before it delivers a finished result. The process is messy and deeply human, shaped by emerging ideas, social negotiation, and shared judgment.

Ideation and prototyping are the phases where understanding turns into action. Ideation explores the range of possible solutions to a user's need, while prototyping translates promising ideas into a tangible form that can be tested and refined. Together, these activities help teams move from loose sketches toward a concrete direction that stakeholders can support and commit to building.

Gestures, when used effectively, can amplify this work because they are part of how people naturally think and collaborate. They allow teams to surface ideas quickly by sketching them in the air, testing how they might work, and building on one another's thinking before anything gets made.

Build the Right Thing, Together

Every product organization wants to build the right thing. The challenge is that the path to get there is rarely clear from the start. For any user problem or unmet need, there are often many potential solutions, each filled with decisions about viability, feasibility, and whether the idea will resonate in the market.

Ideas for solutions rarely arrive fully formed. They come as sparks of inspiration. They live first in the imagination and only become real when you bring them out, build them up with others, and together decide which ones are worth carrying forward. In this way, idea generation is distributed across people, settings, and time, shaped through collaborative exchange. Early in product development, it's your team's job to catch those sparks, nurture them, and advance them toward a prototype that can be built and tested.

This requires teams to iteratively cycle between divergence and convergence. First, you aim wide, imagining a range of possible directions. Then you narrow in on what the team believes is most promising. Ideas are refined and evaluated against constraints like timeline, cost, feasibility, user needs and preferences, and required research and development. Some ideas fall away. Others are set aside. A select few find that sweet spot and move forward.

In this early design work, teams must strike a practical balance between open exploration and the pressure of moving toward a decision. Tools that support quick, low-commitment exploration help teams stay open long enough to assess what is truly worth carrying forward. You already rely on many tools to do this, including sticky notes, whiteboards, and graphic design or modeling tools.

Gestures are an equally versatile tool in this creative process. Because they are always available, require no setup, and can be shaped in real time, gestures give teams a flexible way to explore possibilities while ideas are still forming. They can be picked up and extended by others, modified on the fly, or dropped without cost. This allows ideas to stay loose enough to investigate, yet stable enough to build on before creativity narrows or anything must be committed.

This approach does not replace the design frameworks you already use. Instead, it zooms in on the human fundamentals that make them work. By attending to and using gestures in the creative process, you can follow ideas as they emerge from a group of individuals, quickly share and negotiate them within the group, and carry them forward together toward something the team can build.

Think, Communicate, and Coordinate

When teams advance ideas into something you could one day plug in, download, or otherwise use, the affordances of the thinking, communicating, and coordinating body are fully alive.

Each body contributes something essential. The thinking body does the cognitive work of externalizing and expanding thought. Representational gestures pull half-formed ideas and mental models into the public space where they can be examined, extended, and reshaped. The communicating body projects ideas into shared space. As these gestures circulate, they can be picked up, repeated, expanded, corrected, or layered by others. In this back-and-forth exchange, ideas are refined collaboratively and gain clarity and structure as they move across hands. The coordinating body organizes the interaction, using gestures to guide attention, pace turn-taking, and keep ideas connected as they move across people and artifacts.

When the three bodies work together, they overlap, complement, and reinforce one another. The gestures that matter most when building the right thing together are the ones that help your team do the following:

- **Make ideas visible.** Bring private thinking into the shared space so others can react to it.
- **Explain complexity.** Show details and nuances of a concept (like shape, structure, and composition) when words are insufficient.
- **Develop ideas.** Volley an idea back and forth to iterate and add onto it.
- **Solve problems together.** Explore design alternatives, surface solutions quickly, and make constraints and tradeoffs explicit so they can be discussed productively.
- **Test interactions.** Act out and simulate product interactions and user experience to check plausibility and usability.
- **Align mental models.** Keep everyone aligned on the same product concept and ensure clarity around technical jargon across teams, so everyone operates from a shared understanding of what the product is and does.

When you use your body intentionally as part of your creative process, ideas surface faster than they do through speech alone. You give teammates something they can see and react to, which helps the group align sooner instead of carrying around different imagined versions of the same idea. Assumptions and constraints become visible earlier, when they're easier to discuss and resolve.

This is where gesture consciousness becomes valuable. So, tune it up! When teams intentionally make use of what the body naturally contributes, you explore more of the problem space sooner. You can surface disagreements before they become expensive and move ideas from vague sparks to workable directions more quickly, and with less risk and greater confidence.

GESTURES SPEED UP THE CREATIVE PROCESS

When teams gesture, they think faster, align more quickly, and detect problems sooner. Gestures function as a fast, flexible, information-rich ideation and prototyping medium that can speed up discovery and strengthen shared understanding. Gestures accelerate the creative process[1] because they do the following:

- **Externalize thinking quickly,** making abstract ideas visible before words or sketches can.
- **Offload cognition,** freeing working memory for more flexible, generative exploration.
- **Act as instant spatial models,** allowing people to simulate motion, form, flow, and interaction on the fly.
- **Invite collaborative build-on,** as teammates repeat, modify, or extend a gestured depiction.
- **Expose uncertainty early,** with gesture-speech mismatches and hesitant motions revealing conceptual gaps before resources are spent.
- **Stabilize emerging ideas,** giving teams shared anchors so that promising directions are not lost too soon.
- **Surface usability issues sooner,** as users' hands often reveal friction or breakdowns before they can articulate them.
- **Support rapid, low-cost iteration,** enabling dozens of conceptual trials before committing to higher-fidelity work.

---

1 Goodwin (2000) demonstrated that meaning is constructed through visible, embodied action in interaction, not just through spoken language. His analysis shows how gestures, gaze, and the reuse of others' actions allow teams to build shared understanding and coordinate complex work moment by moment.

Prepare to Build Together

The design path is a generative journey where your team will guide ideas into testable prototypes. Think of them starting out as loose line sketches that gain form and are eventually fully fleshed out (see Figure 7.1). While sometimes ideas sync up easily, more often you will surface different perspectives that you must weigh against real-world constraints.

FIGURE 7.1
Ideas start out loose (left), are refined and built up (center), before being fully realized (right).

As gestures are a natural part of this creative process, you want to ensure that they are used as deliberate tools for innovation. You first want to create the right conditions. A rich, gestural exchange doesn't happen by accident. It comes from intentionally shaping both your team's mindset and the physical environment.

To prepare a space where ideas can emerge, circulate, and be built upon together, you will need to do the following:

- Invite gesture use.
- Prime the team with the problem.
- Set the expectations.
- Prepare the gesture canvas.

When these elements are in place, you can create a space where your team can build on one another's thinking in real time. This allows you to surface and resolve misalignments early, moving forward with greater confidence and speed.

Invite Gesture Use

You want to bring gesture consciousness to the foreground of your creative work. This awareness of gestures now becomes a tool for creative generation. You want to normalize thinking expressed through the body, making it clear that gestures are an integral part of how your team builds ideas.

Activating this awareness can be as simple as prompting a teammate with, "Can you show me what you mean?" This small invitation validates gestural thinking and signals that it belongs in the team's shared practice. But remember gesture consciousness is two-sided: it involves using your own gestures intentionally and actively noticing the gestures of others.

Use your gestures and encourage others to gesture as well. Fragile, emerging ideas often show up first in the body. When you invite the team to use their gestures intentionally, you give them permission to think in rough drafts and show those drafts with their bodies.

Finally, encourage a thoughtful use of gestures. Too many movements creates visual noise; too few can stall the work. Aim for gestures that are clear, purposeful, and easy for others to build on. When used well, gestures keep the collaborative space focused, fluid, and ready for ideas to grow.

Remember that any hands-on activity gets this going too. When people are already moving, like sketching on a whiteboard, arranging sticky notes, or handling a prototype, gestures tend to follow naturally. Bodies in motion tend to stay in motion!

Prime the Team with the Problem

Before weighing any ideas seriously, make sure that the team is grounded in the problem space and its constraints.

Start by immersing everyone in the user's lived experience. Revisit any design principles that emerged from research. If you did not speak directly with users, ask your colleagues which field notes or videos best convey key moments. This is more than reviewing a transcript or an AI summary. Take the time to watch source recordings and observe how people act, struggle, and adapt. Start from a deeper understanding of the people you are building for.

At the same time, gather the materials that will serve as reference points during ideation. This is a cross-functional effort. Bring in technical constraints from engineering, component libraries or brand guidelines from design, and timing or market considerations from product marketing. Track down any early sketches or "PM art" that capture known limits from prior technical discussions.

These images, diagrams, and assets populate the design space (and the gesture space!) (see Figure 7.2). Investing a little time up front reduces rework later and keeps ideation focused. Teams that are properly primed contribute ideas that are not only creative, but viable.

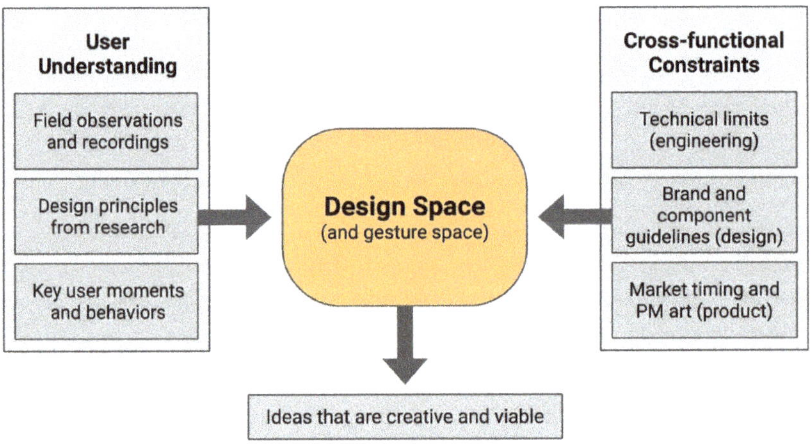

FIGURE 7.2
Populate the physical (or virtual) design space with artifacts that represent both your understanding of users as well as known constraints.

Set the Expectations

You also want to explicitly set the expectations for each creative session. When your goal is to diverge and generate new ideas, set expectations that promote quantity, diversity, and novelty (see Figure 7.3). The classic rule, "There are no bad ideas," helps teams produce ideas in volume. When your goal is to encourage diversity, make it clear that half-baked thoughts and nascent concepts are welcome. Those rough ideas often spark more refined thinking from others.

In these generative sessions, these expectations help early-stage creative work thrive by freeing your team to surface and communicate emerging thoughts without needing to polish them first.

FIGURE 7.3 Ideation is a generative process that encourages both quantity and diversity of ideas.

Prepare the Gesture Canvas

With the right expectations set, you can now set up the physical or digital environment where gestures are visible and available for others to pick up and build on. So, prepare your gesture canvas.

The gesture canvas is the shared, open space where gestures are visible to others and can be picked up, extended, and passed back into the conversation. It's where generative thinking, shared communication, and collaborative sense-making take shape through the body.

Think of the gesture canvas as having two layers:

- **Canvas between people:** The space where gestures circulate among teammates. This is where someone's emerging idea becomes visible, and where another person can mirror it, refine it, or question it.
- **Canvas among things:** The space where gestures interact with artifacts in the environment like documents, diagrams, design tools, sticky notes, and sketches. This canvas lets gestures latch onto reference materials, add detail, or pull in missing information.

To prepare the gesture canvas, in face-to-face meetings clear the visual field between people so gestures aren't hidden behind laptops or bodies. In virtual meetings, split your screens equally between collaborative whiteboard or design tools and other visual artifacts with a generously sized grid of people in the meeting. Then expand the canvas outward by positioning key artifacts within easy reach and clear sight. Keep physical and digital paper, markers, and pens available so the team can create new sketches on the fly, giving gestures a place to land and evolve. For examples of a well-prepared gesture canvas, see Figure 7.4.

FIGURE 7.4
Gesture canvas between people and among things, in person (top) and virtual (bottom).

Deliberately treat the gesture canvas like a dynamic workspace where ideas can be placed, revisited, and reshaped. Here ideas move fluidly from the air into a diagram, from a diagram into someone else's hands, and from their hands back into the shared flow of ideas.

When these pieces are in place, you've set up the conditions for gestures to become a core design medium. They move beyond just something people do to something you intentionally use to think, communicate, and create together.

Turn Sparks into Focused Concepts

Ideation is the bridge between understanding users' problems and generating the first real directions for solving them. This is where teams begin to toss out sparks of an idea that may move forward or fizzle out. These early ideas are quick, rough, and incomplete, surfacing in fragments.

Sparks emerge in many forms during ideation, from sticky notes and quick diagrams to offhand remarks that unexpectedly stick. Gestured sparks often surface even earlier, before words or images are available. They bring pieces of developing ideas out into the shared space where others can see, react, and add to them.

In this phase, gestures function like loose, partially formed line sketches on a shared gesture canvas. Early on, these gesture sketches are exploratory, like laying down rough strokes with a pencil without worrying about the final image (see Figure 7.5). As certain ideas begin to take hold, the same gestures are replayed and added to, giving the team something they can collectively decide to shape or toss.

Now, you'll learn how to use your own gesture sketches and the gesture sketches of others to move ideas from fragile, disconnected sparks toward a shared direction. You'll see how to do the following:

- Catch early ideas.
- Sharpen ideas.
- Sift through ideas.
- Anchor ideas.

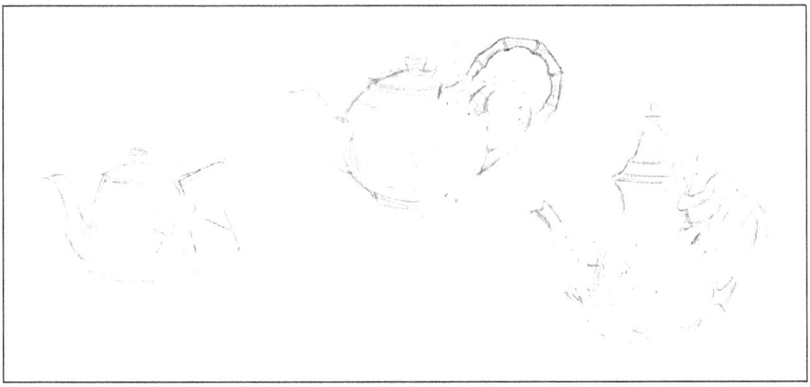

FIGURE 7.5
Gestured sparks are like loose pencil lines on a shared canvas exploring possible solutions to user needs.

Catch Early Ideas

Gestured early ideas are small, partial, and close to the body. You need to be on the lookout for them. They are ephemeral. You will catch them in variations that appear and disappear. You might even hear accompanying phrases like "maybe...," "what if...," or "kind of like..." as you lay down the first strokes of an idea.

It's like when an artist doodles on the paper, starts over, erases, and draws over parts of the image in an effort to bring out their thinking.

To make the most of this phase, you want as many ideas out in the open as possible, because quantity and diversity are essential at the outset of ideation. Each gesture adds another mark to the shared canvas. As more gestures surface, more potential approaches come into view for solving your target user problem.

Catching these raw sparks and bringing them into the shared gesture canvas is the foundational skill in this phase. Doing it well requires you to make your own ideas visible and to watch for emerging ideas of others. Together, these moves give the team a common surface to work on and the shared footing it needs to begin shaping possibilities collaboratively.

Make Your Ideas Visible

Ideas only become useful once they are externalized. This turns private thinking into shared material the team can work with, shape, and advance together. If an idea is never put forward, it can't be developed.

Your team may already use structured activities like Crazy 8s, gamestorming, or charettes to surface early thinking. Gestures can do this work, too. They reveal shape, motion, flow, or intent before words or artifacts are ready, putting the first marks of an idea into the shared space where others can see them and respond.

Once a gestured idea is visible, it becomes material for everyone to work with. Teammates can point to it, repeat it, extend it, modify it, or question it. This is how ideas move across people instead of staying locked inside one person's imagination. To support this, make your gestures intentionally visible by putting them in the gesture canvas.

- Keep your hands where others can see them.
- Gesture high enough and far enough into the shared space for others to catch the idea.
- In virtual sessions, keep your hands in frame—when hands disappear, emerging ideas often disappear with them.

Watch for Others' Ideas

Visibility is reciprocal. Ideation is more than just making your own thinking visible; it is also about receiving the emerging ideas of others. As your teammates gesture through fragments of their thoughts, watch closely.

Consider a team discussing the design of a new, space-saving coffee maker. Customer feedback suggests the previous model is too wide to fit comfortably on a crowded countertop. The team is focused on the water reservoir and how it might be redesigned.

One engineer begins to talk through the problem. "What if we don't really need it?" he says, trailing off mid-sentence. As he speaks, he makes a small pouring gesture close to his body, as if tipping an invisible cup. His gesture shows him imagining a pouring action without a separate reservoir.

A second teammate sees the gesture and responds, "I think people like having this, maybe we just need to move it?" she says. As she says this, she holds her left hand close to her body flat like a surface. And with a small movement, her right hand settles on top of it, as if stacking something (see Figure 7.6). Her gesture depicts a different idea: keep the reservoir but move it to the top to reclaim counter space.

Neither idea is fully articulated nor written down. But both are clearly visible in the room.

FIGURE 7.6
Two teammates gesture different design ideas for the problem of the coffee maker's water reservoir, building off of one another's contributions with gestures.

What began as a half-formed, gesture sketch, becomes a shared idea the team can explore together. In moments like this, gestures make emerging possibilities visible before the group has decided what to do with them. Several ideas can coexist at once, each revealing different ways of framing the same problem.

Early gestures are invitations to collaborate. Small thinking gestures are a natural part of how people work through ideas, but they are easy to miss when attention is divided. Catch them when you can! Watching this natural human behavior helps prevent promising ideas from going unnoticed and not being considered.

When you're not sure what you're seeing, you can rescue a thought on the brink by simply asking, "Can you show me that again?"

GESTURES SUPPORT IDEA GENERATION

Gestures support ideation because they are ephemeral, low-commitment externalizations of thought. Their transient nature reduces inhibition, allowing people to propose, revise, or abandon ideas without the cognitive or social cost of more durable representations. Even brief movements can encode structural information like motion, direction, or scale before a verbal or graphical form is available.[2]

Because gestures are provisional, they remain open to reinterpretation. Others can question or extend them, maintaining conceptual flexibility and reducing fixation. Research on external representations shows that such manipulable forms help teams explore alternatives while managing cognitive load.[3] When a gesture breaks down, it provides immediate feedback about the limitations or incoherence of the underlying idea, encouraging rapid revision rather than fixation.

2 Goldin-Meadow (2003) showed that spontaneous gestures reveal emerging ideas not yet expressed in speech and help people organize and refine their thinking.

3 Kirsh (2010) demonstrated that provisional external representations, including gestures, reduce cognitive load and support flexible exploration by off-loading part of the reasoning process into the environment.

Sharpen Ideas

Once an idea has been caught and made visible, the work shifts from noticing it to sharpening those ideas that hold possibilities and determining whether they can stick or not. Teams already give form to early sparks through talk, drawings, sticky notes, and images. These representations give a loose idea just enough shape for people to figure out whether to spend more time on it or nix it.

This is like when an artist sketches out variations and lands on promising details that they want to continue to develop (see Figure 7.7).

Gesture sketches do this, too. And they do this while contributing something distinctive to this mix. Gestures can also show motion, sequence, space, and dimensionality at the speed of thought, sharpening the blurriness of a nascent idea.

As your team takes up a gesture, assesses their interpretations, and adds shape, the idea grows beyond its initial seed and takes on more coherence and form.

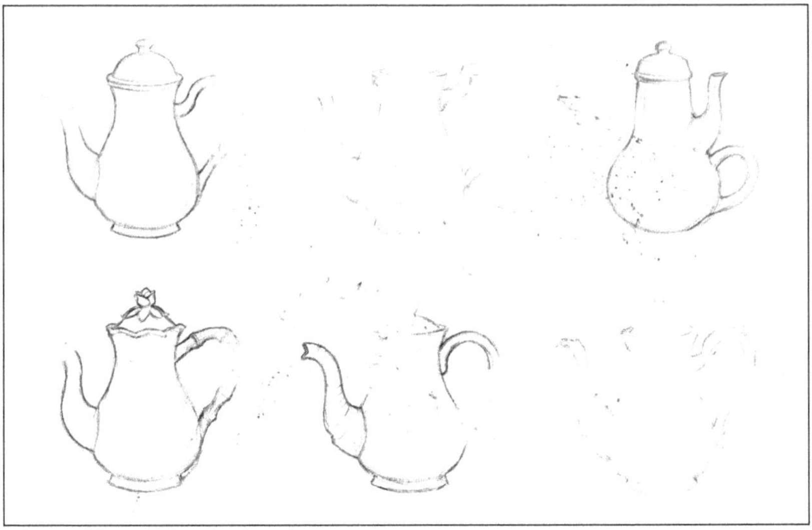

FIGURE 7.7
It's important to sharpen variations on ideas to determine what to spend more time on.

Pick Up and Pass Ideas in Gestures

Gesture sketches are quick and easily dissolved, so you need a way to keep them alive long enough to explore. Picking up a gesture keeps an idea in play and makes it shared. Passing the gesture back and forth helps the team clarify what it means and gradually accumulate precision.

When someone acts out an emerging idea, they offer a rough representation. It gains traction when another person picks it up, literally taking it into their own hands. Once a gestured idea enters the shared space of the gesture canvas, anyone can try out variations or test possibilities. With each pass, small adjustments can add clarity, and as the representation shifts, the idea itself advances with it.

Consider a team developing a new latch mechanism for a modular speaker system (see Figure 7.8). An industrial designer makes a quick hooking motion to represent how a speaker might attach to a base. An industrial engineer picks up the gesture, repeats it with a wider arc, and adds a downward press to show where the lock might engage. A second engineer rotates the motion ninety degrees: "What if the attachment point is vertical?" The designer tries that variant and adds a tightening twist: "That might solve the wobble problem we've heard about."

FIGURE 7.8
Representational gestures are passed back and forth to advance an idea for a design for a latching mechanism.

In under a minute, a simple gestured stand-in of an idea has sharpened through shared contribution. Through being passed back and forth, the preliminary idea of a latching mechanism comes into focus for the team, allowing them to better assess its sturdiness and decide whether it is ready to move forward.

NOTE NATURAL SELECTION OF IDEAS

When a gestured idea gets picked up and passed back and forth, it gathers momentum. When it doesn't, it naturally fades. The circulation becomes a quiet filter: ideas with promise evolve while weaker ones fall away.

As gestures are repeated and modified, they will often surface constraints and opportunities in the process. This provides you and your team an opportunity to see where an idea holds together and where it starts to break down.

Sift Through Ideas

At this point, you and your team have a set of promising ideas that could plausibly meet a user's needs. Now you want to scrutinize them. This is your second pass to further sift through your ideas already on the table and understand them well enough to decide whether they make the cut. The aim is not to round out any one idea into a design concept yet, but to make your ideas concrete and coherent enough to evaluate and figure out if they are worth additional investment.

Sifting happens through an ongoing exchange of clarification and elaboration. You dig into the ideas together, working through them to analyze how they hold up, test their limits, and get a sense of their viability.

Think of this like an artist refining a sketch to decide whether it is worth committing to. An early drawing may be loose and suggestive, capturing many possibilities at once (see Figure 7.9). But at some point, the artist pauses, traces over a line again, adjusts proportions, and holds the sketch steady long enough to really see its structure, its strengths, and what it could or could not become.

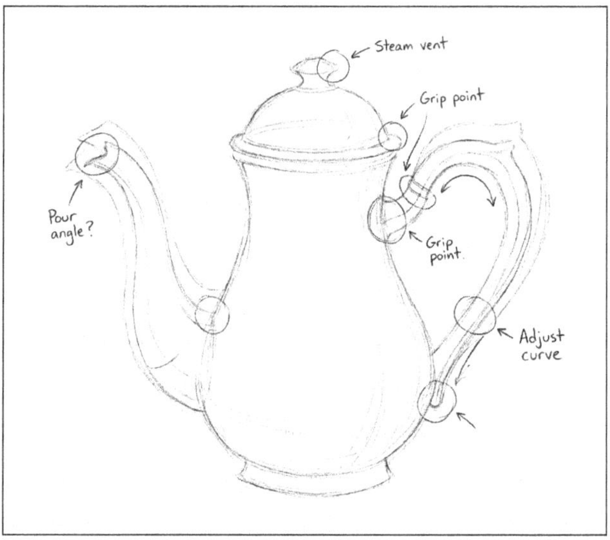

FIGURE 7.9
Sifting through potential ideas for a teapot while keeping it provisional.

At this stage, the team stays with just a few ideas. New ideas are parked. You can tell your team has entered this phase when you hear things like "Let's hold off on new ideas for now." This is where you also want to pull in gestures because they can be created and seen at the speed of thought. This keeps your team's thinking moving.

You may also notice that the rapid appearance of new gesture sketches has slowed and attention settles on a few key ideas. They become more sustained and intentional. Movements are repeated to confirm shared understanding. They are adjusted to sharpen the details. Additional movements are added to explore relationships. Gestures are held in place so the group can examine them together.

When you notice this shift, respond to it. Do not bulldoze past it in search of novelty. These moments mark an opportunity to build clarity and deepen an idea before deciding whether to move it forward.

Clarification plays a central role in sifting through ideas because you don't want to move forward with an idea or toss it out before you truly understand it. You want to be able to identify what is missing, fuzzy, or misaligned. Gestures often signal this need for clarity themselves. Someone may roll a hand forward asking for more information or nod when something makes sense. You may also notice movements trail off or someone hesitate. Gestures and talk also may not quite line up. You will likely hear phrases like, "Here's how I'm thinking about it," "No, it's more like this," and "I don't get it. Can you share more?" So, take time and make sure you all are on the same page before moving forward.

But clarification does not happen alone. Elaboration is always close by. Once you have clarified an idea enough, elaboration takes over. Now you will develop the idea and explore further what it could become without committing to a direction. Your gestures will add, remove, exaggerate, shrink, or rearrange elements to test whether the idea is one you want to keep moving forward or toss. The work gestures will do is they'll probe alternatives and relationships and do so quickly, adding in timing, motion, dimensionality all in a single action. You will hear language like "What if this came first," "How about changing this up?" or, "It might work better/smoother if...." You will see variations that play with structure and detail without locking the idea down.

These moments are important, but they are fleeting. Tune up your gesture consciousness and intentionally work to stay on top of them. Begin by putting the idea in the same gesture space so that everyone can work from the same sketch. Now you want to use that shared material to determine what to sift out. You can do this by doing the following:

- Keeping the idea in a shared gesture space so that everyone works from the same sketch.
- Slowing gestures to highlight flow, order, or dependency.
- Breaking gestures into parts to reveal internal structure.
- Shrinking or exaggerating movements to emphasize key relationships.

- Positioning gestures to show spatial relationships.
- Pairing gestures with nearby artifacts when details need grounding.
- Checking shared understanding ("Are we all seeing the same thing?").

This work of refined exploration and development often gets cut short. Stick with it! Together, clarification and elaboration allow early sparks to develop into shared conceptions. These are mutual mental images that support collective understanding. If you invest the time now, the dividends pay off later by making sure the best and most workable ideas are carried into prototyping.

NOTE **LEVERAGE YOUR RESOURCES**

Gestures don't replace the tools your team already uses; they partner with them. Keep diagrams, screens, notes, and artifacts in play. Moving between these resources helps teams develop clarity and structure together, without locking ideas down too early.

Consider a team mapping the flow of an agentic AI reporting automation tool for a company trying to improve their regulatory compliance. A product manager says, "The nightly cron job rolls up their daily transactions and then those need to get validated," she traces a curved arc in the air everyone can see, sketching how a reporting agent moves the rollup of daily transaction logs from "submitted" to "reviewed." This is clarification because it establishes a shared understanding of the key report states. An engineer picks up the gesture and adds a small, punctuated dip at the midpoint. "It's good practice to have a second agent in the loop to check the work." This is elaboration, adding an important intermediate state between submission and review.

The PM chimes back in, "Oh, good point. And our customer is worried about auditability. So maybe there's . . . " She hesitates and makes a second dip in the arc, followed by tapping her right hand to her chest. Seeing this, the engineer seeks confirmation, "A human in the loop?" The PM nods. This is also an elaboration, by introducing an additional state for a human audit.

The designer then mirrors the arc with the second dip and exaggerates the pause and says "not all the time." The designer is suggesting that the second state with the human review doesn't need to happen every time; it can just be a random human audit to check that the agents are doing the reporting accurately. This process clarifies the designer's contribution and then adds on to it.

Now the loose idea of how a report moves through these distinct states has been advanced together. The team has landed on a concept that integrates requirements from the PM, best practices from the engineer, and smart interaction design from the designer while addressing the customer's need for auditability. Remember this is still just an idea, but it has emerged with more clarity and detail. The team has converged on an idea they can take further and continue to explore.

"IDEABERG" AHEAD!

When you are dreaming up solutions to the problem you want to solve, you want to keep an eye for anything that can sink ideas before they are really explored. Constraints like cost, timelines, and other factors that impact feasibility, can prevent your idea from moving forward. Friction can also present obstacles to your ideas. Sometimes, an idea is hard to scrutinize because it's tangled in technical jargon or uneven understanding across the team. It's important to surface constraints and friction early, while ideas are still loose and shared. Gestures can reveal these issues before people develop strong ownership and before ideas become harder to redirect (see Figure 7.10).

FIGURE 7.10
Constraints and friction always loom, so don't let your ideas run aground.

continues

"IDEABERG" AHEAD! (continued)

Keep an eye out for those gestures that surface these constraints and points of friction. Notice misalignment early and catch feasibility issues before they derail the team. Watch for moments when gestures do the following:

- **Collapse or stop short** because they surface a hidden limit.
- **Move out of gesture space** and are no longer intentionally shared.
- **Hesitate or freeze mid-movement** because they can indicate uncertainty.
- **Show gesture-speech mismatch** because they are an indicator of misaligned mental models.
- **Decrease in frequency amid dense jargon** because the gesture's absence will hamper co-construction of ideas.

When you notice these gestures and sense that the team's momentum is veering into troubled waters, consider the following strategies to respond:

- Reduce a sense of ownership by placing your gestures firmly in shared space to reinforce that you are building together.
- Pull others in by passing the gesture to them to repeat or reshape.
- Don't interrupt people's gestures and let them finish.
- Show interest in their perspective by asking them to show you again.
- Play out the idea in gestures before rejecting it.
- Use your words! Articulate what you think the gestures are conveying, avoid making assumptions.

Above all, remember that timing matters. You want to steer the momentum of your team before it's too late.

Don't let constraints and friction sink your idea! Spot them early and often.

Anchor Ideas

An idea needs to become anchored in order to be durable and able to move forward. Anchoring not only gives an idea staying power, but it also gives it legitimacy. There are many ways to lock in an idea. They can be anchored by giving them a name that people can reference (e.g., "the reporting agent"). You might anchor an idea by sketching or diagramming it out.

This is like an artist confidently outlining the gestalt of an object, then tearing the sketch from the pad and pinning it to the wall (see Figure 7.11). This idea is a go!

FIGURE 7.11
An idea is anchored when it has been vetted and is strong enough to move forward.

Gestures can also anchor an idea or concept by giving it a repeatable motion or action that everyone understands as standing in for a specific design element or overarching concept. It is something the team can return to, reuse, and build on over time.

These anchors become boundary objects—the shared information artifacts that help teams coordinate thinking and work together across different roles and perspectives. You already use many types of boundary objects like sketches and prototypes. They don't need to be finished representations, but they are stable enough to hold an idea in place while people develop them together.

Gestures are also important boundary objects: a looping motion, a branching gesture, or a repeated sweep through space becomes part of the team's shared imagination. It functions like an embodied sticky note that keeps the idea visible and available for the group to build on.

You know you've stabilized and anchored an idea when gestures are as follows:

- Picked up by team members in similar ways.
- Used to fill in for language that explains a concept.
- Given a name informally.
- Referenced in the same spatial locations.
- Show up again when returning to the problem.

When an idea anchors effectively, the team converges on a shared, clear picture of "what it is" and "how it works." This sets you up well for the prototyping that comes next!

Prototype Your Idea

By this point in the work, your team has explored a range of possibilities through gesture sketching. You've also sharpened and sifted ideas worth carrying forward. Now it is time to move into prototyping.

Prototyping turns ideas into a tangible thing that can be inspected, tested, and refined before committing to full-scale and often costly production. Prototypes surface risk early and help teams work out kinks. When you prototype, you have largely settled on a specific direction. You are no longer intentionally searching for new ideas. Instead, you are carrying one idea forward through the fidelity arc.

You may think of the fidelity arc as a continuous spectrum of object development that includes elements like the following:

1. **Proof-of-concept prototype:** Uses low-fidelity sketches or mockups to validate the core idea and confirm that the underlying value proposition makes sense.
2. **"Looks-like" prototype:** Uses high-fidelity visual models to evaluate aesthetics and overall experiential impact.
3. **"Works-like" prototype:** Uses functional mockups, such as clickable flows or physical assemblies, to test interaction and behavior.
4. **Engineering prototype:** Uses production-grade materials or code to represent a near-final system and surface technical risks before full-scale build.

The value of prototypes isn't just the cardboard mockup or the mid-fidelity wireframe. A prototype gives people something tangible to collaborate around. It becomes the focal point where teams gather, test ideas, and make decisions together. In this interaction space, the product—both as an object and an emerging idea—is negotiated and improved through a back-and-forth exchange.

Gestures naturally show up when working with prototypes. As teams handle and inspect a physical or digital mockup, gestures help animate and extend what the object or interface can only partially do. Most of these are movements that teams already use instinctively. Coordinating gestures direct attention to specific parts, like a designer pointing to a button placement on a screen or a mechanical engineer tracing the seam where two components meet. Directional gestures show how an interaction unfolds, like a product manager swiping through an imagined onboarding flow or an industrial designer arcing their hand to show how a lid lifts and rotates open. Spatial gestures map relationships between elements, like a teammate holding one hand above another to indicate a layered menu structure.

Together, these movements bring the prototype to life beyond what the mockup can do, and in turn help everyone on the team inspect behavior, test alternatives, and coordinate decisions before committing further changes.

Gestures also do important work before anything has been built. When a team is exploring ideas together and there is nothing yet to point to or pick up, the hands become the prototype itself.

These are proto-prototypes: embodied, in-the-air gestural stand-ins for how aspects of a design might look, feel, and behave before anything is built. A hardware designer clasps their palm around an imaginary axis to suggest a possible size and grip of a device. A UX designer sweeps a finger through the air to walk the team through an idea of a possible screen flow. An engineer holds one hand steady and moves the other to propose how one service could trigger another in a backend architecture. In this way, gestures take on a representational role and let you depict form, motion, spatial layout, and structure together at the speed of thought—all without needing to build anything first.

Proto-prototypes extend the prototyping fidelity arc backward and give teams a way to make aspects of a potential design concrete enough to work on together before anything is built (see Figure 7.12). Importantly, proto-prototypes don't disappear as fidelity increases. They are present at every stage of the arc. Even when a team is working with sketches, wireframes, or physical models, gestures continue to do proto-prototyping work like testing refinements, exploring alternatives, and pulling existing artifacts into the gesture canvas to build on and revise them before solidifying the next durable iteration.

These in-the-air explorations help you advance your product design because they are fast, require no setup, and can be introduced, reshaped, or discarded in an instant. Without needing to commit to tools or materials, ideas remain flexible and open to development, and the barrier to participation stays low. Anyone can step in, test a change, or suggest an alternative with nothing more than their hands.

In practice, proto-prototyping unfolds through two intertwined embodied processes:

- **Simulating interactions:** Using the body to act out user actions and system responses to test timing, flow, effort, and breakdowns.
- **Extending through gesture stacks:** Layering gestures to add structure, detail, and precision to advance ideas along the fidelity arc.

Together, these processes ensure that prototyping is not just about artifacts, but about the human fundamentals that make ideas real, workable, and worth building.

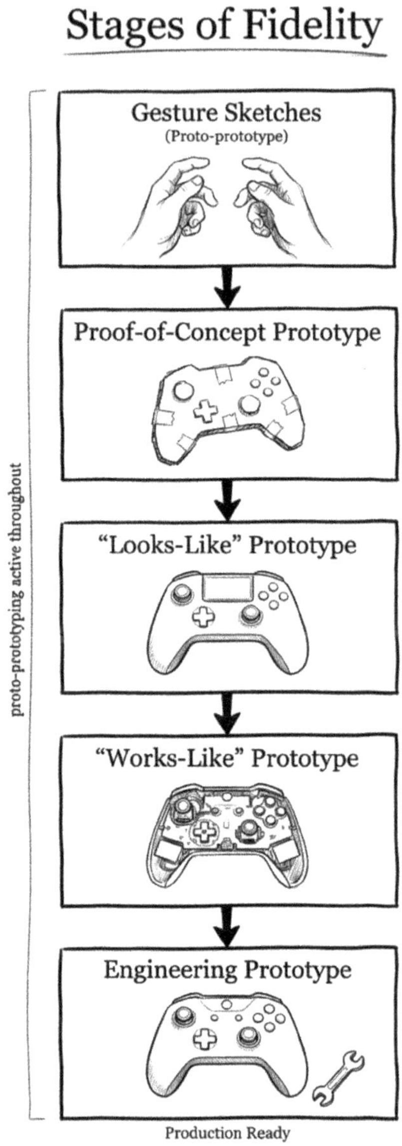

FIGURE 7.12
The fidelity stages of a prototype start with gestured proto-prototypes.

Simulate Interactions

At the core of proto-prototyping is simulated action. This is when you and your team shift from talking about how an idea might work to putting it into action with the body. Rather than imagining a user's experience, a simulated action is the step where you physically enact it. You step into the roles of user, system, and environment and play out how a product or experience will work.

Simulated actions start in the head. When people draw on prior experience to imagine how something might work, they run mental simulations. This is just what humans do!

The artist working on the coffee pot wants to sketch it being used, but senses that the balance of the design is off. To check the physics, he imagines the pour and draws the forces in play and the path of the liquid, using arrows to trace those quantities. When he looks at the diagram, he realizes the coffee pot's handle is too high relative to the center of mass, leading to a gush of coffee that would overwhelm the cup (see Figure 7.13). Time to fix the proportions.

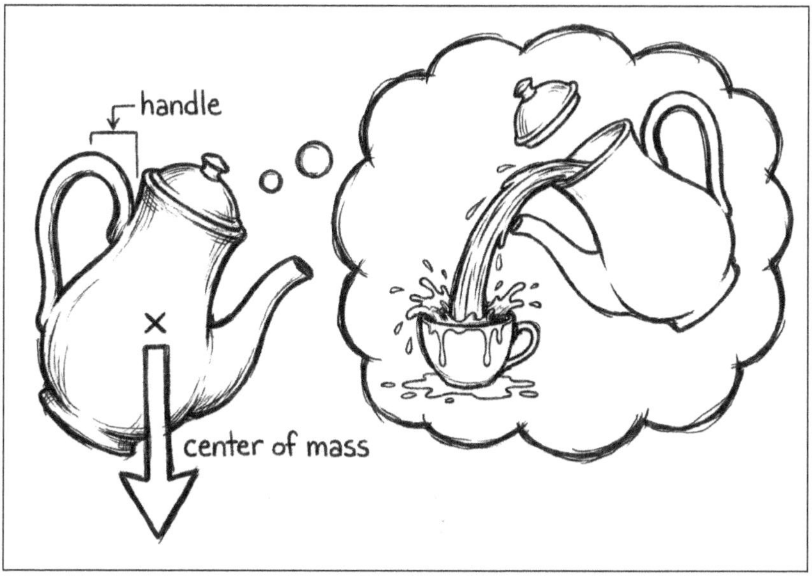

FIGURE 7.13
An idea may not quite work when simulated, highlighting key issues that need further revision.

WHAT IS SIMULATION?

Simulation is a fundamental mechanism of human thought. When people imagine or reason about an object or concept (especially without direct interaction with it), they rely on the partial reactivation of prior sensory and motor experiences to structure information and plan action.[4] This is known as *mental simulation* and includes what you might know as mental and motor imagery, along with other senses.

Simulation, though, is more than just a simple replay of the past. Your mind draws on reusable elements of experience such as shape, motion, force, timing, spatial relations and recombines them to reason about both familiar and novel situations.[5] For example, think of a hot air balloon. Now think of an elephant. Now imagine an elephant in a hot air balloon. You have certainly never experienced such an absurdity, yet you can picture it with ease. Congrats! You just performed a mental simulation. Now keep this scene in your mind and compare it to Figure 7.14.

Whatever you envisioned, you rapidly dreamt up this scene by drawing on simulations of "elephants" and "hot air balloons" and their properties like weight, size, and lift in ways that were not direct replays of past experience. Rather you reactivated simulations of these concepts and their properties to construct your distinct version of the floating pachyderm, instantly evaluating the factors that would render this scene sensible to you. Through simulation, people are able to anticipate outcomes, explore alternatives, and

4 Wilson (2002) synthesized research demonstrating that "offline" thinking—planning, imagining, remembering—relies on body-based simulation, using the same perceptual and motor systems involved in real action.

5 Barsalou (1999) argued that concepts are grounded in perceptual and motor systems, and people represent knowledge by reactivating and recombining elements of sensory and action experience rather than relying on abstract, amodal symbols.

test possibilities without needing to experience them directly. This capacity to assemble embodied knowledge into new configurations underpins human cognition and is fundamental to problem-solving and creativity.

FIGURE 7.14
An elephant in a hot air balloon is something you can imagine even though you've never observed it firsthand.

Simulation allows people to reason about what does not yet exist by recombining what they already know.

But a mental simulation rarely stays in the head. It naturally becomes visible through the body. When a mental simulation moves into the body, you also get another perk. The body becomes a tool for assessment. When a simulation is acted out, people not only can see what you're acting out, but you also get the opportunity to feel it viscerally. Through a simulated action, you experience and feel these properties of the idea.

- **Shape:** The form or structure of something, including its size and contours.
- **Space:** Where elements and objects are located in relation to one another and their environment.
- **Motion:** How elements, objects, and people move and change.
- **Timing:** The order, pace, and rhythm with which something unfolds.

Treated seriously, a simulated action becomes an early feasibility check and a sensing instrument. By physically enacting an interaction, your team can feel whether an idea holds together before committing it to screens, tools, or code.

Here are some common types of simulated actions you can use to intentionally test an idea:

- **Role switching:** Stepping into the shoes of a specific user or persona to test how a design feels from their point of view.
- **Perspective switching:** Taking on the role of the system or an element within it to explore the interaction from the inside out.
- **Representing structure:** Simulating the spatial information in a diagram, such as enacting depth and dimension from a 2D sketch.
- **Animating motion:** Transforming a static concept into a kinetic one by depicting its path or how its parts move over time.
- **Slowing or exaggerating motion:** Stretching time to reveal hidden effort or exaggerating a movement to make subtle issues more visible.
- **Replaying critical moments:** Repeating an interaction or sequence to examine uncertainty, friction, or breakdowns from multiple angles.
- **Comparing alternatives:** Enacting two versions of an interaction side-by-side for immediate, real-time comparison.

To see how simulation can support prototyping, imagine you're part of a team designing a stationary exercise bike that must meet baseline safety requirements to be commercially viable. One requirement is an emergency stop that a rider can activate if they are in distress. During a design review, the lead engineer is reviewing the mid-fidelity 2D sketch made by the design team of the company's newest model. The engineer proposes reusing the safety key mechanism from the company's treadmills. It's inexpensive, familiar, and already approved from an engineering standpoint.

The product owner considers the engineer's idea and then steps into the role of someone using one of their treadmill models. She grasps an invisible set of handles on an imagined treadmill, establishing the shape and spatial position of the runner's body, and then leans sharply backward. "On a treadmill, when something goes wrong, you do this." She traces an invisible tether as she leans, enacting the motion and timing that would pull the safety key free.

She points to the sketch of the bike that is being presented and switches her role to that of the bike rider. She then resets her posture and hunches forward over the imaginary bike. "But on a bike, you start here." She then sits back up and angles her right hand to mirror the posture of the cyclist on the bike, depicting a forward-leaning posture. She hinges her hand forward at the edge of her palm. "If something goes wrong," she continues, "you're falling" and her hand makes a splat sound against her stationary hand to emphasize the downward direction the cyclist would be moving (see Figure 7.15). "It wouldn't pull it out..." she then places her left hand out flat to stand in for the safety key still lodged in the bike. "You'd go like..." and she extends her hand up as the safety key and drops her body, showing the tethered string holding her up by her shirt, the bike still going and the safety key still engaged. The engineer says, "Oh wow, you're right that would be bad. The wheels would still be going," rotating his fingers in a clockwise motion.

In a deft sequence of animated motions, the product owner switches roles between the user and the product, shifts perspective within the system, replays critical moments, and compares alternatives in real time. The simulated actions surface a constraint that discussion alone hadn't revealed: the emergency stop depends on a precise relationship between shape, space, motion, and timing that didn't exist on their current bike concept. Without building anything, the team rules out a seemingly reasonable reuse. This simulated action exposed a feasibility breakdown early before the team became attached to a solution that wouldn't actually work.

FIGURE 7.15

Product owner moves through a simulation to uncover a flaw in the safety key design concept for their stationary bike.

The payoff for including simulated action in your practice is significant. Even before anything is built, proto-prototypes give the team something concrete to gather around. They bring together different perspectives and let the group work through design problems quickly. Issues are resolved in real time and momentum stays high. This helps your team catch feasibility issues early and surface constraints before attachment to an idea sets in. By creating a shared, physical understanding across roles, you reduce downstream rework and can decide more confidently what's worth building—before you

KEEP SURFACING CONSTRAINTS

A proto-prototype is a tool for pressure-testing a design against reality. Building the right thing is an ongoing negotiation, and a proto-prototype makes that negotiation tangible. Your job is to actively seek and surface constraints—technical feasibility, system dependencies, or mental model mismatches—that emerge when a design concept is physically enacted.

If you do not understand what a cross-functional colleague means, press for clarity until you do. Address these constraints as they surface, while the design is still flexible. This allows your proto-prototype to evolve under pressure, rather than breaking later when changes are expensive and attachment has set in.

This is the strategic value of proto-prototyping: ensuring that what you build is not just innovative, but also viable.

build it. Using simulated actions doesn't replace other tools, but it does help you and your team arrive at those tools with better questions and fewer surprises.

Build with Gesture Stacks

Simulated actions let you enact an idea and really feel how it holds up. They make problems obvious. You might notice awkward transitions, interactions that require too much effort, unclear system responses, overloaded moments, or confusion about who is in control. These breakdowns signal that your idea isn't fully baked and needs to be built up more.

When you notice something that doesn't quite work in simulation, you need to fix it. This is where gesture stacking comes in. Gesture stacking is the accumulation of coordinated gestures that add detail and structure as a design is built up. As gestures stack and stick, they build up a new and improved proto-prototype at any point along your product's fidelity arc.

Like the team designing the exercise bike, simulation showed the team that a simple reuse of an existing safety feature would not work. Rather than committing to a flawed solution or jumping straight into higher-fidelity prototyping, the team recognized that the idea needed further work while it was still flexible. This is the moment when gesture stacking becomes useful.

With gesture stacking, you move into a rich process of construction for refinement. Before you reach for tools, you can use your hands to try out potential fixes in real time. Gestures let you respond to glitches and blips by working those moments into a more coherent, usable interaction.

Progress comes from layering building gestures over time. Together, they carry the idea toward a more stable prototype and clearer go or no-go decisions.

Think of the artist redrawing the teapot by drawing layers of possibilities like shorter size and adding hand grips (see Figure 7.16).

FIGURE 7.16
Solving an issue surfaced during simulation can take layers of changes to address.

How to Build with Gesture Stacks

Gesture stacking happens once your team commits to improving a single design concept. You stay with one gestured depiction and move it forward through accumulation like adding elements, reshaping movements, shifting where actions happen in space, and adjusting timing and flow. Each gesture makes a small change, and together these changes give the idea more structure and precision without needing to increase prototype fidelity.

These gestures work together as a system. Each one builds on to another, adding information about what needs to change so a revision addresses the gaps or opportunities surfaced during simulation.

You can often see this process unfolding physically. Gesture stacks tend to form in the center of the gesture canvas, with people leaning in so that details are visible to everyone. One person may hold the core of a gestured depiction while another adds to it. As the idea develops, talk shifts from proposing solutions to refining behavior: "What if this was angled out more?" or "For this part, maybe it could scroll this way?"

Gesture stacks support a different kind of design work. Teams use them to do the following:

- **Add structure** by extending components, roles, and boundaries.
- **Adjust sequence** by refining order, timing, and dependency.
- **Distribute effort** by shifting work between user, system, or environment.
- **Refine behavior** over time by smoothing transitions and emphasizing key moments.

To see how gesture stacks help a team address an issue surfaced during simulation, return to the safety stop design for the exercise bike. The team has already determined that a tethered safety key would not work because a distressed rider would have difficulty pulling it.

The engineer offers a modification: "What if the key were aligned like this..." They lift their right hand from a horizontal to a vertical orientation, holding it steady against the sketch of the bike for others to see. "It could be the same key, just positioned differently."

The product owner sees the gesture and chimes in: "The problem I see is how far someone would have to go before this actually triggers." As they speak, they drop one hand low toward the floor, tilt their head upward, and tug on an imaginary tether from the handlebars to their shirt. The motion makes the issue visible: the rider would need to be nearly on the ground before the key disengaged. "At that point," they add, "it's already too late." The gesture collapses, signaling that the modification doesn't resolve the underlying problem.

The engineer nods, encouraging the team to replay the rider's downward motion, this time slowing it and exaggerating the direction of force. The product owner leans forward and lets her upper body tip down again.

The engineer picks up her forward-leaning motion and builds on it, adding a downward press as if pushing a button (see Figure 7.17). "If it's going that way," he says, pointing down, "then maybe it's not a pull." By layering one gesture onto another, the team sees the problem immediately.

FIGURE 7.17

The product owner enacts gripping the handlebars. The engineer stacks his own gesture to depict a button press, revealing a problem with the design of the proposed safety mechanism.

They begin to explore what that push might require. One person taps an imaginary button on the handlebars, where the rider's hands already are. "Here?" someone asks. Another teammate repeats the gesture but shrinks it, pinching their fingers together and then using their gesture to mimic pressing a button over and over but in random locations. "That's pretty small," she says. The precision required becomes obvious as the gesture tightens. "In an emergency, that would be hard to hit." The stacking of gestured ideas refines possible adaptations.

Someone slides the gesture downward to the vertical bar beneath the handlebars. "What about lower?" They open their hand into a widened palm to suggest a larger surface. The engineer presses downward again, this time with a broad, open palm (see Figure 7.18). "Aiming wouldn't be as important," he says. The group nods. The location, size, and effort all change rapidly through these refinements, bringing the team closer to resolving the issue.

FIGURE 7.18

One gesture places an imaginary button on the handlebars, another critiques it as too small, and a third relocates the button lower and widens it.

Through this stack of small adjustments, like replaying the motion to examine sequence and timing, shifting the gesture's location in space to redistribute effort, and widening the movement to reduce precision, the team adds structure to a user's interaction with the product and refines its design. Each gesture contributes new information about components, their spatial locations, and how they would be used. Together, these stacked gestures move the idea forward into something more stable and usable (see Figure 7.19), without committing to drawings or materials, and prepare it for the next iteration of prototyping.

Because nothing is committed to tools yet, gesture stacks keep emerging solutions lightweight and reversible. Teams can replay, adjust, or abandon a direction easily. They let you explore structure early, align sooner, and avoid costly rework later. Gesture stacks allow teams to stay in low fidelity while still increasing precision. They give shape to timing, effort, and flow without locking ideas into artifacts too early.

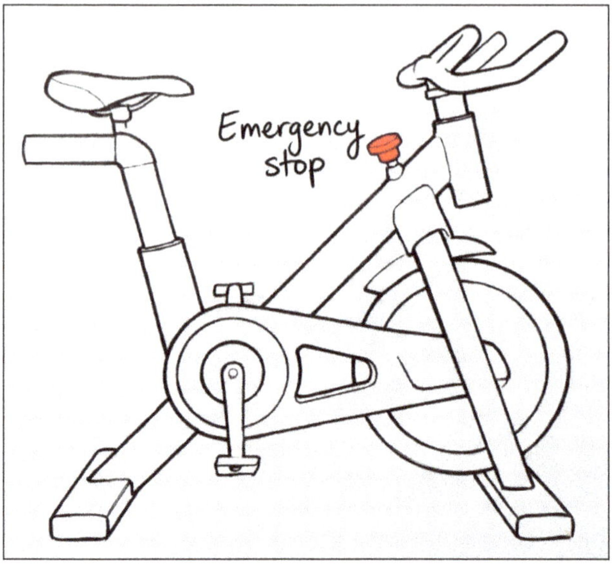

FIGURE 7.19
Gesture stacking helped reposition the safety feature for the exercise bike in a location that addressed concerns from simulated actions.

NOTE PROTO-PROTOTYPE ACROSS THE FIDELITY ARC

Proto-prototyping doesn't stop as fidelity increases. Even when a team is working with sketches, wireframes, or 3D-printed models, gestures continue to build up proto-prototypes. Gestures let the team test refinements and explore alternatives by pulling existing artifacts into the gesture canvas and building on and revising them before solidifying the next durable prototype iteration. This keeps the work lightweight and reversible as you work out design kinks!

Gesture stacks let your team do real, impactful design work together. But remember that it's important for any gestured design concept to be stabilized. Like you saw during ideation, proto-prototypes need to be anchored to be durable and move forward in the prototyping process. You can stabilize gesture-built proto-prototypes like you stabilize ideas. For example, you can give them a name or make a lightweight sketch of them.

HOW TO STACK GESTURES AS YOU BUILD

Gestures are a great tool for building, but they can fall into the background if they are not intentionally treated as building material. Once a gesture enters the space, it belongs to the group. Anyone can refine it, extend it, or reposition it. Keep gestures visible and available to be picked up and worked on. When gestures are treated as shared material, the following practices help teams use them to build up proto-prototypes:

- **Let gestures complete.** Allow others to finish a gesture that introduces a potential refinement before responding. Meaning often resolves at the end of the movement.
- **Replay before revising.** Repeat a shared gesture instead of correcting it verbally. Replaying keeps the idea visible and in play while allowing it to evolve.
- **Rearticulate before moving on.** Pause to "summarize" the current gesture stack to confirm shared understanding before advancing.
- **Stay fluid with perspective.** Shift between roles, such as user, system, or environment, to explore the full range of an interaction.
- **Test alternate variations.** Enact multiple versions quickly to compare pace, structure, or emphasis, rather than settling too early on a single approach.

Used deliberately, gesture stacks turn shared movements into building material, helping teams collectively refine ideas.

From Loose Sketches to the Right Thing

The design path is a journey from a user's problem to a concrete solution. It's rarely a straight line, but you have learned how to navigate its messiest, most uncertain phase by using your body as a precision tool. This process turns fragile sparks into visible gesture sketches, sharpens and sifts those sketches into more refined conceptions, and pressure-tests them as proto-prototypes. By catching, extending, clarifying, and elaborating with your hands, you transform fragmented ideas into a design that your entire team can see, feel, and understand together (see Figure 7.20).

FIGURE 7.20
The final design is complete and brings together your team's best ideas and work.

Ultimately, using gestures in ideation and prototyping changes how your team builds. When you invite this embodied way of working, you leverage an always-available tool that expands creative thinking while reducing risk. Ideas surface earlier, get tested sooner, and fail faster—before they become expensive. The result is a more resilient, innovative culture where teams explore boldly but commit wisely. By using your hands to think, test, and build, you guide your team not just toward a workable solution, but toward the one you can deliver.

Takeaways

- **Build the right thing together.** Ideas are distributed across people, settings, and time. They only become real when you externalize them, build them up with others, and collectively decide which ones are worth carrying forward.
- **Treat gestures as a design medium.** Gestures are always available, require no setup, and can be shaped in real time. They externalize thinking quickly, offload cognition, invite others to build, and surface uncertainty early. That makes them a fast, low-risk way to explore, negotiate, and change direction before anything gets committed.
- **Prepare the gesture canvas.** Invite gesture use, prime the team with the problem and its constraints, set expectations for divergence or convergence, and make the shared space between people and among artifacts visible and available for ideas to land and grow.
- **Move ideas from sparks to concepts.** Catch early ideas before they disappear, sharpen them by picking up and passing gesture sketches back and forth, sift them through clarification and elaboration to test their limits and viability, and anchor what survives so it can persist and move forward as a shared concept.
- **Proto-prototype before you build.** Before anything is sketched or coded, the hands become the prototype. These proto-prototypes let teams simulate interactions and build up ideas through gesture stacks.
- **Simulate to pressure-test.** Simulated actions let teams physically enact an interaction to feel whether an idea holds together before committing it to screens or materials, exposing feasibility breakdowns early.
- **Stack gestures to refine.** When simulation surfaces a problem, gesture stacking lets teams add structure, adjust sequence, redistribute effort, and refine behavior through layered, coordinated movements.

FIELD NOTES FROM STEPHANIE

Dane and I spent much of our writing time on video calls together, a shared document usually filling most of the screen. Our faces sat in small boxes in the corner. That worked fine when we were reading a sentence or moving a paragraph around.

When we were trying to develop an idea together, the small boxes were not enough.

"I can't see you." "Make your camera bigger." "Wait, I need to show you this with my hands!"

We said some version of this so often it became a running joke. The book about gestures kept demanding that we actually gesture at each other.

I remember one session where we were trying to work out the product journey metaphor in Chapter 1, "The Need to Go Deeper" (see Figure 7.21). The idea of paths through a journey sounds simple enough, but we kept getting tangled in what the paths actually meant. Were they sequential? No, that wasn't right. They overlapped, ran in parallel, circled back. And the gestures that mattered happened when you bumped into people along the way, headed toward the same goal, and in those moments of intersection something got pointed toward, or handed off, or redirected.

We had to gesture it to know if it was working. I started moving my hands through the air, tracing one path forward, then another branching alongside it. Dane reached in with his own hands and crossed one path over the other. "But they're not just parallel," he said. "They converge here." He brought his fingertips together at a point in the space between us. I picked that up and added the moment of contact, two hands meeting briefly before moving on in different directions.

That was the metaphor. Not the words we had been writing, but what had just happened between our four hands in the air.

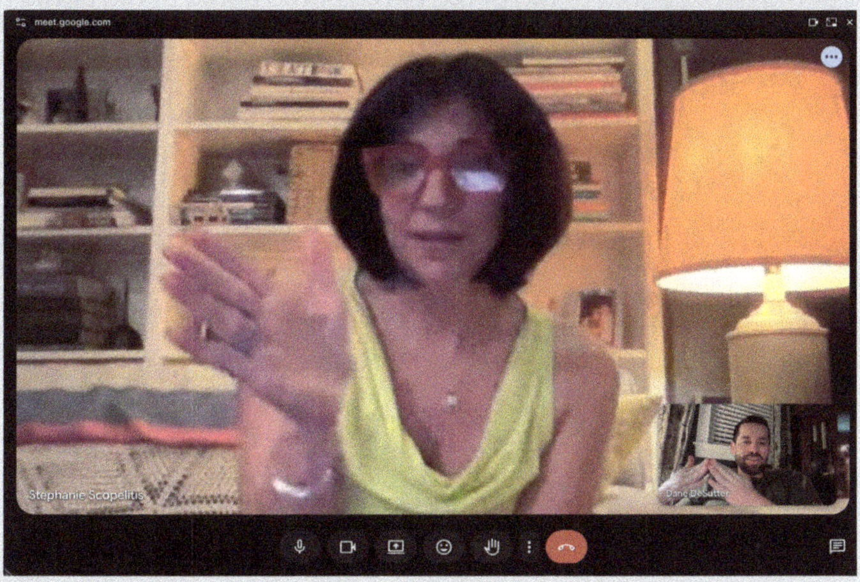

FIGURE 7.21

Stephanie and Dane on video using gestures to develop an idea together.

We noticed it working the other way, too. Sometimes we would both reach for the same gesture at the same moment without planning it, our hands landing in nearly identical shapes. When that happened, we knew we had found something solid.

Then we would go back to the document and try to write what we had just worked out. The words came after the idea had already been handled a little. And when it got fuzzy again, one of us would stop typing.

"Wait. I need to see you."

FIELD NOTES FROM DANE

My good friend, Caroline, and I had been talking about my kitchen renovation for years. The layout was a tight U-shape with a single-entry point (see Figure 7.22), and I had a concept to open it into an L with an island and a banquette along the far wall. I had sketched it out, done the measurements, and felt pretty confident about the direction.

Then I sat down with Caroline, who has a sharp eye for how spaces actually get used, and things got interesting fast. We were talking through what the kitchen would feel like in the evening, when dinner was winding down and someone was loading the dishwasher while others were still sitting at the banquette. Caroline paused: "You know, the banquette is pretty close to the sink and dishwasher." The clanking dishes, the running water, the dishwasher cycling would make it difficult for people to enjoy the last bit of their evening.

I put my hand up and traced a line from the end of the banquette straight to the ceiling. "Something could go here," I said, gesturing a partition splitting up the space.

Caroline nodded but leaned forward and used both hands to show what a full wall would feel like: enclosed, cut off. "You'd lose the light. The space would feel smaller."

So, I kept the partition in my gesture, but opened it up, spreading my fingers to suggest something with gaps. "Slats, maybe?" Caroline picked that up immediately, her hand moving along the line I had drawn, pausing at intervals to hang imaginary plants. "You could stagger them at different heights."

What had started as a noise problem had become, through a few minutes of gesturing at nothing in particular, a design detail we both could see and assess. Each gesture built on the last, a stack of small refinements that moved the concept from a vague partition into something with form, texture, and purpose.

This sequence of gestures eventually made it into the renovation prototype (see Figure 7.22). Whether it makes it into the final renovation may depend on a constraint Caroline and I forgot to simulate: the budget.

FIGURE 7.22
Dane's kitchen renovation progressed from an original U-shaped layout (top) through an early concept render (middle) to a final design featuring the slatted partition with plants separating the banquette from the sink area (bottom).

Oh, they have one of those new robots!
Remember you like it even.
Somehow I doubt either of us gets what we actually want.
WELCOME TO ESPRESSO YOURSELF DANE. ANOTHER LA GRANDE?
LA GRANDE
Can I have a...
...small flat white latte, half oat, half whole milk. A quarter pump of vanilla (but only if it's house-made) and a heart design in the foam. I love hearts!
I think his smile is telling us to get lost.
Don't you have something in your bag I can throw at it?
ESPRESSO YOURSELF
ESPRESSO YOURSELF

CHAPTER 8

The Body Points the Way

Throughout this book, you've learned to see and use gestures as tools for thinking, communicating, and coordinating. But it wasn't lost on us that "gesture" also shows up in computing, where it's often a synonym for the swipes, taps, and pinches of modern operating systems.

This isn't a disconnect; it makes perfect sense. Computing is built on metaphors that bridge the physical and digital worlds. You organize files, you toss items in a trash bin, and you drag and drop objects into place. This reliance on physical metaphor is part of how this technology grew up. Because in order to build for people, you must start with what they already do. The more we talked about it, the more we realized that gestures feel so at home in computing *precisely because the body has always shaped it.*

Look at the history of computing and you'll see this has always been the central design challenge: how do you bridge the physical, human realm with the digital? This challenge is more critical now than ever. As the pace of innovation accelerates in the age of AI, understanding this history is essential to avoid alienating the very people you're building for. The past is littered with examples of places where technology succeeded and where it failed, and the body is always somewhere in the mix. Some of the most successful products that you still use today were shaped by the quiet, persistent movements of the human body. In that sense, technology-coupled gestures are not just a means of interaction. They are what make technology feel intuitive, reachable, and human!

As technology evolves along the innovation path, the human body remains your constant anchor. To ensure what you build stays human-centered, it's helpful to first look back.

The Body's Trace on Computing

Since the 1950s, computing has taken a long journey from specialized labs to everyday life. You likely know the headline moments—punch cards, Xerox PARC, the Apple II. But beneath those milestones is an interesting product story: one where designers and engineers have continually worked to make computing feel more natural by aligning it to the body.

This has been as much a design challenge as a technical one. The body doesn't change much, but user expectations for how technology should feel and function definitely do! As technology moves faster, it becomes important to intentionally keep the body in mind and avoid the trap of innovation for innovation's sake that can leave the body behind.

Over the decades, product designers have searched for ways to make digital systems feel like intuitive extensions of physical action—something you can touch, move through, or manipulate directly. When you look at the history of computing, the push and pull is everywhere as a constant negotiation between what technology can do and what the body will accept.

From early pointing devices to the rise of today's immersive augmented reality (AR) and virtual reality (VR) systems and robotics, the arc of computing has followed a consistent path: to bring the machine into alignment with human reasoning, social norms, and embodied expectation. Each new generation of interfaces and consumer products tries to close the gap between how people move in their physical and social space and how they navigate digital systems. What makes an innovation human-centered is explicitly reckoning with the body's formative role from the start: Is it consistent with how people already move? Does it fit the body that people have? Is it aligned to people's social expectations?

IT'S MORE THAN HARDWARE

You've probably used an emoticon before :) Those early combinations of text characters weren't just clever—they filled a gap. People needed a way to express emotion in written messages where tone, face, and gestures were missing. Emojis grew out of that same need. They gave you a formalized, visual language for what text alone couldn't do. And look closely: many emojis are the body.

- Facial expressions (😘😭🙄🥺😐🙃)
- Hand gestures (👍👏🤞🤟🙌🤘)
- Full-body actions (🤷🤦💁🙅)

These aren't just illustrations. They're stand-ins for physical presence, carrying intent, feeling, and social nuance.

Even in pixels, you're reaching for the body to communicate what words can't! 😍

So don't take the body for granted!

Technology evolves, but the body is the anchor that doesn't. When you lose sight of it, products quickly feel clunky, and people decide whether to find a work-around or abandon it altogether. What people do with their bodies produces an ongoing trace of how they make sense of the world, offering a valuable source for innovation. Keeping the body in mind isn't optional. It's a reliable way to achieve true convergence and keep design human-centered.

Experience at Arm's Length

There's an inescapable human instinct to reach out and touch. Developmental psychologist Jean Piaget observed that infants begin understanding the world by acting on it: grasping, reaching, pushing. These physical actions form the foundation of sensorimotor development and allow children to build mental models of space, cause and effect, and the objects around them.

Before language, there is motion. Before concepts, there is contact.

That same principle has been a driving force in the evolution of computing. Direct manipulation is the design commitment that digital systems should respond in ways that feel as immediate and physical as acting on the world around you. Pointing, dragging, tapping, pinching—these are design hooks that connect the body's natural actions to digital abstractions.

These hooks don't just make interaction easier; they echo how you use your body. For example, dragging a file to the trash doesn't just mirror a physical behavior. It maps a digital task onto the embodied cognitive process of making a decision and expressing closure. Similarly, a pointing gesture on a screen borrows its logic from the way you point in the real world. In this way, direct manipulation routes the logic of the body through the screen.

But achieving that alignment isn't always seamless. Designing digital experiences that feel truly embodied is an ongoing process of trial, adjustment, and compromise—always negotiating between what feels natural and what the system can actually achieve.

NOTE **THE TERM DIRECT MANIPULATION**

The phrase *direct manipulation* was coined by computer scientist Ben Shneiderman in the early 1980s. It refers to interfaces where users interact with visible objects directly—like dragging a file or tapping a touchscreen—rather than using abstract commands. His work helped formalize a principle that had already shaped decades of design. The term *manipulation* is rooted in the Latin word for hand (manus), underscoring this fundamental connection between digital action and physical experience.

Direct Manipulation: The First Push and Pull

Two of the earliest technologies to bring direct manipulation to users were the light pen and the touchscreen. Both offered the promise of more intuitive, physically grounded interaction by letting users point and select directly on a screen. However, these early attempts represent the first chapter in an ongoing story: a push and pull between technological ambition and the body's physical realities.

The light pen, introduced in the 1960s, gave people the ability to interact directly with their display. Users held a wired stylus and touched it to a cathode ray tube (CRT) monitor, selecting or drawing directly on the surface (see Figure 8.1). For its time, it was an elegant technical solution that offered users a thrilling taste of direct manipulation. But the light pen quickly ran into a limitation that made long-term use uncomfortable.

FIGURE 8.1
Light pens let users point and interact through a physical stylus with content on CRT monitors.

The flaw was predictable if you were spotting gestures that matter in the wild. Think of an eager student in a classroom with their hand raised. After a minute, they inevitably use their other arm as a kickstand for support. This simple gesture reveals a fundamental truth: unsupported limbs fatigue quickly. The light pen's designers focused on the directness of pointing but missed this crucial insight. The result was "gorilla arm," a muscular strain that made the interaction unsustainable. It was a classic disconnect between the tool's demands and the body's natural limits. Though the device technically worked, the body pushed back.

Around the same time, another now-familiar interaction model was taking shape: the touchscreen. In contrast to the light pen, the early touchscreen succeeded conceptually because it aligned with a fundamental human instinct: you touch things to act on them. For the air traffic controllers using E.A. Johnson's 1965 design, tapping a blip on a screen wasn't an abstract command; it was a direct, tactile response to a potential threat. This was an early example of letting the human body lead the design.

However, this conceptual alignment was ahead of its time. Early touchscreens had their own trade-offs, as seen in experimental systems like PLATO IV (see Figure 8.2). They were often imprecise and laggy. When you touch something in the physical world, you expect an immediate reaction. The technology's delay created a new kind of disconnect—one between embodied expectation and digital reality. It would take decades for the hardware to catch up, but the core idea was sound.

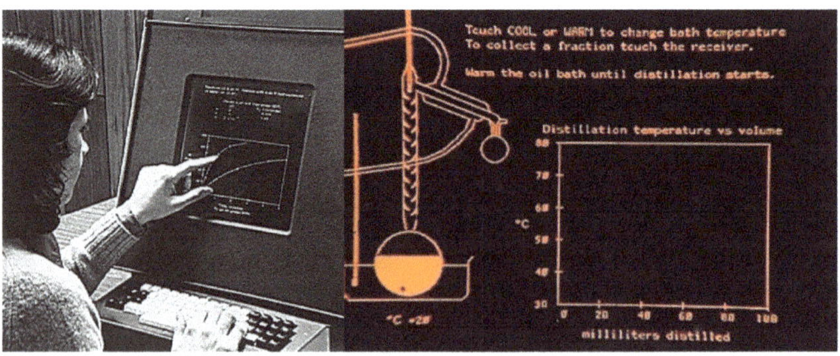

FIGURE 8.2
User taps on a graph in the PLATO IV touchscreen system.

These early attempts revealed a crucial lesson. Direct manipulation made interactions feel simpler and more connected to the physical world but designing for intent alone wasn't enough. The light pen and early touchscreen showed that truly intuitive design involved trade-offs governed by the entire body. Interfaces must not only align with natural movement but also remain responsive, comfortable, and sustainable over time. This was the first of many lessons in the push and pull between technology and the body, a cycle of one step forward and half a step back that continues to shape the product journey today.

Bringing the Body to the Desktop

These early attempts at direct manipulation revealed a core tension. The promise of intuitive interaction was compelling, but the physical cost of "gorilla arm" fatigue showed that the body was already pushing back. For the product journey to continue, a refined approach was needed, one that could solve this bodily disconnect.

That solution arrived in 1968, when Douglas Engelbart revealed a suite of tools in a demonstration later known as "The Mother of All Demos." The star was a device no one had seen before: a small wooden box with wheels and a cord, which he called a *mouse* (see Figure 8.3). It offered a new kind of interaction that was fast, spatial, and physical. Not a typed command, but a gesture.

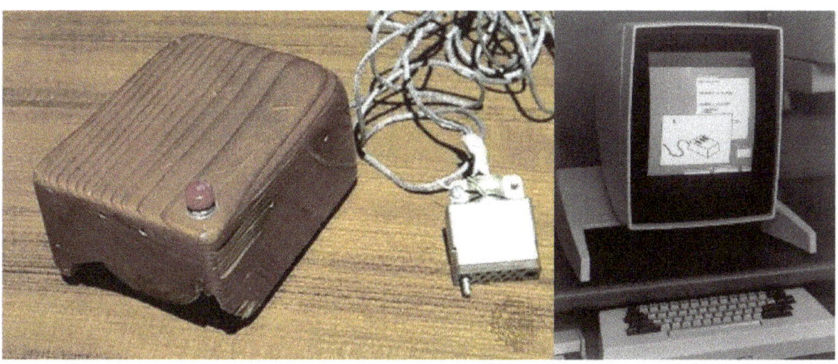

FIGURE 8.3
Engelbart's first mouse design (left); Xerox PARC Alto computing system with its pioneering GUI (right).

The genius of the mouse was moving the body's interaction from the vertical screen to a horizontal surface. Instead of holding an arm aloft, users could rest their arm comfortably, often on the arm of their chair or desk, using small and efficient movements. This was a critical insight for the intended user: an office worker who needed to interact with a computer for hours a day. The mouse made direct manipulation not just possible, but sustainable.

In the early 1970s, many of Engelbart's collaborators moved to Xerox PARC, where they paired his mouse with a bitmapped screen and a graphical user interface (GUI). The team unveiled this combination in the Xerox Alto, but the Alto's most transformative idea was its use of metaphor. The GUI borrowed visual logic from the physical world: desktops, documents, folders, and trash cans. You could open a file or drag it to a trash icon, mapping digital tasks onto familiar physical actions. This was more than just an improvement to usability; it created a bridge from embodied knowing to digital doing. By making digital interactions feel physically grounded, the GUI helped users externalize intention, track spatial logic, and coordinate action.

The mouse and the GUI were a perfect partnership. The mouse provided the comfortable physical means for interaction, while the GUI offered the familiar cognitive map to navigate the digital space. While Xerox pioneered these concepts with the Star, it was Apple that brought them to everyday users with the Lisa and, later, the Macintosh. For many people, this was their first experience controlling a computer through movements that felt familiar.

That shift marked a fundamental alignment of digital systems with how people physically operated in space—what their bodies were used to doing, and how they already managed objects in everyday life. The GUI didn't replace complexity but rather restructured it into something visible and grounded in bodily experience.

The success of the mouse and GUI is an example of what happens when the push and pull between technology and the body bridges the disconnect to arrive at a durable partnership. Products that are created not just to be used by the body, but to *work with it,* create a meaningful alignment that is both physically comfortable and cognitively intuitive. This is an essential move in the human-centered direction that has shaped computing to this day.

SKEUOMORPHISM IN DESIGN

One of Apple's most consistent design commitments has been to make digital systems feel like extensions of physical life. This approach, known as *skeuomorphism,* designs digital elements to mimic familiar physical objects so that users intuitively understand how to use them.

In the original Macintosh GUI, skeuomorphism took the form of desktop metaphors: files, folders, trash cans, all visually styled after their real-world counterparts. In later decades, it reappeared in iOS with interfaces like the Notes app (which looked like yellow legal paper) and the Bookshelf in iBooks (which mimicked wooden shelves). Even as Apple has shifted toward cleaner, flatter interfaces, the principle still holds: use the body's existing experiences to help people feel at home in digital space.

Skeuomorphism isn't just about style, but bootstrapping users through their embodied experiences. ✌️

Reach Out and Grasp

Pop culture has long dreamed of stepping inside the computer. From the neon wireframes of *Tron* to the plug-in portals of *The Matrix,* there's been a shared cultural obsession with a future where digital space is not just visible, but inhabitable. It's the fantasy of reaching beyond the glass to touch code and move through data.

But this fantasy is about more than science fiction. It reflects the ambition to design products and systems that think with the body. The goal isn't just to control digital experiences differently, but to build a bridge for natural, embodied ways of thinking to enter the digital world. What if you could sculpt data with your hands or walk through a complex system to understand it spatially?

When the body engages, you connect everyday cognition and behavior to the digital world. This blue-sky vision of immersive computing builds on a long convergence between human and machine. Earlier products focused on how the body acted on the world, like dragging a file to the trash can, for example. Immersive computing pushes further, treating the body not just as a control mechanism but as the medium for experience and understanding. But delivering on that promise has proven fiendishly difficult.

Data Gloves

One of the most ambitious attempts to bring the body into digital environments came in the form of the data glove. This wasn't just about adding another input device; it was an effort to take the body seriously by establishing a high-fidelity connection between the hand's movements and a virtual world. How people use their bodies not only reflects thinking, communication, and coordination, but it also supports it. The data glove, in this sense, represents pulling the cognitive body into connection with the digital to elevate embodied reasoning.

The first major version was created in 1982 by Thomas Zimmerman and later refined at VPL Research. The glove used fiber optic cables or resistive sensors to measure the flexion of each finger and the orientation of the hand. When connected to a computer, it allowed users to perform actions like pointing, grabbing, or signaling in virtual space. The goal was to make digital interaction feel as natural as interacting in the physical world. It's no coincidence that the term *virtual reality* was coined during this era.

The value of this approach to align technology and bodily experience was so clear that NASA and other research institutions saw the potential. NASA developed a glove-based input system for high-stakes training called the *Virtual Interface Environment Workstation* (VIEW) (see Figure 8.4). With these systems, they weren't just training the mind; they were training the body, building muscle memory for complex tasks.

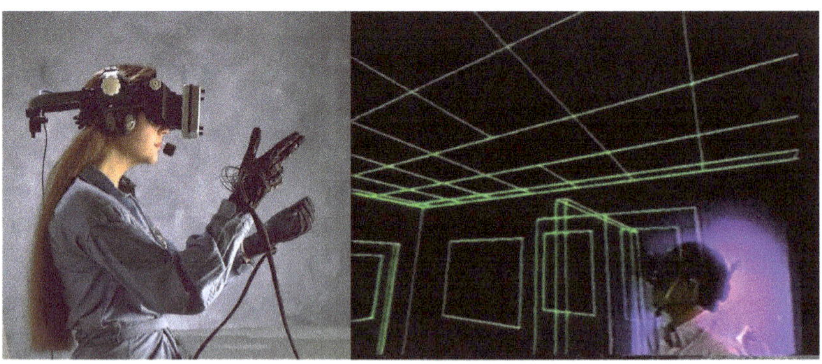

FIGURE 8.4
The Virtual Interface Environment Workstation (VIEW) developed at NASA was an early virtual reality environment pairing a head-mounted display with a data glove for gesture control.

Data gloves became a symbol through VR of using the full human experience in design. But despite the push forward this represented, broad commercialization was constrained by several factors. For one, the hardware was finicky and difficult to set up quickly. Scene cameras and sensors required careful calibration and the glove was often unreliable with different hand sizes. Though the technology aimed to enable the body (good work!), it faltered in adapting to the physiology of different users (not quite there yet!).

It also was incredibly expensive. Even in the late 1980s, VPL's Data-Glove cost $9,000 and when bundled with an EyePhone and other hardware, a single setup could set you back around $200,000.

Beyond sheer cost, the computing systems of the time were also limited. They couldn't create immersive environments that responded smoothly to user actions. This created a sensory disconnect—a lag between the user's physical movement and the virtual feedback. While the glove captured the hand, it failed to account for the entire bodily experience of seamless, real-time interaction. This disconnect rendered the data glove a steeply expensive curiosity with limited utility.

THE ARTIST'S HEAD START

Art emerges from human experience and that's exactly what makes it a valuable source of inspiration when building something new. An artist's mission is to capture, represent, and connect with some facet of human experience. That freedom makes art a rich source of inspiration for human-centered innovation, especially when it explores new technologies.

The spark for many ideas in immersive computing was first explored through hybrid digital and physical installations. Myron Krueger's Videoplace (1975–1983) let participants move their bodies in a camera-tracked space to interact with projected virtual scenes with physical presence (see Figure 8.5). David Rokeby's Very Nervous System (1982–1991) used a camera to translate movement into sound in real time, turning an empty room into an invisible, ambient instrument. Just movement and music were woven together in a way that blurred the line between physical movement and digital experience.

continues

THE ARTIST'S HEAD START (continued)

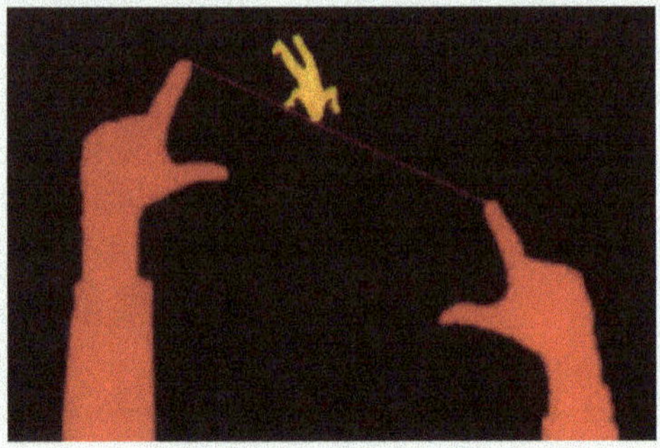

FIGURE 8.5
Videoplace lets exhibit visitors interact in surreal video spaces where digital representations of the body could interact with simple physics over exaggerated scales.

These installations were products in their own right and also grappled with the same foundational questions that human-centered innovators must ask: How does the body want to move? What does presence feel like? How do people naturally reach out and connect?

When you're at the frontier of innovation, look to art for inspiration and clues.

Multisensory Immersion in VR/AR

The data glove left an important trace on the product path of technology, but it also revealed a fundamental challenge: the closer products get to full immersion, the more factors they must get right. Both virtual reality (VR), which replaces the physical world with a simulated one, and augmented reality (AR), which overlays digital information onto the world you're already in, attempt to dissolve the boundary between person and interface.

To deliver on the promise of full-body interaction, immersive technologies have had to tackle a wide range of challenges to create intuitive sensory and embodied experiences. These include the following:

- **Visual fidelity:** Rendering environments fast enough and realistically enough to maintain spatial coherence
- **Auditory immersion:** Delivering directional, spatially-aware sound to enhance realism and feedback
- **Touch and haptics:** Simulating force, pressure, and texture through gloves, vests, or vibration
- **Motion tracking:** Following head, hand, and body movements in real time, without encumbering the user

- **Balance and proprioception:** Supporting people's sense of orientation, posture, and presence in 3D space
- **Ergonomic wearability:** Accommodating different body sizes, physiologies, and energy levels
- **Social presence:** Enabling expressive avatars, eye contact, and comfort in shared spaces

The illusion of immersion is fragile. Each sensory layer adds complexity, and when any one of them falls short, it doesn't take much for the experience to unravel. The history of these technologies is a practical lesson in how even a single failure in this complex sensory web can create a disconnect.

For decades, the promise of virtual reality remained trapped in research labs, held back by immense cost and technology that couldn't keep up with the human senses. The modern era of VR began in 2012 when the Oculus Rift debuted. Thanks to cheaper motion sensors, it could track head movement with high accuracy, making the experience feel more intuitive. But this breakthrough success also threw the body's other needs into sharp relief, revealing several new disconnects.

First, the Rift required a wired connection to a PC, creating a physical disconnect that limited a user's motion. Later models like the Oculus Quest cut the cord (see Figure 8.6), but this only revealed more subtle challenges. A persistent issue was motion sickness. Even a small delay between head movement and visual update created a sensory disconnect, triggering nausea as the body's visual and motor systems fell out of sync.

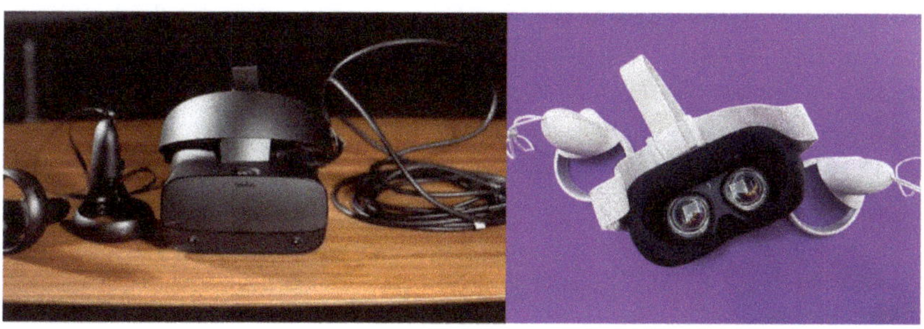

FIGURE 8.6
Oculus Rift (left) required a wired connection to support graphics rendering. This was later solved by the Oculus Quest (right).

Another problem was ergonomics: early headsets with fixed lenses set to the average interpupillary distance (IPD) of adult men created a physical disconnect for many women, making the devices uncomfortable and disorienting. These weren't just UX bugs; they were moments where the body's own feedback revealed a fundamental design misalignment.

AR systems approached the problem of fidelity differently. Rather than trying to completely supplant the physical world, they sought to complement it. This strategy, however, encountered its own set of disconnects with the body.

Microsoft's HoloLens, first released in 2016, targeted enterprise contexts with a high-precision headset that allowed professionals to visualize and manipulate 3D digital models directly in their real-world environment (see Figure 8.7). But users often described the experience as "looking at holograms through a small mail slot." This created a perceptual disconnect by failing to meet the body's expectation for an expansive, unobstructed visual field.

Google Glass (Figure 8.7), on the other hand, stumbled into a social disconnect. It promised seamless, heads-up computing, but its hardware violated the unwritten social contract that governs how bodies interact. Designing with the body in mind means respecting the space between people—the nuances of eye contact and shared presence that build trust. Because the device felt invasive and raised fears of surveillance, users were dubbed "glassholes." Its failure wasn't just about hardware; it was a failure to understand that when you disrupt the humanness of interaction, the body pushes back—not with physical strain, but with social rejection.

Consider now the current wave of "spatial computing," which attempts to synthesize the lessons of VR and AR. In 2023, Apple released the Vision Pro (see Figure 8.8), which promised a refined platform with advanced gesture control and eye tracking. It even tried to solve the social disconnect with its EyeSight feature, an outward display showing a rendering of the user's eyes.

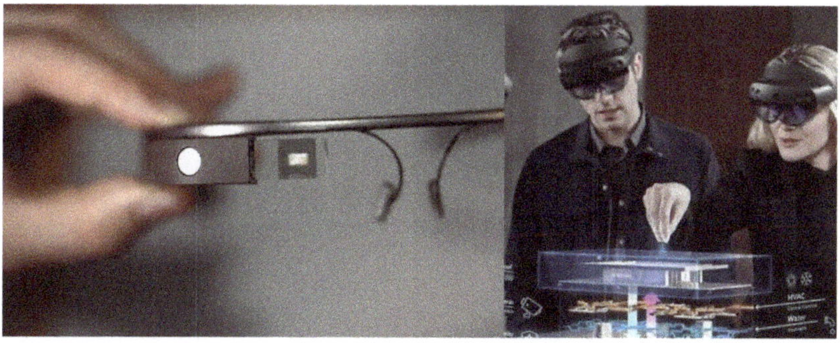

FIGURE 8.7
Google Glass aimed to be a mass market AR augment to the smartphone (left), whereas Microsoft's HoloLens focused on more technical applications (right).

But solving for old problems revealed a new one: a utility disconnect, encumbering the physical body. The Vision Pro asked users to perform familiar 2D workflows in a complex 3D space. In doing so, it risked forgetting a key lesson learned from the era of "gorilla arm": the body thrives on comfort and efficiency. By requiring users to control and extend their limbs for gesture controls, it moved interaction away from the supported desktop and back into the air. This not only reintroduced potential fatigue but it also failed to account for the vast range of human bodies, assuming a level of dexterity and mobility that excludes many due to age, injury, or ability. It displaced a lightweight laptop with an isolating headset with few compelling use cases.

FIGURE 8.8
Apple's Vision Pro offered front-facing video feed of the user's eyes (left); the visionOS mostly brought a translucent desktop experience to 3D space (right).

Despite these setbacks, the push toward immersive computing has sparked meaningful innovation. But for these technologies to truly take off, they must continue to close the gap between what's technically possible and what the body finds intuitive, comfortable, and canny. Each chapter in this story—from VR's sensory conflicts to AR's social stumbles—teaches the same lesson. It is not enough for technology to be powerful; to succeed, it must keep the body and the entirety of its experience in mind.

Gaming as a Stage for Innovation

The journey to creating truly innovative products is a constant push and pull between technological ambition and the body's realities. But what if there was a world where the market pressures were different? Where experimentation was the main attraction, and awkward software and hardware could be forgiven if the experience was fun enough?

That world is gaming. Unlike productivity software or enterprise tools, games can be weird, experimental, and fun. That creative freedom makes gaming an important stage for embodied innovation, and some of its most influential design patterns emerged from pushing on the relationship between the body and the experience of play.

Gaming's relationship with the body goes back to the earliest days of the industry. Sega's *taikan* cabinets—meaning "body sensation"—were fixtures in arcades throughout the 1980s and gave players control of game mechanics by leaning side to side on a motorcycle rig or engaging controls in a cockpit. Players felt a visceral sense that they weren't just playing a game but actually riding a motorcycle or flying a plane. What these early designs understood was that connecting familiar physical movements of the body to these novel gaming experiences made them feel more real and that made them more fun.

Nintendo was the first company to bring body-based gaming to a home audience. Early products like the NES Zapper, a plastic point-and-shoot gun, and the Power Pad, a floor mat with hot spots you could hit with your feet to control a character's running, showed that players will use their bodies if the experience is engaging enough. Nintendo then pushed this further with the Power Glove (see Figure 8.9) in 1989 as a mass-market offshoot of the earlier DataGlove. It was a wearable glove that fit directly onto a player's hand and featured bend sensors and ultrasonic tracking to allow them to control game mechanics by moving and flexing their hand in natural movements.

While its tracking was crude and the software support was weak, it offered a shift and made a novel idea about embodied interaction tangible: What if your hands became the controller? The Power Glove captured the imagination of gamers even when the hardware couldn't fully deliver. Its real contribution was opening a new design space, one where the body itself was the starting point for how a game could be played.

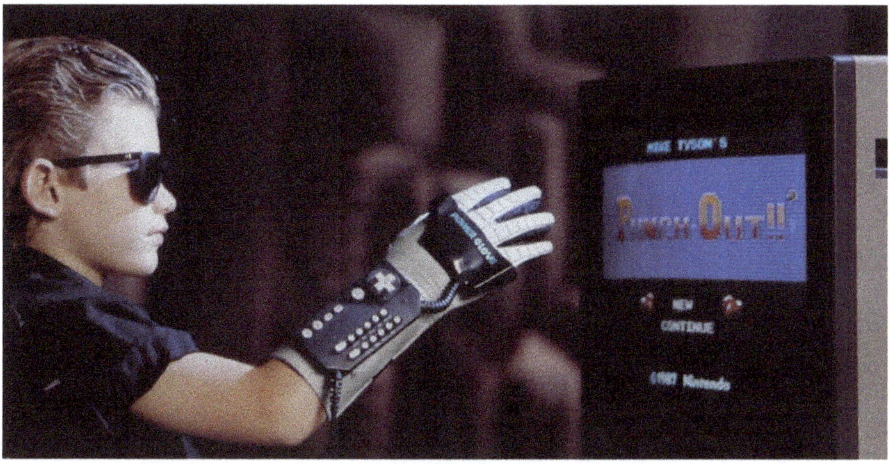

FIGURE 8.9
Nintendo's Power Glove was crude and a general commercial flop but lived large in the gamer's imagination.

Game controllers then evolved rapidly through the 1990s, bringing analog sticks, vibration feedback, and ergonomic two-handed gamepads that let players engage their hands more fully, extending game play beyond fingers and clicks.

But a real leap change came in the 2000s, when gaming entered the full-body era. The Nintendo Wii introduced motion control to the masses in 2006 with the Wiimote. By waving a wand-like controller that sensed movement, players could mimic actions like bowling, swinging, and fishing. The Wii worked because it recruited movement patterns people already knew. Importantly, they realized that the actions performed with the Wiimote didn't need to be high fidelity to be fun. For example, a bowling motion didn't need to replicate the weight of a ball; it just needed to feel familiar enough to make the interaction natural and enjoyable.

The result was a runaway hit. By letting people operate the game through the body they already knew how to use, the barrier to entry dropped, and gaming opened up to players of all ages and backgrounds who had never picked up a controller before.

The 2010s brought even more body into the loop. Microsoft's Kinect ditched controllers altogether, using depth-sensing cameras to track the player's whole-body orientation (see Figure 8.10). Players could dance, jump, or navigate menus with a wave of the hand. Sony's PlayStation Move followed with a hybrid system combining button-based input and camera tracking. Where the Wii had recruited familiar body movements through a physical controller, these systems removed the intermediary entirely. The body was no longer operating a device! It *was* the device.

FIGURE 8.10
Game systems like those offered by Nintendo (left) and Xbox Kinect (right) found ways to connect the body to digital experiences.

Gaming has proven to be an important incubator for exploring the intersection of the body and human-centered products. Each generation of body-based controllers carried the imagination of fuller bodily engagement forward, pushing on what was possible even when the technology couldn't fully deliver. What that experimentation revealed is something worth taking seriously well beyond gaming: people respond deeply to experiences that engage the body in ways that feel recognizable, natural, and worth showing up for. When you take that seriously, something shifts. The body is no longer just a vehicle for operating a product. It becomes the source material for design.

THE ALGORITHMS OF GAMEPLAY AND THE BODY

The push and pull of the body has clearly driven innovation in hardware. But what gets far less attention are the indispensable software innovations that had to happen in parallel. Every new attempt to bring the body into the digital world required new algorithms to make sense of what the body was doing.

A depth camera is just a sensor without the software to interpret what it sees. Motion control is just noise without the algorithms to distinguish a bowling swing from a casual wave. Gaming provided a proving ground for some of that development. The algorithms developed for games, especially in vision-based tracking, have shaped everything from VR systems to gesture recognition libraries. Camera-based motion capture, facial analysis, pose estimation, and object detection—many of them now open-source—were refined through the demands of making game interactions feel responsive and natural.

The algorithms of gameplay are a valuable part of creating human-centered experiences.

The Body as a Feedback Loop

A growing ecosystem of hardware, software development kits (SDKs), and open-source tools now makes it easier to capture and analyze nonverbal behavior. Whether you're processing real-time interactions or reviewing recorded video, it's now possible to use software algorithms (sometimes in conjunction with specialized hardware) to track gestures, movement, and bodily expression with just a few lines of code.

Body-tracking tools typically fall into a few broad categories:

- **Computer vision:** Algorithms that detect and track objects, posture, and body movements in both live and recorded video.
- **Vision-language models:** Tools that combine computer vision with large language models (LLMs) to label complex behaviors, gestures, or interactions in context.
- **Wearables:** Physical devices, including smartwatches, smartphones, and purpose-built sensors, that use onboard hardware to measure motion, orientation, and physiological signals.

- **Eye tracking:** Systems that detect and map gaze by measuring light reflected off the retina and cornea, often used to understand attention or visual search behavior.
- **Audio processing:** Algorithms that extract nonverbal signals from voice, such as pitch, tone, and timing or detect anomalies in conversational patterns.
- **Embedded environmental sensors:** Hardware in physical spaces that can detect presence, proximity, touch, and movement across surfaces and environments.

Computer Vision

Computer vision emerged in the late 1960s at AI research labs, where the goal was to teach machines to see and interpret images the way humans do, starting with basic shapes and edges and building toward full scene understanding. Early applications were limited, but the field changed dramatically with the rise of deep learning in the 2010s. Convolutional neural networks (CNNs) have made it possible to detect faces, hands (see Figure 8.11), and full-body poses with far greater accuracy, even in messy, real-world environments.

FIGURE 8.11
MediaPipe hand tracking algorithm detects the orientation of the hand and maps a mesh to 21 unique landmarks.

These tools make it easy to parse raw video footage for various body landmarks, including applications in facial expression recognition, which is the automated detection and classification of expressions like surprise, disgust, or engagement from facial movement.

Some computer vision tools that are worth exploring include:

- **MediaPipe:** Developed by Google, this library offers real-time tracking of full-body pose, hand landmarks, and facial features and is lightweight enough to run on a phone or laptop.
- **OpenPose:** Tool for multiperson pose estimation, tracking body, face, and hands simultaneously across video (useful for analyzing posture or group interaction).
- **OpenFace:** Focuses specifically on the face, tracking landmarks, head pose, eye gaze, and basic expressions.

Vision-Language Models

Vision-language models (VLMs) emerged from the convergence of computer vision and large language models. By the early 2020s, advances in both areas made it possible to combine them into systems that could interpret images and video using natural language. The result was a new kind of tool that didn't require fixed labels or predefined categories. Rather, you could simply describe what you were looking for, and the model would locate the image in video frames.

This extends the benefits you get from computer vision to a broader range of objects through the flexible use of the large language models (LLMs). This can make it possible to scan large data sets for specific gestures and bodily actions, supporting analysis that extends beyond words.

Some popular vision-language models include:

- **Grounding DINO:** An open-source model that detects and labels objects and regions in images based on natural language prompts, making it a flexible tool for locating specific moments of interest across a dataset.
- **BLIP/BLIP-2:** Multimodal models for image-text understanding, well-suited for open-ended scene interpretation and captioning large volumes of video data.
- **OWL-ViT:** Google's open-vocabulary object detection model that identifies objects and regions described in natural language, useful for searching video for specific interactions or behaviors.

GESTURE DETECTION WITH HAND-TRACKING

We've experimented with using hand-tracking in interviews to identify when gestures occur in video data (see Chapter 4, "Understand Users' Gestures"). Since gestures often follow a predictable structure—starting from rest, moving through a stroke phase, and returning to rest—it's possible to flag likely gesture moments by detecting significant deviations from a baseline hand position. Some of the quantified gesture data from the Chapter 4 case study is presented in Figure 8.12.

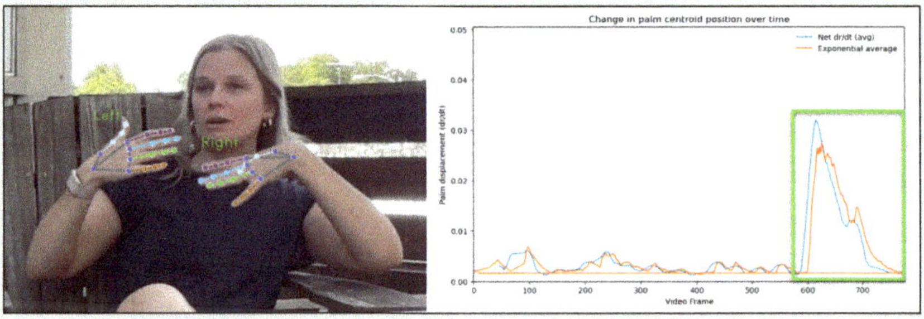

FIGURE 8.12

The MediaPipe framework being used to track hand movements from Carmen's interview.

With some computational processing, these flagged moments can surface segments worth closer scrutiny. However, it's important to set error thresholds. Hand detection algorithms can produce false positives due to incorrect handedness mapping, background motion, or interference from other people in the frame.

Careful calibration is necessary to maintain data quality and ensure that signals are reliable. ☝

Wearables

Developed in research labs in the late 1990s, early Inertial Measurement Unit (IMU)-based systems offered a portable alternative to bulky optical motion capture rigs. As miniaturization advanced, sensor fusion algorithms made it possible to track movement with increasing precision outside of controlled environments. Now, wearable sensing spans a wide range from research-grade hardware to the smartphone in your pocket. In that span, the technology has become one of the most accessible ways to capture how the body moves in the real world.

This makes wearables a flexible option for capturing how the body moves, responds, and shifts over time in naturalistic settings. Unlike video-based tools, wearables provide continuous streams of motion data that can surface patterns in rhythm, physical engagement, and spatial movement that might not be visible on camera. Research-grade IMUs, typically worn on the wrist, ankle, or torso, capture detailed motion data at high precision and are well suited for analyzing subtle or repetitive movement (see Figure 8.13).

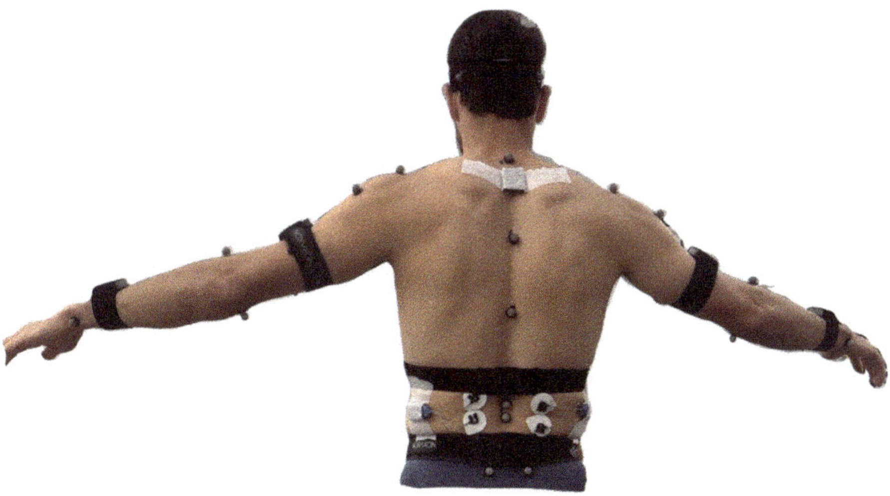

FIGURE 8.13

Participant in a study on spine joint kinematics wears a series of IMUs to track movement at various joints.

Consumer devices like smartphones and smartwatches offer a more accessible alternative, using built-in accelerometers, gyroscopes, and GPS to track how someone moves through space in everyday life (see Figure 8.14).

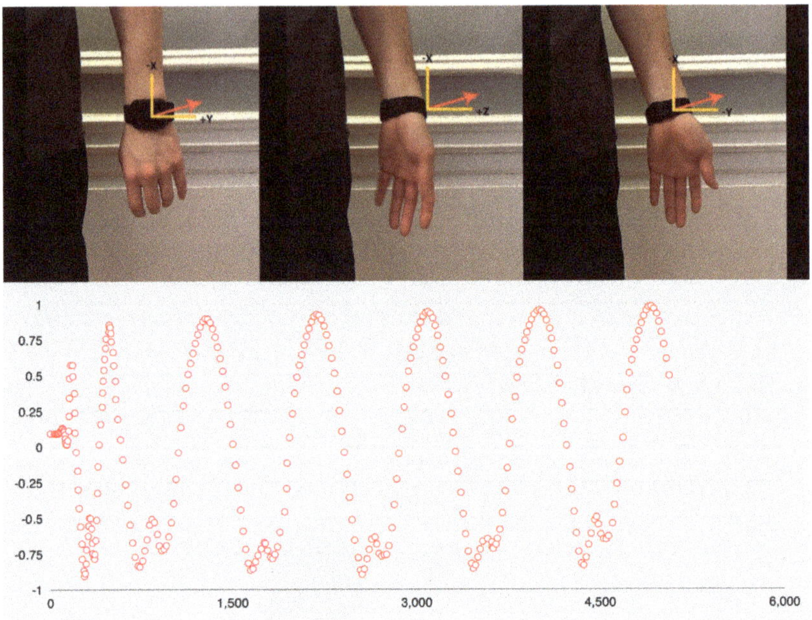

FIGURE 8.14
Example of data collection from one of the spatial axes that you can track using WatchKit for the Apple Watch.

Some popular wearable tools include:

- **Xsens:** Research-grade IMU platform used for full-body motion capture, tracking joint angles, orientation, and movement in real-world environments without the need for cameras or fixed infrastructure.
- **Apple WatchKit/Core Motion:** Apple's SDK for accessing accelerometer, gyroscope, and activity data from Apple Watch and iPhone, useful for tracking movement patterns and physical engagement in naturalistic settings.
- **Android Sensors API:** Google's framework for accessing motion and position sensors on Android devices, providing accelerometer, gyroscope, and step detection data for consumer-grade motion tracking.

PHYSIOLOGY IN PSYCHOLOGY

While IMUs and smartwatches are often used to track movement and posture, other wearables are designed to measure physiological signals and offer a complementary view into how people react emotionally or physically to an experience. Devices can capture a range of physiological signals including the following:

- **Skin conductance:** Galvanic Skin Response (GSR) and Electrodermal Activity (EDA) are both used as a proxy for stress or arousal.
- **Heart rate:** Heart rate and Heart Rate Variability (HRV) are both linked to sustained attention, mental effort, and emotional regulation.
- **Respiration rate:** Can reflect calmness, anxiety, or cognitive load.
- **Skin temperature:** Sensitive to emotional arousal and recovery from stress.

These tools are used to surface shifts in emotional state that might not be obvious in facial expression or behavior alone.

As with all sensing tools, they don't tell you why someone responded the way they did, but they can help you locate moments of physiological change that are worth a closer look. 👀

Eye Tracking

Eye tracking has been used in research since the late 19th century, when scientists first began studying how the eyes move while reading. For most of its history it was an expensive, lab-bound technology that required specialized hardware and careful calibration. That changed significantly in the 2010s, when advances in infrared sensing and computer vision brought the cost down and made the technology practical for UX and product research. Today, eye tracking is available in everything from dedicated desktop hardware to AR and VR headsets.

Eye tracking measures where someone looks in a visual scene—whether on a screen, in a physical environment, or inside a headset. By dividing the scene into defined areas of interest (AOIs), it is possible to track how long a person focuses on each region and how often their gaze shifts between them. These movements, called *saccades*, help reveal where attention is concentrated, how it shifts, and when a user looks away. One common output is a gaze heatmap, which visualizes aggregated viewing patterns across individuals, helping to identify which elements draw attention first, what gets overlooked, and whether the visual design supports a meaningful flow of attention (see Figure 8.15).

This can help you track the gaze shifts.

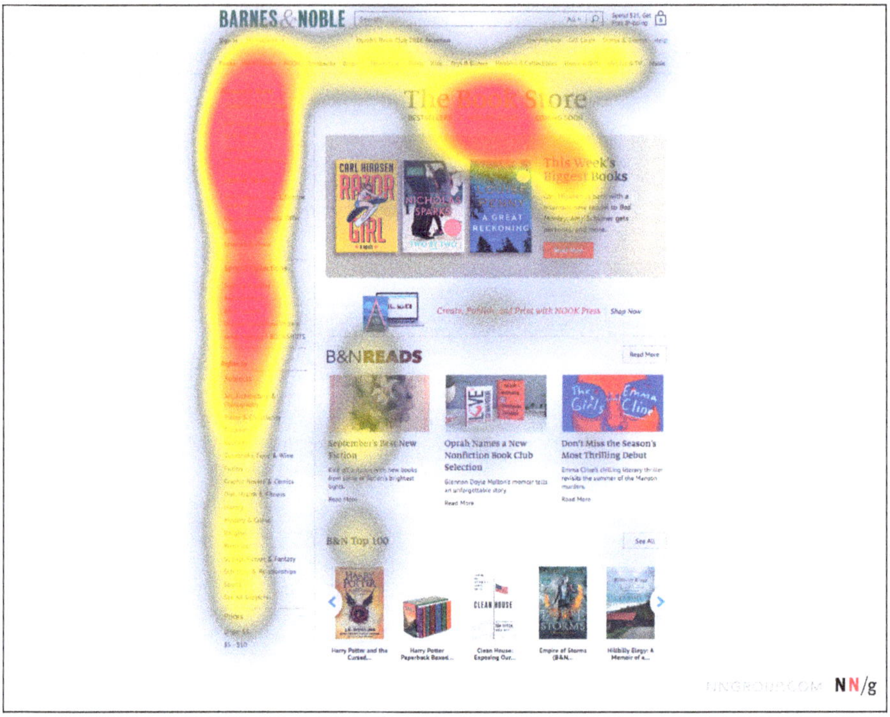

FIGURE 8.15

Heatmap generated from multiple participants scanning the Barnes & Noble homepage.

As the technology has moved into AR and VR headsets, it has also become an input modality. Apple's Vision Pro, for example, uses eye tracking (see Figure 8.16) to allow users to select and interact with interface elements simply by looking at them.

FIGURE 8.16
Apple Vision Pro headset alternates flashing light on the eyes as part of its eye-tracking technology.

Some popular eye-tracking tools include the following:[1]

- **Tobii:** Eye-tracking platform across both research and UX contexts, offering hardware ranging from desktop-mounted trackers to wearable glasses, paired with software for heatmaps, AOI analysis, and gaze replay.
- **Gazepoint:** More affordable desktop eye-tracking system well suited for UX and usability testing, with built-in tools for heatmaps, AOIs, and pupil diameter measurement.
- **iMotions:** Integrated biometric research platform that combines eye tracking with other physiological signals like facial expression and skin conductance, useful when you want to study attention alongside emotional response.

Audio Processing

Speech is not separate from the body. It is something the body does. The voice is produced through a complex choreography of breath, muscle, and movement. Like gestures, it carries meaning that goes well beyond the words themselves. Tone, inflection, rhythm, and volume shape how spoken language is interpreted in ways that a transcript cannot capture.

You already notice this instinctively. Say these two sentences out loud, placing emphasis on the italicized word each time:

- The *quick* brown fox jumped over the lazy dog.
- The quick brown fox *jumped* over the lazy dog.

1 For a comprehensive guide to applying eye tracking in UX practice, check out Aga Bojko's *Eye Tracking the User Experience* (2013)..

The words are identical, but the emphasis shifts the meaning of the sentence. In real-time conversation, these vocal cues help listeners understand what is important, emotionally charged, or uncertain. They also work in concert with gestures. With the right tools, you can extract these features from audio recordings and use shifts in pitch, speech rate, pause length, and intensity to surface moments worth a closer look.

This is the domain of sentiment analysis, where tools attempt to infer emotional state from vocal features. Some popular audio processing tools include the following:

- **Praat:** Open-source tool for phonetic and prosodic analysis, capable of tracking pitch contours, speech rate, intensity, and pauses across recordings.
- **openSMILE:** Open-source library for extracting low-level acoustic features like pitch, jitter, and speech rate, used in affective computing and emotion recognition from voice.
- **ELAN:** Multimodal annotation tool that allows you to align and analyze speech alongside gesture and behavior in video, making it particularly useful when you want to study how vocal and bodily cues work together.

Note that sentiment analysis systems, tools that attempt to infer emotional state from vocal features, have well-documented accuracy limitations. Performance varies across accents, speaking styles, and demographic groups, and what registers as frustrated or negative in one context may simply be directness in another. They also exhibit known racial and gender bias. For that reason, use them as a starting point, but don't overrely on their outputs!

Embedded Environmental Sensors

Environmental sensing emerged from building automation and retail analytics, where the goal was to understand how people moved through and occupied physical spaces. Early systems used simple motion detectors and infrared beams to count foot traffic and detect presence. Over time, more sophisticated tools like depth cameras and thermal sensors made it possible to track multiple people simultaneously and map movement patterns across larger spaces.

This gives environmental sensors a different lens than the other tools in this section. Rather than tracking individual bodies up close, they offer a macro-level view of how people behave in aggregate like which paths they take, where they linger, and which areas they avoid. For designers of physical spaces, exhibits, or any product where the environment itself shapes behavior, this kind of ambient data can reveal patterns that no interview or usability test would surface.

Some common environmental sensing approaches include the following:

- **PIR sensors:** Passive infrared detectors that register presence and movement within a defined zone, useful for understanding traffic patterns and dwell time in a space.
- **Depth sensors:** Devices like Intel RealSense that use structured light or time-of-flight technology to track the position and movement of multiple people simultaneously without capturing identifiable imagery.
- **Footfall analytics platforms:** Integrated systems like Density or Verkada that combine sensor hardware with software dashboards to visualize occupancy, flow, and spatial behavior over time.

Keep Yourself in the Loop

The tools in this section represent a genuine expansion of what is now possible when tracking the body and human behavior. It is possible to detect bodily signals at scale and automate the process of scanning hours of video in order to flag moments of hesitation, locate bursts of movement, or surface shifts in gaze across large datasets. That is a meaningful capability. It changes what you can realistically look at and where you can direct your attention.

But detection is not interpretation. A gesture is not simply a data point but an action unfolding within a human interaction. Algorithms can help identify when and where movement occurs, but understanding what that movement contributes still requires human judgment. These tools can help you narrow down to a set of interesting gestures, but only you can determine which gestures matter for your goals and will drive innovation.

HOW SPOOKS SENSE PEOPLE WITH WI-FI

Experimental systems have also been developed to translate ambient signals from Wi-Fi routers into real-time presence tracking. Researchers from Carnegie Mellon have demonstrated how DensePose can interpret the reflections of radio signals from common wireless routers to accurately detect the number and position of people in a space even without a direct line of sight (see Figure 8.17).

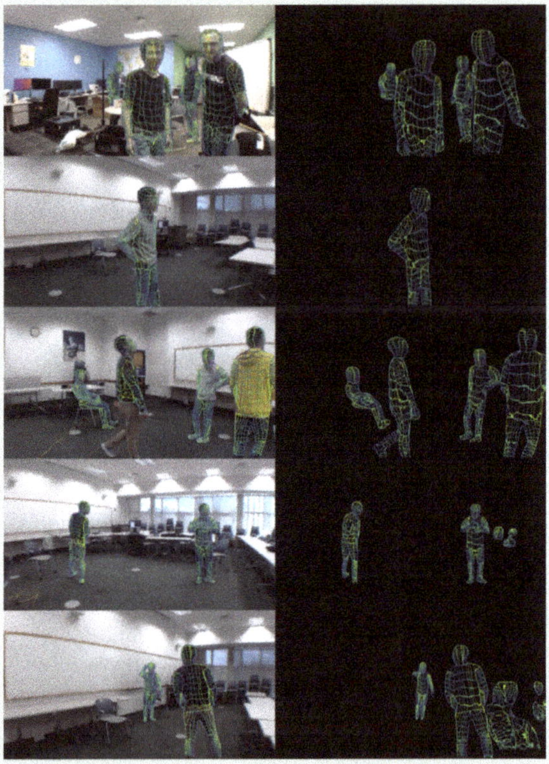

FIGURE 8.17
Demonstration of how DensePose is able to detect humans in a space without visible light.

By analyzing how wireless signals reflect off bodies and move through space, machine learning models can reconstruct rough silhouettes and movement patterns. These systems offer a low-friction way to gather behavioral data across large or sensitive areas, such as healthcare settings or public buildings.

The Next Push and Pull?

The push and pull between technological ambition and the body's realities has quietly shaped which products succeed and which ones people reject. As innovation moves forward, where will that dynamic play out next?

Robotics is one space where the push and pull are already visible. Robots have been a scientific curiosity for decades and a fixture of factory assembly lines. But a convergence of cheaper components, more sophisticated hardware, and more capable algorithms has made them commercially viable in ways they never were before. Labor shortages and aging populations have positioned robots as a solution to some of the most pressing challenges ahead. As they move out of controlled environments and into the streets, homes, and workplaces where human bodies already live, the push and pull will begin in earnest.

The contours of that push and pull are already taking shape, and appearance is one place where it showed up early in the history of the technology. One way robotics have tried to ease integration is by making robots look and act like people—giving them skin-like textures, expressive faces, human posture, and gestures that mechanically mirror what people do naturally. The instinct is clear: human likeness feels familiar and approachable.

Robots like Sophia, developed by Hanson Robotics in 2016, demonstrate the appeal of this approach (see Figure 8.18). Designed with a human-like face capable of expressing emotion and holding conversation, Sophia became a global phenomenon and appeared on talk shows, spoke at the United Nations, and became the first robot granted legal citizenship anywhere in the world.

But the same features that can draw people in also raise expectations. The roboticist Masahiro Mori argued that as robots become more lifelike, small imperfections and gaps in their behavior from what humans do become magnified, tipping familiarity into unease (what he called the *uncanny valley*). This is the push and pull of appearance in action: the more human a robot looks, the more people expect it to behave like one. When they don't behave like humans, it strikes at an innate fear programmed into the brain through eons of evolution.

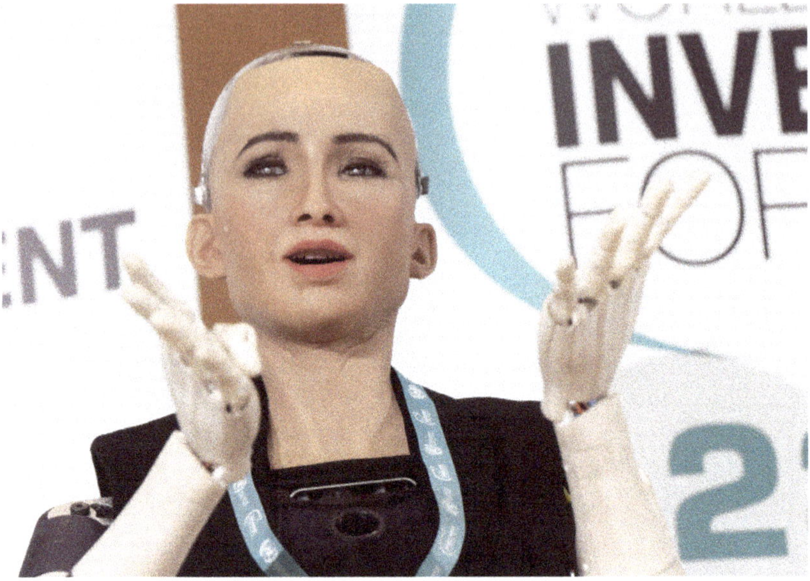

FIGURE 8.18
Sophia the robot developed by Hanson Robotics, seen here at the World Investment Forum in 2018.

So, although human likeness can ease integration, when pushed too far, it becomes a liability. The body does not respond to resemblance alone. It responds to coherence that is learned over a lifetime of interpersonal interactions. When that coherence breaks, acceptance can quickly turn to rejection.

But appearance is only one layer of the push and pull. Robots must also be compatible with the human social systems they enter. Food delivery robots have made this tension visible. Many have been vandalized at high rates, a signal that sharing public space with machines does not come naturally. The push and pull here is social as much as physical. People are not just reacting to how these robots look. They are also reacting to what their presence implies about shared space, balance in the labor market, and social order.

HERD BEHAVIOR

When dozens of food robots were filmed gathered at a docking area outside a building, a viral video followed that gave a deeply unsettling sense of collective, animal-like organization (see Figure 8.19).

WWW.INSTAGRAM.COM/REELS/DTDBRZJGFXK

FIGURE 8.19

Food delivery robots gathered at a staging area in Chicago.

Importantly, no individual robot evoked this reaction. Rather, it was an emergent phenomenon when these delivery drones took on a different presence within the broader social ecosystem.

Innovators have responded directly to that pushback. Cute faces trigger care rather than threat. A slight rotation of the wheels before moving signals intent the way people naturally do when navigating shared space. These are not arbitrary choices. They are deliberate responses to the body's push and pull shaping design in real time.

As robotics evolves, the challenge is not whether robots can appear human, but what aspects of human-like presence are appropriate and where that threshold begins to break down. Adoption depends on how well robots support rather than undermine what people recognize as fundamentally human.

Though robots may approximate human behavior, humanness is not a set of features to be copied or convincingly rendered. It is a complex, lived condition. It is fundamentally relational, embodied, and dynamic. It is enacted through continuous coordination between intellect and sensation, action and response, self and other. Without the lived integration of body, environment, and relationship, what appears human will remain only a simulation.

This is where the deepest push and pull lies. Robots can reproduce gestures, expressions, and even patterns of interaction. But the body is a site where meaning is made, where thought takes shape, and where interaction unfolds. How far technology can go in replicating that—and whether it should—will shape this era of innovation.

An Evergreen Source of Insight

Neil Postman offered a provocative idea in the late 20th century: that much of what is called "human progress" is actually a misunderstanding.

Since the Industrial Revolution, it has been common to speak about the advancement of humankind. But Postman argued that it is not people who are evolving. It is the environment around them. Technological change, in this view, is *ecological*. It transforms the conditions people live and work in, but it does not fundamentally alter how people think, feel, or relate to one another.

In other words, technology evolves quickly. People not so much.

People engage their changing world through the constant of their physicality. They act on the world, make sense of it, and connect with others through gestures and embodied action. The environment may shift around them, but the body remains as the enduring bridge between people and the ecosystems they inhabit.

And that is exactly why attending to gestures and the body matters. When the environment changes faster than the people living in it, the body endures as an evergreen and reliable guide. It operates on ancient principles that remain remarkably stable—how people make sense of situations, express meaning, and organize action in the world. Every nod, reach, pause, or shift offers a glimpse into that ongoing human work. It was true long before the first interface was designed, and it will remain true long after the next wave of technology arrives.

Let Gestures Do Their Work

To build innovations that fit seamlessly into people's lives, move beyond the primacy of language and let gestures do their work. When you look to the body, you extend what words do not capture and you arrive at a fuller understanding of the range of human experience. This is when meaningful innovation begins.

Gestures do not stand alone. They are performed in human moments and unfold within a context of words, things, intentions, actions, and relationships. A quick flick of the hand might signal frustration. The same movement might demonstrate how a product component rotates. Or it might be an invitation for you to continue. But it might not matter at all, just a reflexive movement to shoo away a mosquito. What matters is the work they do and how you can make use of them.

Gestures widen the field of what is available to think with, communicate through, and coordinate around. It is this interplay of the affordances of the three bodies—thinking, communicative, and coordinating—that makes it possible to go deeper, to move past the surface, and to grasp the underlying why and how of the people you are designing for and the people you are designing with.

Let gestures shape your product journey. You'll make better decisions. You'll build with greater precision. And you'll create innovations that actually fit into the lives they are meant to serve.

Tune Up Your Attention

But never forget that you already know how to do this.

If there is one thing you carry forward, let it be this: learning to see and make use of gestures does not require mastering a new discipline. It simply means turning up your natural gesture consciousness and committing to attend to gestures more deeply.

Maybe doing so reshapes how you conduct interviews and observations. Maybe it changes how you interpret what users show you as they explain their experiences. Maybe it helps your team develop ideas together, using gestures to explore possibilities and coordinate action around a prototype. Maybe it helps your team create something that has never existed before in human history and quietly reshapes everyday life. *Body Talk* is a lens you can bring into any space where people think together, communicate meaning, and coordinate activity.

Like any skill, this awareness deepens with practice. The more you look, the more you will notice. You will begin to ask better questions about what people are doing with their bodies and why. Technology can help you broaden your view or locate patterns you might otherwise miss. But your attention, judgment, and empathy will always lead the way.

That kind of attention and how you respond is already part of how you move through the world. The cashier waves you forward, and you step up. Your child slides back in a chair with crossed arms and you begin negotiation. A neighbor quickly peeks over the hedges, and you close your blinds. That fluency is already yours and it is part of how you work. You spot patterns. You analyze moments. And then you act. Attending to gestures expands the dimensions of how you engage in the world and your work. Gestures expand your toolkit allowing you to see, think, and do more.

As technology becomes more intelligent, more ambient, and more embedded in everyday life, the body will remain a steady guide. Gestures offer a thread to hold onto, one that keeps your work human-centered, grounded, and attentive to how people actually live and work.

This is where we leave you. Carry that gesture consciousness into every process, product, and team that you help build.

The body always has something to say. The work is simply to listen.

Takeaways

- **The body has always shaped computing:** Technology has continuously evolved by trying to align digital systems with human movement and embodied expectation. When products feel intuitive, it is because they fit the body that people already have.
- **The push and pull between technology and the body never stops:** Every major computing innovation involves a negotiation between what technology can do and what the body will accept. Products succeed when they close that gap and fail when they ignore it.
- **Designing for the body means more than designing for intent:** Interactions must also account for physical comfort, endurance, and sustainability over time. When they do not, the body pushes back in ways that make even technically capable products fail.
- **The body's social expectations are as important as its physical ones:** People do not just respond to how a product feels to use. They respond to what its presence implies about shared space, trust, and social order. Innovations that disrupt those expectations face rejection even when the technology works.
- **Detection is not interpretation:** Body-tracking tools can help locate moments of interest at scale, but they cannot deliver meaning on their own. Gestures only become insight when a human interprets them in context, grounded in intention and situation.
- **The body is an evergreen source of insight:** Technology changes quickly, but the body does not. Gestures and embodied action remain a stable, reliable guide for keeping innovation human-centered, no matter how fast the surrounding environment shifts.

FIELD NOTES FROM STEPHANIE

I was on a video call explaining an idea, and like I often do, I lifted my hands to shape what I meant. One hand marked one part of the idea. The other showed how it connected to the next. In the middle of my explanation, the platform decided I was celebrating. Suddenly, confetti burst across the screen (see Figure 8.20).

Everyone laughed. My hands were not cheering. They were working. They were helping me explain, organize, and make an idea visible. The program recognized the movement, but not the meaning of the movement in that moment.

And then it happened again. And again. The video screen was a spontaneous, ongoing celebration for a bunch of nothing.

FIGURE 8.20

My hands were not celebrating. They were trying to make an idea visible.

FIELD NOTES FROM DANE

When we started creating the cartoons for this book, I decided to experiment with AI image generation tools to produce the illustrations. I had played around with early versions of Stable Diffusion back when you had to train your own custom embeddings. It has come a long way since then.

Text-based image generation is genuinely appealing: describe what you want, get an image back, iterate from there. For simple things, it worked reasonably well. A coffee shop interior. A table with laptops. Background details that didn't need to be precise.

But when I tried to describe specific physical poses, things got complicated fast. Every time I needed something particular, an arm extended in a specific direction, a hand reaching rather than pointing, a body leaning with intent, the results came back close but not quite right. A torso turned the wrong way. A limb positioned just slightly off.

The irony was not lost on me. I had spent years studying how language falls short and how people use gestures to fill that gap. Now, I couldn't describe my own characters' bodies well enough for a model to render them. All that fluency in analyzing and describing movement, and I still couldn't put it into words precisely enough to matter.

To work around this, I had to get clever. So, I built a small tool that lets me position a digital representation of an artist mannequin. I can position it with 3D controls, capture the pose, and then use that image directly as grounding in my prompt (see Figure 8.21). The results improved immediately. What I learned is that AI, just like people, is just more efficient when it gets information through the modality of the body.

FIGURE 8.21
The mannequin pose provided the model with a clearer guide than words alone.

INDEX

Numbers

A

B

C

D

E

F

G

H

I

J

K

L

M

N

O

P

Q

R

S

T

U

V

ACKNOWLEDGMENTS

This book exists because of a chance encounter. Paula Bach, you were so kind to give us the floor at that Quant-Qual Bridge meeting where we introduced this quirky new topic to a group of industry researchers. That gave us the confidence that gestures were something new, interesting, and relevant for this audience. We also want to thank Lou Rosenfeld for spotting the potential in our ideas. Every professional success is built on someone taking a chance on someone else, and we're ever grateful to both of you for that.

To Marta Justak, our intrepid editor and product manager, you always knew when our words and what we meant were telling different stories. Thank you for your diligence and earnest feedback. It made the work better. We look forward to having that sangria with you as we look back and laugh.

To Siri Mehus and Rebecca Evanhoe, who consistently offered incisive observations that deepened our argument. To Steve Portigal, thank you for taking the time to write our foreword and for doing so with such characteristic generosity and wit *[both grinning widely, heads shaking slowly in delight, index fingers extended in Steve's direction, eyebrows raised "this guy"]*. You instantly saw what gestures add to the craft of interviewing and product work and encouraged us to share our knowledge far and wide. Siri, along with Nick Smarrelli, Beth Ard, Thérèse Dugan, Vera Haussler, Michelle Cortese, and Cheryl Platz, also offered testimonials that helped us understand how these ideas land in the hands of practitioners. To Chris Waltemate, who brought visual clarity to Dane's illustrations.

We're especially grateful to the researchers, designers, product managers, and teams who took time to talk with us, answer our questions, and give us feedback on early drafts. You helped us understand how these ideas land in practice and where we needed to be clearer. And to the hundreds of participants and groups who let us interview and observe them over the years: this book is built on what your bodies revealed. Thank you all for your generosity and honesty.

We also want to acknowledge colleagues at the University of Illinois at Chicago, University of Washington, and Northwestern University, who shaped our thinking over the years and challenged us to ground our work in rigorous observation and real human activity. Specific thanks to Mike Stieff and Matt Lira from UIC and to Reed Stevens and Betsy Cooper at UW. Dane's colleagues at Microsoft's Power BI Research team, Guoping Ma, Erika Devine, Todd Haskell, and Lynda Osborne, who helped him understand how products get built across large, complex organizations. To Brian Arneson, Tim Smith, Jamie Caras, and Kim Taylor at Catalyst Education who gave Dane the latitude to wear multiple hats across research and product.

On the personal side: Alex, Stephanie's husband, kept her steady and fed through the long stretches of writing. Her children and siblings forfeited time together. Carmy, Dane's dog, understood that some weeks meant fewer walks so that Dane could focus.

Most importantly, we're grateful to each other. This book exists because we found a way to think more fully together. That collaboration was messy and generative, sometimes frustrating but always punctuated by laughter. We pushed each other's thinking in ways neither of us could have done alone. We wrote the book we needed to write, and we needed each other to write.

Dear Reader,

Thanks very much for purchasing this book. There's a story behind it and every product we create at Rosenfeld Media.

Since the early 1990s, I've been a User Experience consultant, conference presenter, workshop instructor, and author. (I'm probably best-known for having cowritten *Information Architecture for the Web and Beyond*.) In each of these roles, I've been frustrated by the missed opportunities to apply UX principles and practices.

I started Rosenfeld Media in 2005 with the goal of publishing books whose design and development showed that a publisher could practice what it preached. Since then, we've expanded into producing industry-leading conferences and workshops. In all cases, UX has helped us create better, more successful products—just as you would expect. From employing user research to drive the design of our books and conference programs, to working closely with our conference speakers on their talks, to caring deeply about customer service, we practice what we preach every day.

Please visit rosenfeldmedia.com to learn more about our **conferences**, **workshops**, **free communities**, and **other great resources** that we've made for you. And send your ideas, suggestions, and concerns my way: louis@rosenfeldmedia.com

I'd love to hear from you, and I hope you enjoy the book!

Lou Rosenfeld,
Publisher

ABOUT THE AUTHORS

Dane DeSutter is an embodiment and gesture scientist who has spent over a decade studying how the body externalizes and supports complex cognition and putting those insights to work in product development. He uses spontaneous co-speech gestures to probe the fine details of people's mental models across domains as varied as spatial reasoning in science, physician-patient dynamics in clinical environments, wearables, developer experience, and human-AI interaction. He is currently a Senior Product Researcher at Microsoft.

Dane earned his doctorate in Learning Sciences from the University of Illinois at Chicago, where he studied the embodiment of spatial thinking as people reason with scientific visualizations. His work has contributed to multiple products including pedagogical chemical simulations, critical infrastructure visualization for Argonne National Laboratory, visualization of learning analytics data and telemetry, and AI grading support for instructors.

Dane presents his research at venues including the International Society of the Learning Sciences, Quant UX Con, Advancing Research, ICMI, and CHI. He also volunteers with Out in Tech to mentor early career queer UX practitioners. He also holds a B.S. in Applied Physics from Purdue University.

When he isn't in research mode, Dane bikes along Lake Michigan, hikes, swims, and follows his dog Carmen (Carmy) Sandiego wherever she leads. He hopes that someday she leads them both to the foothills of the Alps.

You can find Dane online at danedesutter.com.

Stephanie Scopelitis is an educator, learning scientist, and qualitative researcher. Her life as a professional dancer carried her into a deeper study of human interaction and the body. She has built her work on a fundamental belief: we understand and navigate the world through our bodies.

She designs experiences that pull from her life as an artist, educator, and researcher to help people think, create, and solve problems together through deliberate use of gesture and embodied interaction.

Her main home is where teaching and learning happen. She teaches and mentors across learning spaces and subject matters, from prisons to K–12 and higher-ed classrooms, in courses on social entrepreneurship, creative thinking, ethics, pedagogy, and arts integration. She brings interdisciplinary and multimodal approaches to all her work, treating gesture and the body as cognitive, communicative, and interactional resources.

Her practice spans research labs, community arts programs, and product teams—including collaborations with educators, designers, organizations, and the healthcare sector. She helps them recognize and make deliberate use of gestures and embodied interaction to move learning, collaboration, and creative work forward. She shares this understanding through teaching, consulting, workshops, publishing, and conference presentations.

You will often find Stephanie engaged in gesture-filled conversations dotted with phrases like "Why do you suppose?" "What if…?" and "I have an idea." She can't stop herself from turning the gestures she observes into quick dance sketches on the spot. Challenge her with one—she loves it.

Stephanie holds an MFA in Dance and a PhD in Learning Sciences from the University of Washington. She completed her undergraduate studies in English and Philosophy at Indiana University, after dropping out four times. She also studied at Yale Divinity School, examining the body as a theological text.

www.ingramcontent.com/pod-product-compliance
Lightning Source LLC
Chambersburg PA
CBHW040739120926
51354CB00028B/286
9781959029250